D0881179

We Say No

Also by Eduardo Galeano

We Say No

CHRONICLES
1963 / 1991

Eduardo Galeano

Translated by Mark Fried and others

W · W · Norton & Company

New York   London

Due to a lack of space, permissions appear on page 317.

Translation copyright © 1992 by Mark Fried
Copyright © 1992, 1989 by Eduardo Galeano
First American edition, 1992.
Printed in the United States of America

The text of this book is composed in 11 on 13.5 Simoncini Garamond
with the display set in Simoncini Garamond
Composition by PennSet, Inc.
Manufacturing by Courier Companies, Inc.
Book design by Margaret M. Wagner

ISBN 0-393-03150-0
ISBN 0-393-30898-7 (pbk)

W. W. Norton & Company, Inc.
500 Fifth Avenue, New York, N.Y. 10110
W. W. Norton & Company Ltd.
10 Coptic Street, London WC1A 1PU

1 2 3 4 5 6 7 8 9 0

To Susan Bergholz, my literary angel

Contents

CONTENTS

I am part of the sun as my eye is part of me.
That I am part of the earth my feet know perfectly,
and my blood is part of the sea. . . . There is nothing
of me that is alone and absolute, except my mind,
and we shall find that the mind has no existence
by itself, it is only the glitter of the sun on the
surface of the waters.

—D. H. Lawrence

We Say No

We Say No

Pelé and His Retinue

MONDAY, 9:00 P.M.

In the lounge of the Columbia Hotel, a diplomat friend argues loudly that this interview will really be worth it. Calm as can be, Don José Ozores, "Pepe el Gordo," Pelé's Spanish manager, administrator, custodian angel, father, brother, publicity director, and agency of public relations, says: "All right, already. The embassies. He is more ambassador than all of the ambassadors put together. People speak of Him in places where they've never even heard of Brazil. And what does Brazil give Him? Taxes. That's what they give Him."

So you are his attorney, I say.

He explains, "He lives with me, He eats with me, I take care of Him, I take care of His business. As if He were my son." He stops speaking Portuguese and switches to Spanish, so that there be no mistake: "Yes, *Life* also wanted to do a story like that, and a long one. I charged them a few dollars. If they let a 'nigger' onto the cover, with all the discrimination, it's got to be because it makes them a lot of money. So, He has a right to a piece of it. In any country, a magazine with His face sells by the ton. In popularity polls, He's always first, everywhere. Then come Jacqueline Kennedy, Khrushchev, de Gaulle, and all the others."

I enumerate 137 differences between *Life* and *Marcha*, my Uruguayan review.

"Okay, okay, okay, I understand. But He is upstairs resting. He doesn't want to hear about anything. There are always so many journalists and photographers. Think about it, He's tired, a prisoner of His name. Trapped by glory. Edson Arantes wants to be a man like any other, but they won't let Him. He's condemned to be Pelé, and that's why He's going to retire from soccer."

The diplomat stops talking and smiles. He knows that Pelé won't retire from soccer. He'll be Pelé until He can't go on, until the years or the hostility of His rivals knock him out. Pelé: the black panther that eighty million Brazilians idolize and who electrifies crowds all over the world. A little boy at the summit of a mountain of money and glory.

I turn my head and see Him, squinting at a painting by Vicente Martín that has certainly doubled in value since He laid eyes on it. I move closer, a cloud of journalists with me. Flashbulbs pop. I give up. An artist tries to sketch the Black Marvel, but it's impossible. In the doorway I hear the protests of my angry colleagues: "It's easier to do a story on Jango Goulart [president of Brazil at that time] than this man! I spent half an hour with the president chatting in the embassy. Aren't I right?" And my diplomatic friend tries to calm them: "But Jango is Jango. And Pelé is the greatest leader of America. . . ."

TUESDAY, 9:00 A.M.

I have breakfast with Pepe el Gordo. "Uruguayans sure can eat," he says. "We Brazilians . . ." Brazilians? "I was born in a village in Pontevedra [Galicia], the truth be said. But I've been in Santos for ten years." He tells me that he's been with the King for four years. "Since He was fifteen, He's played soccer: field and ball, ball and field. Now He's twenty-three, but He never had time to grow up." And he adds, fatherly: "He needs someone."

Someone like Pepe el Gordo, I suggest.

"It was Zito who said: Pepe is the man. Zito is my partner in the construction company. And from then on I've been with Him."

Why do they call Him Pelé?

"Nobody knows. They've always called Him Pelé. Ever since He was a poor skinny kid living in the Santos camp doing errands for the veterans and washing the floor."

I'm interested in how He was discovered. How God was revealed to man.

"Like a slave in the time of the slave trade," he says, wrinkling his brow and his mustache. "A civil servant from Baurú noticed Him. And he told the mayor of Santos: 'If you get me transferred from this office to São Paulo, I'll bring you a marvel.' And he brought Him, against the wishes of His mother, who didn't want Him to be a soccer player. She knew what that was, because His father was also a player, in Baurú. She never wanted a famous son. She's still the mother of Dico, the child, her baby," he says, and he opens his hands: "The Mother: A saint on the altar, who starts walking."

The reporter falls silent. Someone takes away the empty glasses.

Pepe el Gordo insists: "Like I tell you. A saint."

Doña Celeste, mother of the world-renowned miner from Três Corações, sees her son only by chance. The road trips to other states of Brazil and to other countries take up seven, eight, nine months a year, and in the other months Pelé plays in São Paulo or He rests, in the protective embrace of Pepe el Gordo, who does not leave His side in the sun or the shade. Journalists and admirers run up against this wall from Galicia, who knows everything you ought to know, and much more.

Manager? "Friend, father, brother." Does the team pay you a salary? He becomes indignant: "No! I am not an employee

of the Santos. If the Santos were to pay me, there wouldn't be
enough money. No. He who takes money is not a friend. I told
the kid: The day that you try to give me just one cruzeiro, I'll
punch you."

He's sleeping in the room next door. He didn't go to practice
this morning, because He didn't feel well. "Constipated," explains Pepe el Gordo. "What's more, He doesn't need to practice." Pelé eats little and sleeps a lot. When He eats too much,
He has nightmares and talks in His sleep. So Pepe el Gordo
doesn't let Him eat more than "a few mouthfuls of meat and
cheese, and one or two glasses of fruit juice." Object of universal
admiration, source of euphoria or misery for millions and millions of people, He must be cared for. It could be fatal to ignore
the lesson of one of the divinities who preceded Him in history:
Buddha died of indigestion from eating pork.

TUESDAY, 10:30 A.M.

We go on a tour of the old city in Montevideo, the edge of the
city, by the river. I carry a copy of the Rio daily *O Cruzeiro*,
which of course mentions Him. I tell Pepe el Gordo about the
article. He shows me a photo: an enemy dressed in black. "This
referee is a hermaphrodite," he explains.

The morning is burning with sun. Lover of vistas that I am,
I look and I comment. But Pepe el Gordo asks about prices:
"That's expensive, really expensive." And he talks, as always,
about the glory he has in his hands, because "God is in heaven,
and Pelé on earth." Two times world champion, He has the
enormous apparatus of Brazil's press, television, radio, and movies at His feet. Politicians court Him and the brands of coffee
or automobiles or drinks pursue Him relentlessly, because He,
His name or His signature or His face, will sell. Atma, a plastics
factory, prints Pelé's autograph on the balls it makes, and they're
a sure success. The book *I Am Pelé* was a best-seller in Brazil
and is being translated into English. In Germany, the first edition

caused a furor and is already sold out. On the second edition, Pepe el Gordo won't get a thing: "I didn't accept any royalties. I charged a certain amount for the rights and goodbye. I detest complications." And then the Argentine, Christensen, made a movie about the Great Subject, *O Rei Pelé*, which also added a few cruzeiros to the mountain of millions. Pelé and Pepe el Gordo are partners in several powerful firms, and all this is just the "extras."

I think of Baltazar, a star already waned, who now carries bags in the port of Santos. And I think of Garrincha, another star who I understand has fallen into disgrace. I tell him. Pepe el Gordo points to his forehead: "Pelé has soccer and good judgment," he says. "Garrincha doesn't." Details about the case: "He abandoned his wife and their eight daughters. That singer has been his ruin."

I tell him I think Elsa Soares is well worth the mess. There is a lamentable misunderstanding and Pepe el Gordo tells me yes, He goes to mass every Sunday. And He says the rosary two times a day. A good Catholic. A fervent Catholic, who likes to follow the commandments. All of them. "He wouldn't ruin a virgin. There you have the kid's personality." He doesn't smoke. He doesn't drink. He avoids the nightclubs. He loves children and old folks. "He is a son. Who turned up in my house. And that is my problem: I can't rest until I see Him on an altar or as a statue, like that one," he says, pointing to the monument to Garibaldi.

TUESDAY, 12:00 NOON

Columbia has received reinforcements. Verdoux, Mansilla, and Casimiro Rueda in a throng. Introductions. We go up. He's asleep, still. We talk in the next room, facing the sea.

"Make yourselves at home," says Pepe el Gordo, with his shoes up on the windowsill. "I was telling my friend here that He, if He hadn't been born a person, He would have been born a ball. He's the best soccer player of all time." I don't contradict him—I would feel uncomfortable—but he was really telling me that Pelé is a prisoner of soccer, and is unhappy.

Mansilla runs off his mouth with a few exotic words. He says at the going price of twenty-four-karat gold, about $1.15 a gram, Pelé is literally worth a lot more than he weighs. Pepe el Gordo doesn't like such calculations, and declares: "There is not enough money or gold to pay Pelé. He plays because He likes to. He has no need of that."

Of course, He's had plenty of offers. When the Santos toured Europe, the Juventus of Turin offered him 800 million cruzeiros, about $800,000. Some managers favored the trade, and He talked to Pepe el Gordo. "I told Him: If you promise me you'll never leave the Santos, I'll make sure they pay you even more in your own country. Then, in '61, the Internationals of Milan offered the club a million dollars, another million for Him, and two hundred thousand more for me to convince Him, besides the monthly payments which I thought of asking for. I told the boy, and He asked me: What about our commitment?"

Mansilla shifts around in his chair. "Then," he says, "you're willing to do business."

Pepe el Gordo grumbles, "There is not enough money in the world to buy my word. Most journalists think I'm exploiting Pelé's name and fame."

Verdoux cuts him off politely: "But that's outrageous. My colleague was not suggesting anything like that."

"There you have it," says Pepe el Gordo, "The world today is more materialist than spiritualist, and it's hard to admit that someone does something in vain. I used to be free; not anymore. I used to live better; I went where I wanted; I owned myself. But this new job is a cross to bear: I have eighty million Brazilians who distrust me because I'm a foreigner."

And he tells the story of the offer from the Milan Internationals. A Mr. Ricci showed up, and Pepe el Gordo, who smelled a bribe, hid a tape recorder behind a window and put the

microphone in the curtain. Later he played the undignified prop-
osition on the radio.

Casimiro Rueda looks serious. "If Pelé were to leave Brazil,
there would be a revolution."

*"You have said it: He cannot use His talent outside of where
God put Him."*

But Mansilla insists. He rolls his eyes, saying how much he
admires the devotion and friendship of Pepe el Gordo for Pelé,
but that human virtues are like shoots of grass in the sun, fragile
and easily burned.

"Money doesn't stick to my hands," insists Pepe. "No one
buys me."

And they get locked in a discussion which reminds this reporter of the apocryphal dialogue between George Bernard
Shaw and Samuel Goldwyn, in which Shaw comes to the conclusion that they could never understand each other because
he, Shaw, was only interested in money, while Goldwyn was
only interested in art. Pepe el Gordo saying that money hadn't
saved his father from a stomach ulcer, that no money can buy
love, that the human condition cannot be reduced to material
conditions, and that Pelé, He, the boy, is not merchandise. And
Mansilla responding that he shouldn't be so hard on money,
that it can be a good tool in saintly hands, that Von Braun and
other geniuses worked for cash and not for democracy, and
saying,

"It's human."

"It's evil, yes," responds Pepe el Gordo, *"You have said it."*

Verdoux, meanwhile, looks skeptical and yawns in his easy
chair.

TUESDAY, 2:00 P.M.

At last He appears. No altar: a cat, not very muscular, who
offers me a peach. "Ours are smaller," He says, "and the juice
doesn't spray like this." He still looks sleepy, sounds as if He

has a cold. He says little, in correct Spanish, and He smiles, with a certain melancholy. "The Mozart of soccer," the Europeans called Him, astonished by His rhythmic and elegant style on the field. In Rio de Janeiro they sell out months in advance when He is going to play, and the papers in all Brazil write about Him on the editorial pages. Trumpets announce His passage through the capital cities of the world. But He doesn't seem to notice: He isn't turned on or off by glory, He simply puts up with it, because that's the way things are.

Pelé can't be this average human being. There must be some mistake. This can't be Pelé, this timid boy who tells me Dondinho, His father, was "much better than me," although this reporter has been told that he was only mediocre, and who confesses humbly that He crosses himself before every game "so that they won't hurt me," and after every game "to give thanks." This isn't Pelé, this boy with an ingenuous stare who doesn't understand why people venerate Him and hate Him at the same time.

"I'm never pitied," He says. "On Brazilian fields, the other is always right. The referee or the adversary." The hostility of the referees is worse lately, especially in Pacaembú stadium. The better He plays, the more whistles, insults, and boos He gets from the São Paulo public; when Pelé wears the shirt of a team from another field, He sells His soul. The Santos, a team which is not from the state capital, has won several national and international championships, and Pelé is their star of pure gold. The public from the capital will not forgive Him. "I don't deserve that," He says defensively. "It wasn't me who started people saying that I'm the best player in the world. I've got nothing to do with it. Believe me, I'm not faking. I believe the greatest player hasn't been born yet. He'd have to be the best in every position: goalie, defense, forward."

I tell him that recently He's shown himself to be a magnificent goalie, and that He's proved himself in almost every position.

He shakes his head, shrugs His shoulders, looks at me without understanding why I insist on believing that Pelé is Pelé.

I ask Him if He's really bewitched: once after a match He wanted to burn the bus on which He was riding, screaming, "Witch! Witch!" His smile molds His face as if it were rubber. "The Italians started that story," he says. "They said I had a little magic machine and I put pictures of the people I didn't like inside and they would die." And is it true? "Nooo . . ."

What happened to the Independiente in Buenos Aires? "We don't know what happened either." But five goals . . . "That happens in soccer." Didn't Rolán hit you very hard? "Hard, yes, but he meant no harm, eh, write that he meant no harm." Don't you feel trapped sometimes on the field? Don't you feel that the player you face seeks fame at your expense? He makes a face: "When a hard player hits Pelé, he's twice as hard." Is that why you believe in God? Because you're afraid? "I believe in God because it's my faith. And God protects me." And aren't you afraid of Peñarol? "In friendly matches, the Santos play to play, and the opponents play to win. That's what happens. I don't take risks in friendly matches. When I think something might happen to me, I don't take risks."

What is the stupidest question you've ever been asked? "So many stupid questions . . . If I like to play soccer." And do you like it? He laughs. "When I was little, I wanted to be a pilot." What book are you reading now? They say you like to read. "I like it. Yes, I do. Especially didactic books; none of those about the Wild West and such, no. Now I'm reading some stories by Mariazinha and *Problems Between Parents and Children*." Tell me the titles of some of the books you've read recently. He thinks a moment and lists: *On Love and Happiness in Marriage, The Book of Nature, On Failure and Success, Human Relations*.

Don't those books bore you? "Pepe el Gordo buys them for me," He says. "He buys the books for me to read." Pepe el Gordo? "That's right, my attorney." Why do you live in his house? "Because he understands me. It's strange that I would reach such an understanding with a foreigner. Because you know I have a difficult temperament." Is that why you haven't married yet? "Too early." I ask Him if he's not married to soccer. He says, "Soccer used to be my love. Now it's my profession."

And then He takes it right back: "Of course, there must also be love, because without it you can't do it." You can't do what? "Play." So you wouldn't let them trade you to a foreign team? You'll wear the Santos shirt until the end? "For now, I'm not thinking of leaving. Later on, who knows?"

And finally Pelé, the friend of Jango Goulart, makes a sympathetic comment on Goulart's reactionary enemy Lacerda in response to my question: "I know him, yes, but I've never spoken to him. He seems like a man who likes his work and knows what he wants." And politically? "I don't know anything about that either."

Pepe el Gordo, who has left Him alone for too long, reappears behind Him. "That's enough. You've got to rest," he says. "You shouldn't wear yourself out." And Pelé, resigned, goes upstairs, walking slowly toward His room. Tens of thousands of spectators have paid high prices to see Him play against Peñarol, and He doesn't have the right to defraud His fans or the curious or His enemies. That cold must be nipped in the bud before the match, and it will be, no doubt. That's what Pepe el Gordo is there for, with cold tablets in hand.

TUESDAY, 3:00 P.M.

The task is complete. Leaving the hotel, I run into a few kids kicking a ball against the hotel wall on Misiones Street. Their voices pursue me: "Here he comes! Here he comes!" "It's yours!" "Kick it, Pelé!" "Let it go! Let it go!"

The sun hurts my eyes, but a breeze is just beginning to blow off the river.

(1963)

The Thrice-Born Emperor

I interviewed the last emperor of China in Beijing twenty-five years ago. The story was published in Marcha toward the end of 1963. The worldwide impact of Bertolucci's film about him perhaps justifies resurrecting the reportage at this time.

A mishap occurred that was not mentioned in the published text. I paid scant attention to it at the time, but today it seems quite amusing, to say the least. At the end of our chat, when I asked the emperor if he was or would like to be a member of the Communist Party, the translator committed a gaffe or a slip of the tongue in transmitting the reply. Instead of using the Spanish word honor, *he said: "The Emperor says, 'For me, it would be a great* horno [furnace].' "*

On February 12, 1912, the *New York Times* printed a laconic wire from Beijing: "Today, 267 years of rule under the Manchu Dynasty came to an end." Pu Yi, the last of the Ch'ing, would go down in history as a unique case: the only emperor of China whose head remained on his shoulders after he had been overthrown. It may well be said that he was born three times: first, as the head of the Celestial Empire; second, as the puppet emperor of Manchuria; and, in a third incarnation, magically incorporated into communist ranks, glowing with gratitude, starry-eyed in his enthusiasm.

The past still lives in this enchanting country in its objects and people: the ancient alleyways of Beijing, the high walls of the Forbidden City, legendary pagodas and palaces that reveal themselves from behind the mists of time or a dream. Memory of age-old China merges with the reality of new China. One discovers the traces of ancient oppression, for example, in the bound feet of women over fifty who seem to be walking on stumps. Male predilection for small feet imposed this custom of atrophying the feet of little girls. And one finds the traces of foreign domination in the architectural styles of the structures raised by the dominating nations in the concession zones. From the high rooftops of Shanghai and Wuhan, I can recognize the architecture of each country: up to this point, the Japanese were masters, the North Americans until here, the French over there, farther over the British and the Germans . . . China, a juicy fruit, sliced into chunks and distributed.

The cities and the people bear witness to the old humiliation.

THE FORMER DRAGON'S MEMORIES

Emperor Pu Yi opens our talk with a lengthy harangue in support of China's position in the dispute with the Soviet Union. He says exactly what I have just heard from another Chinese, Tang Yeng, who was a slave in Tibet until 1959, repeating the same slogans against contemporary revisionism, the Titoist clique and social turncoats.

Pu Yi then tells me his story of how the mightiest man of a mighty country was transformed into a humble worker at the service of his people. The flamboyant robes of silk and gold exchanged for the plain cotton uniform buttoned up to the neck. From the Sutras to *Capital*—a long road.

"Let's go back," I say to him, "to before your fall, and even before that. To your earliest memories, to your life in the palace." But he, too, wants to know things, and so I pay my tithe by speaking first. "Montevideo? Yes, the city that leans over the estuary; my people." He would like to know Latin America. We will be expecting you, I tell him. He lights a cigarette and offers me one. "No, thank you." And I explain that I smoke Tian Shan, the Chinese equivalent of Republicanas, a strong dark Uruguayan brand.

The threadbare cuffs of his shirt peep out of the sleeves of his uniform. Pu Yi bears no resemblance to the man I had expected to see. I had constructed a character out of the vapors of imagination, and I can't deny that I feel rather disappointed now that I see him in the flesh. I had anticipated clouds of melancholy and imperial dignity hovering about him, sad resignation in the bowed head, the long, bony fingers. . . . Not at all! This emperor seems rather a civil servant, a bureaucrat satisfied with his lot. He smiles throughout the two-hour conversation and talks in torrents. As I listen, an image of a few days before comes to mind: the tormented branches of the sophora tree from which the last emperor of the Ming Dynasty hanged himself at the foot of the Hill of Coal.

I ask the last emperor of the Ch'ing Dynasty if he had known his aunt, the Empress Tz'u Hsi. I know that the images will never fade from my mind of the luxurious halls of the Summer Palace, which she had expanded with the many millions lent by the mandarins to build a fleet. China had no navy, which it needed. Instead, a lake was made to appear at the foot of the Sacred Hills of the West, an island rose in the lake, and on the shores were built pagodas and new residences for the empress. The white keel of a great marble ship guarded by dragons made its appearance. "My fleet? There it is," said the Empress Tz'u Hsi, according to the story. I wish never to forget that throne surrounded by lions carved out of birch-tree roots; the Halls of Beneficence and of Long Life where the old ogress hidden behind gauze curtains received her mandarins; the vessels of bronze and gold for burning incense and sandalwood; the immense carved tables where she would eat a bite from each of 270 dishes served there every afternoon. There, trembling, the privileged mandarins waited for Tz'u Hsi to toss them a scrap of food—the greatest possible honor.

But the story interests me particularly because I feel as though I can see her fighting off death. Everywhere in the palace, the metal turtles and cranes give testimony to her immortality. On the altar of a tiny chapel was an oil painting of Tz'u Hsi by a North American artist of no talent. She was seventy years old at the time it was done, but on the canvas she looks twenty—the last Lady of the Celestial Empire fighting against time.

Yes, Pu Yi knew her. He knew her at the time she was dying. "She sent for me to take the throne when I was a child of three. I saw her only once. The experience was so frightening that it left a deep mark on me for the rest of my life."

His first recollection, the memory of tears. He wept and wept. "When the empress decided that I should be emperor, I was warned that I could never again see my mother, nor my grandmother; that I could never again leave the palace. When I went into the palace, I saw many men. I had never seen so many together before. I remember that."

It isn't hard to imagine: mandarins and courtiers making way for the tiny creature sent by the gods, dragging his glorious cape and barely able to hold up his head under the overwhelming crown of pearls edged with threads of gold, as he made his way toward the throne reserved for the Children of Heaven. And after the ceremony, he went into the bedroom and saw her, raising his eyes he saw her.

"Everything was in shadow. The emaciated face, as of death. It scared me, and I began to cry. The empress ordered that I be given a candy. I threw it to the floor. Yes, strange that I should recall all that. I was so little. But I remember."

"Did she resemble the portrait?"

"I don't know. She was very skinny."

Pu Yi draws the proper conclusions. The tiny Dragon who witnessed the death of the Phoenix is today "a real man, because the Communist Party saved me."

And he explains to me: "You see, under the feudal system, human feelings didn't count . . . they tore me from my mother's arms. But later, I began to enjoy it. I was a child and I felt more powerful than all my elders. All of them were at my feet. I was most sublime; above anybody. My father wielded the real power, although another aunt, the honorary empress, made the weightiest decisions."

I ask about his father, Shai Fung.

"He died in 1950. But after the Revolution of 1911, he was no longer concerned with politics. He spent the entire time at home."

RENDING HIS CLOTHES

Pu Yi, however, did not spend his days at home. He did not give way to resignation. Only 267 years of the Ch'ing Dynasty? Didn't it deserve a few more centuries?

He wished to restore the empire. The Japanese thus had their man. "I was a traitor. The Japanese instituted a policy of aggression against China and sought to use Chinese to dominate the Chinese. I was living in the city of Tientsin when my contacts with them began. They were interested in dividing China to facilitate an invasion. They and I were of the same mind, because I wanted to go on dominating the people of the Northeast and the country as a whole. Then they made me emperor of Manchuria. I was on the throne in Changchun from the year 1932. I was emperor for fourteen years. At least I held the title, if not the power. I was an international pretext, if you know what I mean. The restoration was a smoke screen, an instrument of Japanese domination."

"A puppet?" I ask, anticipating the interpreter, for once.

Pu Yi, ever smiling, nods. He beats his breast along with his words. "If everybody had acted like me, there would be no socialism in China today. Our country would have remained under imperialist occupation."

HALLELUJAH, HALLELUJAH!

There is a large white building on the outskirts of Beijing. Visitors cannot but be surprised when they are told that it is the Institute for Rehabilitation of the Bourgeoisie.

Gaily, Pu Yi intones his *mea culpa* regarding his own experience in reeducation. "I couldn't have imagined it even in my wildest dreams. The Communist Party is so great that it does not annihilate the person physically, in the flesh, but rather annihilates mistaken ideas. And so it made me distinguish truth from lies. I was reeducated. They treated me very well."

He strokes his neck. "Little by little I discovered the truth. I admitted my crimes. I visited the whole country several times for the purpose of comparing the old China with the new China that is being built by the party of the proletariat. I learned that the thing to do is to base oneself in the people."

He was granted provisional freedom. And now? I tell him that I had read an article by Field Marshal Montgomery a couple of years ago in which it was said that he was a gardener.

"No longer. I am now working in historical research."

"On your own history?"

"That, too. I wrote an autobiographical book. Too bad you can't read Chinese! I'll send it to you when it's translated."

CHERCHEZ LA FEMME

Pu Yi informs me that he got married recently, last year. "On the first of May," he says.

"To whom, if it is not an indiscretion to ask?"

"To a nurse from the hospital."

"Tell me, tell me."

Pu Yi's first marriage was out of his hands. When he was a child, his parents arranged the engagement to a young lady of a noble family. He doesn't even want to recall it. "In the beginning, my parents decided. Later, the Japanese."

However, he says that he was in love with his second wife, a student from Beijing. When the Japanese learned that he intended to get married, they sent a general to Changchun. They warned him that he could not marry before they had made the respective investigations. Finally, the commander in chief of the Japanese army approved the marriage. That bride hated imperialism, Pu Yi recalled. She fell sick and was treated by Japanese physicians. She died.

"In that period, the commander in chief of the Japanese army had installed himself in my palace. He came to express his condolences to me. In one hand he held flowers, in the other sheafs of photographs of Japanese girls for me to choose from. But I did not want to marry a Japanese. They stuck their noses into everything. They wanted to run my life, to control my every action. I obeyed them, but not always. I told them I would marry whom I wanted to marry. They then presented me with photographs of young Chinese girls. I again rejected them and on my own chose a fifteen-year-old student. I was satisfied with her because she was obedient to me in all things. But afterward, I got divorced."

Pu Yi's sparks of rebelliousness were never long in being snuffed out. He was afraid the Japanese would replace him with his brother or nephew. "I was afraid of losing power. I wanted to preserve my interests."

And, as though it could not be otherwise, he drew his moral: "Characteristic of my class, the exploiting class."

THE INCOMPARABLE GLORY

I ask him if he is a member of the Communist Party. No, he is not. Would he like to be?

"Oh! The title of Communist is a most noble title. I am still very far from attaining that incomparable glory. I still have a lot of studying to do. I must finish changing my ideas if I am to reach such an elevated goal. It would be a great honor for me."

The emperor insists on my having a fourth cup of jasmine tea.

The dragons on the porcelain surface are fighting.

(1963)
Translated by Asa Zatz

El Che Guevara:
Cuba as Showcase or Spark

1

"Traitor," I told him. "You're a traitor." I showed him the clipping from a Cuban newspaper: he had on a baseball uniform, he was pitching. I remember that he laughed, we laughed; if he said something, I don't know what it was. The conversation bounced like a Ping-Pong ball from one subject to another, from one country to another, from one memory to another, from nostalgia for home and experiences of the revolution, to jokes: "What's happening to my hand? It's cursed." Damned? "Of course. It shook Frondizi's hand and Frondizi [Argentine president, 1958–62] fell; it shook Janio Quadros's [Brazilian president, 1961] hand and the same thing happened to him." It's a good thing I have no place to fall from, I responded with a worried look, and he laughed, furrowed his brow, sat down, stood up, walked about the room, let the ash fall from his *cazador* cigar, and pointed at me with it, at my chest. He'd go to the blackboard to explain a complicated thought, more like a debater than a teacher, scribbling it out with chalk: the polemic on economic calculations and the validity of the law of value in socialist society, or the system of paying people by production norms. He was caustic like people from the

River Plate, aggressive, and at the same time fervent like a Cuban, sincere: generous with the truths he had discovered, but on guard, ready to bare his teeth to defend them. A profound and lovely strength flowed from inside him incessantly; as with everyone else, his eyes gave him away. He had, I recall, a pure, clean gaze, like the dawn: the look of a true believer.

2

He believed, all right: in Latin America's revolution, in its painful evolution, in its destiny. He had faith in the new human condition that socialism *ought* to engender. When he talked about such subjects, one got the impression that the temperature of his blood rose, but whenever I started jotting down notes he kept his enthusiasm on a short rein. Then, his eyes fixed on the Bic dancing on the paper, he'd blow out two or three dense lungfuls of blue smoke between thick mustache and scraggly beard, and, smiling, he'd make some mischievous and cutting comment. Being a journalist was awful. Not because I had to go to work after so many incoherent nights and days of vertigo without sleep, nor because of how nervous all that made me, but because the flow of communication that burst forth spontaneously every so often would always get cut off. "We're talking among Cubans and Uruguayans," Che would then lie, to avoid an indiscreet question. Yet everything about him showed that the passion vibrating in him, shining throughout him, had broken down the borders others had invented for Latin America, and that he of course did not believe in them. Talking with that man you could not forget that he had come to Cuba after a pilgrimage throughout Latin America. He had been—and not just as a tourist—in the whirlwind of the nascent Bolivian revolution, and in the convulsive agony of the Guatemalan revolution. He carried bananas in Central America and took photos in the plazas of Mexico, to earn life; and to risk life, he threw himself into the adventure of the Granma.*

3

"One day they came by," he wrote in his farewell letter to Fidel, "asking who they should notify in case of death, and the real possibility that it could happen hit us all. Later on we discovered that it was true, that in a revolution (if it's real) either you win or you die." In search of new victories, or of his own end, he left Cuba. Yes, there in the middle of the tempest and the fight, you win or you die: "under other skies" now. Others, friends, so many friends had fallen along the way: they would continue to fall. El Patojo, for example, who had been on the run with him during the rough times in Mexico and ended his days shot full of lead in the Guatemalan jungle. (Don't trust, don't trust, Che had advised him: he died betrayed by a high school friend.) Another one was the Argentine Masseti who got lost, badly wounded, in the woods of Salta.

Che was not made for a desk job: he was a *creator* of revolutions, and it was obvious; he was not, or he was in spite of himself, an *administrator*. In his words and gestures under his apparent calm, you could sense the tension of a caged lion that would have to spring free.

4

He missed the mountains. I don't mean to imply that he was of no use in the peaceful rebuilding that follows armed victory. Very much to the contrary, Che was also an exemplary revolutionary in this sense, a worker who never tired in any of his posts of great responsibility. People suspected that he, like Fidel,

* The Granma was the yacht that carried Fidel Castro, Che Guevara, and eighty other revolutionaries from Mexico to the coast of Cuba to begin the guerrilla war.

never slept: day and night there were complicated matters to be resolved, and difficult tasks to be undertaken, above all in the struggle to industrialize the country. At the end of each workday, and each workday lasted an entire week, he would go on Sunday to cut cane as a volunteer. He would still find time, inexplicably, to read, write, and debate. And to fight with the relentless asthma that had plagued him during the guerrilla war. ("The order to set off," he told us, "arrived suddenly, and we all had to leave Mexico just as we were, in groups of two or three. We had a traitor among us, and Fidel had ordered that once the order was given we should leave with whatever we had in hand, to get away before the traitor had a chance to notify the police. That traitor . . . we still don't know who it was. So that's how I ended up leaving without my inhalator, and during the crossing I had a ferocious attack. I thought I would never arrive."

He was totally committed, "as it should be," to the difficult task of building socialism in Cuba. Of all the leaders, he was the most austere and, because of his capacity for sacrifice, the most like the image of a Christian in the catacombs. Obsessed with the notion that the mystique of socialism, the faith in the new world being born, should spur development, he refrained from the excessive use of material incentives or systems of payment that might give someone hopes of "becoming a Rockefeller." The possibility that upholding the law of value—in which he did not believe—might lead to a return to capitalism ("other cases prove it") made him indignant. In this regard he was inflexible. "The gentlemen of the INRA [Agrarian Reform Institute]," he would say, referring to those who wanted to carry out a different revolutionary economic policy. His famous article answering Charles Bettelheim ends, for example, "Those who defend economic calculations fit the old saying 'I'll take care of our enemies, I hope God will protect us from our friends.'" On the next page of the same issue of *Cuba Socialista*, the first paragraph of an article by Joaquín Infante warns that "economic calculation is the method of economic policy used in socialist companies in the USSR and in other socialist countries and in popular democracies. . . ."

Criticized perhaps correctly by certain economists for "idealizing" the revolution, Che Guevara always used his biting capacity for polemics to illuminate *Cuba's* problems. It had nothing to do with the Sino-Soviet split, as some erroneously believed. "We're not going to get involved in that," he told us to explain why Cuba didn't publish a text by Paul Baran that referred to the conflict between Moscow and Peking. Any analogy could only be made by extension, but Cuba, its destiny as the advance guard of the Latin American revolution, was at the center of his concerns. "I'm not interested in discussing these things outside Cuba," he warned us when he referred to the controversial issues of the rhythm of the revolution, the keys to its development, the interdependence of domestic and foreign policy, issues on which the leaders took different positions. Che was the outspoken leader of one side, with clearly defined stances not only on economic calculation and the law of value, but on the relative importance of industrialization, the conflict between the budget system and decentralization, and Cuba's role in the broader scope of continental revolution.

As much as he was prone to argue, he did not hesitate to admit his own mistakes, which were the mistakes of the revolution itself: lowering sugar production, or "attempting to substitute for too many imports by making finished products with all the tremendous complications that importing intermediate products brings."

5

Che, not born of their land but vitally involved in the challenge of their revolution, touched the Cuban people with his example. He lived just as he preached; everyone knew it, and on top of loving him, they admired him. Candela, the driver who took us through Cuba at the wheel of a luxurious expropriated Cadillac, liked to call him "horse." This supreme praise *a la cubana* was applied to only three people from Candela's mouth: Fidel, Che, and . . . Shakespeare. The efforts to bring theater to the people bore fruit in this unexpected way: every so often, Candela would go into a trance and out would rush a torrent of comments on the Elizabethan playwright ("It is pronounced several ways; the Americans say Chéspir") and of his work: "Oh, yeah. That was a real horse, chico. A horse: very philosophical his writing, and very didactic, yes sir."

All down the length of Cuba, wherever we went, Reina Reyes, Julio Villegas, and I, we met peasants, workers, technicians, students, officials, all quoting Che as frequently as they quoted Lenin or Fidel:

"Monoculture means underdevelopment; Che explained it clear as could be."

"The revolution is won by sacrifice, chico, like Che says. Or do you think everything is a party?"

Cuba was like an enormous resonating box for his essential message, the most important of all, heard by all, understood, incorporated, spread: the revolution is a force that purifies people, pushes them beyond selfishness. And purity earned must be defended, with bullets, study and work, as if it were life itself.

6

In Santa Clara, which a poet once called the city "of red and multiple roofs," Candela showed us the walls still bitten by lead, the exact place where Batista's armored train had been derailed and attacked, the police station besieged by Vaquerito who fell once and for all at the head of a suicide squad. He told us about improvised alleys through garden walls, Molotov cocktails, blood and fire; Che Guevara, his wounded arm held by a rag, was the hero of the stories. "It's going to be six years," Candela said. "And it hasn't rained here since then." But the images were still alive in the retinas of the witnesses and protagonists, and the scars were visible, they still burned: history, which had no need for the passage of time to turn this into legend, was still occurring, the enemy attacking, the revolution battling on, and death was still something that could touch anyone at any moment.

7

Che's irreverence was the irreverence of the revolution. But in another style, more like ours in the River Plate, sober and sarcastic. Perhaps it was nostalgia for his lost home, half vengeance and half homage, that made Argentines the butt of his most acid comments: he would remind them that revolutions are made and not said, that the mission of communist parties is to be at the vanguard of the revolution (a satisfied smile) . . . but lamentably in almost all of Latin America they are in the rear guard (indignant silence). When a well-known Peronist got mad because he had been kept waiting more than a month for an appointment, Che patted his back: "But you've waited eight years to make the revolution. . . ." And other wicked comments: once he suggested that to raise money for the revolution, they buy certain people from Buenos Aires for what they were worth and sell them for what they *thought* they were worth.

8

The image of the guerrilla Che in Santa Clara foreshadowed that of Che struggling in the inhospitable Bolivian jungle, and it got confused with the memory of Che at the Punta del Este conference, brilliant statesman, economist, somber prophet: that refined intellectual, who read poetry anthologies in the Sierra Maestra, knew by heart much of Neruda's *Canto General*, spoke admiringly of the novels of Carpentier, and laughed at socialist realism. But through all the images, or adding them together,

one emerges. It was Che at a press conference, answering the
question of some idiot who wanted to know if he was Argentine,
Cuban, or what:

"I am a citizen of America, sir," he said.

When we spoke in Havana, I told him, "The destiny of Cuba
is intimately linked to that of Latin America's revolution. Cuba
can't get confined within its borders; it works like an engine of
continental revolution. Right?" And he answered:

"There was a chance that wouldn't be the case. But we have
eliminated such chances. If Cuba agreed to stop being an example for the Latin American revolution, then the Latin American revolutionary movements would not be directly linked to
Cuba. The simple fact of being alive does not make one an
example. In what way is it an example? The way the Cuban
revolution approaches its relations with the United States and
the spirit of struggle against imperialism. Cuba could become
a purely economic example."

"A sort of socialist showcase."

"A showcase. That would safeguard Cuba up to a point, but
would divorce it from the Latin American revolution. We are
not a showcase."

"And how can you spread the strength of an example and
not end up simply contemplating your achievements? Through
solidarity? How far can that reach? What are the limits? How
would you define what's needed for solidarity between Cuba
and the liberation movements of Latin America?"

"The problem of solidarity—yes, yes, of course you can write
this down—consists of doing all that's feasible for the Latin
American revolution within a legal framework, and that framework is the relation between countries on the exchange of ideology or politics, on the basis of mutually respected accords."

"A situation which only exists with three countries."

"With two. Bolivia broke off relations this afternoon."

He took it for granted that it would not be long before
Uruguay would do the same.

I had the impression, I said, that Chile's decision to break relations surprised the Cubans. "What do you mean it surprised us? It did not surprise us a bit." But the people in the street seemed truly astonished. "The people, maybe. The government, no. We knew what was coming." I asked him what he thought of certain statements of Chile's FRAP [the leftist Popular Action Front] on Cuba, shortly before Frei's victory.* "Well, we thought they were terrible," he said. I suggested that it could be the result of the circumstances: the inevitable zigzags on the electoral road to power. He declared: "Power in Latin America is taken by force or it is not taken." He shook his head and added, "Put it down as 'generally speaking.'" So let's say the road to the government, not to power, I said. To confuse one with the other could have serious consequences, right? That happened in Brazil, didn't it?

But then Che remembered that he was with a journalist: spontaneity and caution chased each other without respite during three hours of conversation.

9

"Suppose new revolutions occurred in Latin America. Would that produce a qualitative change in Cuban–U.S. relations? The possibility of a coexistence accord has been mentioned. But if the fire spreads and imperialism is forced to throw water on the flames, what will happen to Cuba, the spark?"

"We define the current relationship between Cuba and the United States as an automobile and a train moving more or less at the same speed. The car has to cross the tracks. As the crossing gets closer, so does the possibility of a crash. If the car—which is Cuba—crosses before the train, that is, if the Latin American revolution acquires sufficient depth, then we'll already be on

---

* Chile's Popular Action Front (FRAP) was an alliance of six leftist parties formed in 1956, a precursor to Allende's Popular Unity (UP).

the other side: Cuba will no longer matter. Because imperialism is attacking Cuba not out of spite, but because it is important. I mean that if the Latin American revolution gets to the point where a large number of U.S. troops have to be deployed, then a number of territories will no longer matter. We will have already passed the railroad crossing. We deepen our confrontations with the United States every day, objectively and fatally as the situation in Latin America worsens—and the best of it is how bad it is. Now if the situation gets so bad that the United States has to send in lots of troops and equipment, by its own weight Cuba's importance will disappear. The fundamental issue will not be Cuba as a catalyst, because the chemical reaction will have already occurred. The unknown is whether we will cross before the train. We could step on the brakes, but that is unlikely.

"From this perspective, is coexistence possible?"

"The point isn't about Cuba, it's about the United States. The United States is not interested in Cuba if the revolution doesn't gel in Latin America. If the United States manages to dominate the situation, what will it care about Cuba?"

10

"And suppose the Latin American revolution doesn't get off the ground. Would it be possible for Cuba to continue moving forward?"

"Of course it's possible."

"In the long run?"

"In the long run. The worst of the blockade is over."

"I'm not only referring to physical survival. I mean, couldn't cutting off Cuba from its source of Latin American nourishment cause other sorts of problems—internal deformations, ideological rigidity, ever stronger ties of dependency? A Latin American revolution would undoubtedly enrich Marxism: it would allow for the theory to be best applied to our particular reality. And if the revolution becomes Latin America–wide, it would allow Cuba to resume its natural framework of existence. This isn't a statement; it's a question."

"It sounds a bit idealistic to me. We can't speak of sources of nourishment. The sources of nourishment are Cuban reality, no matter what that may be, and the correct application of Marxism-Leninism to the Cuban people's way of being, under given conditions. Isolation may cause many things. For example, we might fail to understand the political situation in Brazil; but distortions in the march of the revolution, no. Of course, it's much easier for us to speak with a Venezuelan than a Congolese, but we would definitely understand the Congolese revolutionaries perfectly, even though we have yet to speak with them. There is an identity in the struggle and in the ends pursued. A revolution in Zanzibar could also give us new things, new experiences; the union of Tanganyika and Zanzibar; the struggle in Algeria, the struggle in Vietnam. We have the Indian apron of our American mother, Martí liked to say, and that's fine, but a long time ago our American mother went through successive changes. And these are becoming more and more worldwide: a world capitalist system and a world socialist system. The fact that Algeria is free strengthens Cuba. We keep one thing always clear: Cuba's identity with revolutionary movements. In spite of the racial, religious, historic relationships, Algeria is closer to Cuba than to Morocco."

"And closer to the USSR than to Morocco?"

"That's one the Algerians will have to answer."

11

"When you referred to the 'world socialist system' you mentioned countries that are not part of the socialist bloc. Nationalist movements inclining toward socialism have placed their own stamp on those countries."

"The final result will necessarily be either a move toward

socialist integration or a return to the capitalist camp. The Third World is a world in transition. It exists because dialectically there is always a camp between opposites where contradictions sharpen. But it cannot remain there isolated. Algeria itself, as it deepens its socialist system, little by little leaves the Third World."

"Couldn't we speak of a Third World that cuts across the socialist bloc? The conflict between the Chinese and the Soviets, no longer silent, was analyzed by some Marxist thinkers like Paul Baran as a consequence of the contradictions between socialist countries with different levels of development and different degrees of confrontation with imperialism."

"The death of Paul Baran left me deeply moved. I held him in great esteem; he was here, with us."

Imperturbable, he moved his Havana cigar in silence; he watched my pencil as if it were an intruder taking part in our dialogue; I decided to put it away. From then on, Che Guevara answered a shower of questions on economic issues. From the Geneva Conference ("Some people have the answers, others have the things") to the mistakes made in the domestic economic process, Che Guevara spoke patiently and at length.

Until an enemy broke into the room to remind the minister of industries that his rival had been waiting for twenty minutes by the chessboard on the floor below. And he wasn't about to lose the tournament just like that.

(1964)

Magical Death
for a Magical Life

"I believe armed struggle is the only solution for peoples who are struggling to be free, and I live in accordance with my beliefs. Many will call me an adventurer, and I am. Except I'm an adventurer of a different sort, one who risks his skin to test his beliefs. This adventure might be the definitive one. I'm not looking for it, but it falls within the logical calculation of probability. If that is the case, here is a final embrace. I've loved you very much. I just haven't known how to express my affection. I'm extremely rigid in my behavior and I think sometimes you did not understand. It wasn't easy to understand me. But if only for today, believe in me. I've polished my will with the delight of an artist, and it should sustain these flaccid legs and tired lungs. I will do it. . . . Remember every so often this little twentieth-century *condottiere*."

Che Guevara wrote these lines to his parents a short time before he dropped out of view. By the time the letter arrived in Buenos Aires, his mother, Celia, had already died without seeing her son. She did not receive this "final embrace," this goodbye that foretold the news that has just shaken the entire world. "In the laborious work of revolutionaries, death is a frequent accident," Che once wrote regarding the death of an intimate friend. His letter to the Tricontinental Congress ends with a salute to impending death, as long as death announces "new cries of war and victory." A thousand times he said dying was so very possible, yet so insignificant. He knew well: after his successive deaths and resurrections, he himself claimed to have seven lives. He used up the seventh as he had planned. *He entered into death asking neither permission nor forgiveness*: he led his men forth to face the bullets of the surrounding army in the dusty ravine of Yuro. Machine-gun fire pierced his legs but he kept shooting for a while, seated, until a well-placed blow blasted his M-1 from his hands. A large group of soldiers captured him alive, despite the efforts of the few surviving guerrillas who from the middle of the afternoon until nightfall found the courage to fight hand to hand for the wounded man. Later they were exhibited at his side, their heads destroyed by gun butts, their bodies slashed open by bayonets. After the battle, after a full night and day in the Higueras Valley military camp, the wait grew unbearable. Finally, the order arrived from the government palace to kill the prisoner.

Still warm, the body was tied to the runners of a helicopter and carried up through a cloudless sky over the inhospitable sun-beaten terrain where the mountains open toward the Amazon Basin. In the Lord of Malta Hospital in the village of Valle-grande, Che's body was shown to a group of journalists and photographers. Later it disappeared, along with a chubby bald man who gave orders in English. He had injected the body with a liter of formaldehyde. Bolivia's President Barrientos said Che had been buried, while General Ovando said he had been cremated—in a place without the means to do it. They announced that they had cut off his hands. The Bolivian government ended up with a few embalmed fingers and a photocopy of the guerrilla's diary; the destination of the body and the original diary is secret or legend.

So filled with hallucination and mystery were his life and

death that innumerable legends have been woven about this hero of our times. Several legends, a few, are the fruit of the boundless capacity for infamy of certain fools who threw themselves like crows on the memory of dead Che, although they would never have withstood the gaze of Che alive. Others, nearly all, grew out of the people's imagination, which celebrates the immortality of the fallen hero on the infinite and invisible altars of our Latin America.

"At that moment, when everything seemed lost, I started thinking about the best way to die. I remembered an old story by Jack London in which the protagonist, leaning against a tree trunk, prepares to end his life with dignity." Che wrote this remembering a decisive moment amid the butchery that followed the landing of the Granma on the coasts of eastern Cuba. Eleven years have passed since that first brush with death. Now I look at the wire-service photos one by one. They present the body from all angles, the holes where the lead penetrated his flesh, the ironic and tender smile, proud and full of compassion, which more than one fool confused with a rictus of cruelty. I can't help but stare at that wonderful face of a Jesus from the River Plate. And I want to congratulate him.

The day of his baptism by fire, in a place called Alegría de Pío in Cuba, Che made a decision that would forever mark his destiny: "I had a knapsack full of medicines and a case of bullets. Together they weighed too much to carry. I picked up the bullets, leaving the knapsack behind as I crossed the clearing to the canefield." In the farewell letter to his parents, Che himself wrote that "almost ten years ago I wrote you another farewell. As I remember it, I regretted not being a better soldier or a better doctor. I'm no longer interested in the latter. As a soldier I don't do badly."

He chose to be on the front lines of the revolution, and he chose it for keeps, without even allowing himself the benefit of the doubt or the right to repent. *This is the unheard-of case of a man who abandons a successful revolution he made along with a handful of crazies, to throw himself into launching another.* He didn't live for victory, but for the struggle, the ever-necessary unending struggle against indignity and hunger. And he didn't even turn his head to look back at the lovely fire rising from the bridges he had burned.

His asthma wasn't the cause, as one Buenos Aires daily claimed, nor was it the oblique and sophisticated resentment of an impoverished patrician, as a widely read magazine insinuated: Che's embrace of solidarity can easily be traced in his life. And that word, *solidarity*, offers the only key to understanding him, even though it is absent from the dictionaries used by the scribes of the system.

An infinite number of possibilities lay before the eyes of young Ernesto Guevara when he came down from the sierra of Córdoba to the asphalt of Buenos Aires. He worked twelve hours a day, six to support himself and another six as a volunteer. He was a brilliant medical student, but at the same time he read treatises on advanced mathematics, wrote poetry, and began ambitious projects of archaeological research. When he was seventeen he started writing a "Dictionary of Philosophy," because he found that he and other students needed one. In 1950, a photograph of Che, who at that time signed his name Ernesto Guevara Serna, appeared in an advertisement in *El Gráfico*. The ad quoted a letter he had written to Micrón, a company that made motors for bicycles. In it, Che reported that he had traveled four thousand kilometers through twelve of Argentina's provinces, and that the motor had worked well. Now Armando March, a union leader and boyhood friend of Che's, recalls that while Ernesto was a student, his mother had an operation— they suspected a tumor on her breast. Ernesto set up an improvised laboratory in his home and experimented feverishly with guinea pigs and pipettes and oil solutions to try to save her life. Che and March had wanted to go to Paraguay to fight against the dictator Morínigo. Intelligent and multifaceted, with an innate seductive power that his life would only confirm and augment, young Ernesto Guevara was not a coddled and resentful kid. He was a young man open to adventure, with no clear political ideas and with a marked inclination to prove to himself that *he could do everything he could not do.* The continuous asthma attacks, which for years obliged his father to sleep sitting up so that his son could spend the night leaning on his chest, did not keep him from playing soccer and rugby, though at the end of the game his teammates would often have to carry him from the field. Asthma kept him from going to school after the fourth grade, but he managed to take his exams on his own, and later on in high school he got excellent grades. The war against asthma was the first war Che fought and won: he won it insofar as he never let asthma make any decisions for him.

This great warrior of Latin America was rejected as unfit for military service by the Argentine army. That was when Che crossed the Andes on a motorcycle and, drawn by the legend of Machu Picchu, reached Peru by foot. The residents of a leper colony then built a raft for him and his friend Alberto Granados, which they rode from the heart of the Brazilian jungle to Colombia. In Iquitos they worked as soccer coaches. Che got deported from Bogotá and ended up on a plane carrying thoroughbred horses to Miami. Some time later he made a second trip through Latin America, to Bolivia, to the streets of La Paz, where miners were marching triumphantly with dynamite caps in their belts—and later to Guatemala. "We couldn't see Che in Ernesto Guevara," Guatemalan revolutionaries who had known him told me years later. He was nothing more than a bureaucrat in the agrarian reform ministry, or an Argentine lying sick in his bed in a rooming house full of Peruvian exiles from APRA, Peru's eternal opposition. However, in Guatemala, Ernesto Guevara discovered Che. He discovered himself in the euphoria and defeat of the Guatemalan revolution, in the achievements and mistakes of a process of reform in progress, and in the helpless rage that accompanied the fall of Arbenz. Paradoxically, it was a ship of the United Fruit's White Fleet that took Guevara to Central America, where his true passion for socialism emerged.

He could have been a distinguished doctor in Buenos Aires' elegant Barrio Norte, or a prestigious specialist in blood or skin disease, a professional politician or a highly esteemed expert in any technical field. He could have been a fascinating café charlatan, as brilliant as he was derisive and excessive, or a jaded adventurer for adventure's sake. Years later, he could have remained the idolized leader of a revolution consecrated by success. The right always loves to put revolutionaries on the psychoanalyst's couch, to diagnose rebelliousness by reducing it to the clinical analysis of some original frustration, as if militancy and commitment were nothing more than the result of some bottle not being served on time, or the impossible love for Mommy. But Che was a living example of how revolution is the purest form of fraternity and human dignity, and also the hardest, the most difficult. His was not the pathological catharsis of a lad from a wealthy family in decline, but an act of continuous generosity: very few people in the history of our time have renounced so much so often, in return for one or two hopes, and he asked nothing for himself but to be the first at times of sacrifice and danger, and the last at the moment of recompense and security. Very few men have had such good alibis with which to soothe the conscience: the asthma that harassed him ceaselessly or the very important role he played in the construction of socialism in Cuba. Even he admitted how hard it was for him at times to climb a mountain during the days in the Sierra Maestra. "At those moments, I remember how hard the peasant Crespo worked to get me to walk. When I couldn't go on and I'd ask them to leave me behind, he would use that special vocabulary of our troops: "Shitty Argentine, walk or this gun butt will make sure you do." Despite the asthma, Che became a minister of the revolution capable of cutting cane or driving tractors with his face swollen from cortisone and an inhalator tied to his belt. In the same way, he was the revolutionary instructor Colonel Bayo's best student in Mexico, when Fidel Castro's men were training for the invasion. (In Mexico, Che earned a living taking children's pictures in the plazas and selling little stamps of the Virgin of Guadalupe; when the government tried to deport him, he fled from the airport and made contact with his comrades again.)

Before Mexico, he had already begun another secret war, the struggle against cynicism and the inability to believe which seems inherent to the excessive spirit of the people of the River Plate, particularly the *porteños* of Buenos Aires. When he heard a loud bunch of Cuban youths in a café in Costa Rica talk about the attack on the Moncada and the coming revolution against Batista, Che commented, "Why don't they tell another cowboy story?" In Mexico some time later, those same young people introduced him to a big man who had just been released from Isle of Pines prison. His name was Fidel Castro.

Recently, in Buenos Aires, I had the unwarranted privilege of reading the letter that Che's mother tried to send him shortly before her death, and that never reached him because Che had already disappeared. As if sensing her own impending death, in that letter the mother announced that she would tell him what she had to as naturally as she could and that he ought to answer the same way: "I don't know if we have lost the frankness with which we used to speak, or if we never had it, and we've always spoken in that somewhat ironic tone characteristic of everyone who lives on the shores of the River Plate, aggravated by our own family code that is even more closed. . . ." Che must have insinuated something about his next destination, because in the other paragraph Celia says, ". . . Yes, you would always be a foreigner. That seems to be your destiny."

A close friend of Che's mother defined it this way: "Che's intimates and girlfriends in Córdoba are now a legion, if you are to believe them. At two kisses a doorway, it would have taken him his entire life. But the truth is that he had tremendous magnetism. You know what I mean? That boy who listened to Vivaldi, read Heidegger, and set off to see America was tempted by practically every path. I think it was Trotsky, I'm not sure, who said that the most revered revolutionary is he who could have chosen something else instead of the revolution, and yet *prefers it*. Ever since then, solitude somehow became an obligation. The only profound relationship he could accept was with the revolution itself. He always had a deep need for completeness and purity."

This man who had all the doors of professional and personal success open to him became the most puritan of Western revolutionary leaders. In Cuba, he was the Jacobin of the revolution: "Watch out, Che's coming," Cubans would say in jest, but meaning it. That need for completeness and purity became, then, an incomparable capacity for personal sacrifice. He was intransigent with himself to the extreme of not allowing himself a single weakness, a single step in the wrong direction, so as to be able to demand as much from others. He didn't have the flexibility of Fidel Castro, who proved his aptitude for political negotiations by dealing with God and the Devil long before he took power. After he became a guerrilla, Che seemed to live according to the motto *All or nothing*. It's not hard to imagine the exhausting battles with the temptations of doubt this refined intellectual must have fought to achieve at last that steely certainty, that astonishing rigor.

"He is perhaps the most fascinating Latin American legend since El Dorado," writes the *Times* of London. A Falangist daily in Madrid compares him to the conquistadores in the huge scale of his undertaking, and *Azul y Blanco*, the organ of right-wing nationalism in Argentina, affirms that he was "a hero of the nineteenth century." Fidel Castro says he never will be able to speak of him in the past tense, and General Ovando himself admits that he was "a hero in any part of the world." Bolivia's President René Barrientos, wisely termed "an idiot" by Che in his war diary, declares that "an idealist has died." The priest Hernán Benítez, who was Evita Perón's confessor, exalts the figure of the fallen leader in these terms: "Like the Jews of the Old Testament who believed the prophet Elijah to be alive, the Spaniards of the Middle Ages and El Cid, the Galicians and Artús, it is also possible that in years to come the guerrilla soldiers of the Third World will believe they feel the hallucinating presence of Che Guevara amid the clamor of battle."

The pens for hire, meanwhile, have not lost the opportunity to exhibit their capacity for infamy. One Argentine magazine suggests that Che was the assassin of Cuban revolutionary leader Camilo Cienfuegos; another affirms that he's better dead than alive, since that way it's clear that terror is not the road to progress for Latin America; a third expresses surprise that guerrillas are not the product of the West, but of "communist countries." I imagine Che, with a slightly bitter smile, setting aside all this luxuriously printed verbiage that offends both one's intelligence and one's sensibilities.

I think of those true words of Paul Nizan: "There is no great work that is not an accusation of the world." The life of Che Guevara, so perfectly affirmed by his death, is, like every great work, an accusation of our world.

(1967)

Perón, the Sparrows, and Providence

One man set off shouting *"¡Viva la revolución!"* He had an Argentine flag rolled up under his arm. I stopped him at the door and I asked him what he was up to. He answered, "I'm taking a flag to the boys, sir. . . ." Inside the flag was a typewriter.

—*From Juan Perón's account of the Revolution of 1930*

1

The journalist moved through the whirlwind of kids playing on a sunny street in the southern working-class part of Buenos Aires. It occurred to him to ask a boy, who must have been ten or twelve, what he thought about the elections coming up in March: this was 1962, and the boy's response might be useful for the story he was writing. The snot-nose jumped several times on some tin cans; between jumps he said, "Elections aren't worth a thing." And then he shouted, "Here, we're waiting for the Man!" A few days later, the Man's candidates, Andrés Framini and others, won the elections by a landslide. But the kid was right: the will of the people is just fine so long as it doesn't contradict the will of the military. The generals rose up and on their own they elected the provincial governors and the new president; the Man's candidates got dropped along the way.

This was not the last time the generals would do this, but the slums of Buenos Aires have yet to stop waiting for the Man: the myth feeds off its enemies. For many long years, legend has promised that one day a black airplane will cross the sky as the sun goes down, and Juan Domingo Perón will set foot on Argentine soil once more, igniting it with his presence.

2

A caudillo is like a magnet: he lives to the extent that he attracts. Twenty-one years ago, that smile, so like the tango singer Gordel, that now extends its invincible charm to welcome my friend electrified the crowd packed into the Plaza de Mayo. That night in October 1945, the hand that now shakes mine rose up many times to underline with defiance his last few words, or to acknowledge with grace the passionate ovations. During that hopeful and tumultuous year, through the voice of this man the Argentine working class confusedly assumed a collective awareness of its destiny. When the children of the gauchos moved to the factories on the outskirts of Buenos Aires, they brought with them an old rage which first expressed itself politically on the concrete pampa. Eleven years ago [1955], defeated more by his own contradictions and weaknesses than by the doubtful coherence and strength of his enemies, this man fled: the Paraguayan gunboat, the hydroplane, through Asunción and the Caribbean, the pact with Frondizi and a third marriage, leading up to his definitive exile in Madrid. The defeat left behind a decade of government that was not over. Peronism remained the most powerful movement in Argentina, an immense encampment without borders, even though General Perón was no longer sitting on the throne at Rivadavia, and even though he would not return to the homeland he deserted.

3

From the moment Perón fell, the successive military coups have been nothing but homages paid out of fear to this truth: when elections are free, the Peronists win. The Peronists are still, by commission or omission, the arbiters of Argentine political life, and Perón is a guest of stone who decides by his absence: his victory in the March 1962 elections cost Frondizi the government; the possibility of his winning in March 1967 brought down Illia's government before its time.

4

I spent four hours with Perón at the end of October 1966. Major Vicente, his loyal aide-de-camp in other days, requested and obtained the interview. In the incessant drizzle of that autumn morning, we went to see him at his mansion in Puerta de Hierro on the outskirts of Madrid. He received us in his study, with his dogs at his feet, shelves of books behind him, the most recent work by Argentine historian Jorge Abelardo Ramos open on his desk.

"Power makes you ignorant," he said, smiling, his face alight with good humor. "Only now, in exile, do I have time to read."

Since then the dictatorship of General Onganía has accelerated the denationalization of Argentina, selling off the country at bargain-basement prices. Vital parts of the nation's industry are falling into the hands of foreign monopolies. The state is losing control of essential services. A law has been signed allowing Standard Oil and Shell to keep all the oil and gas and everything else they find underground or under water. U.S. Steel benefits from systematic official sabotage of the state steel industry. Political parties have been dissolved, the university brought under control; unions are being attacked and strikes fiercely repressed. Terror is being institutionalized in a way that would make McCarthy pale: the law repressing communism makes a leper of any Argentine who dares to think; it jails anyone who has the audacity to disagree with the regime or doubt it in public.

A comment Perón himself made about General Onganía during that interview has become even more current with the passage of time. He told me, "In the army we say there are four types of officers. The intelligent hard worker: that's a useful man, you'll have no problem with him. The intelligent loafer, who has to be made to work. The stupid loafer: with him there's no problem because he's worth nothing. And lastly, the stupid hard worker: that's the dangerous one. That is Onganía."

He also told me that very difficult times were coming. "Look," he said, "this is a dummy with his own ideas. He's going to fight. He's not going to simply walk away, no. He'll provoke a civil war between nationalists and colonialists. We can calculate now that the war will cause the death of a million Argentines. Because there is a proportion that's constant in that type of war. And in Argentina we have a population of more than twenty million. Calculate it yourself."

5

Ever since Perón fell, the Argentine people have known nothing but humiliation and swindles and economic anguish and broken promises. From 1955 to today, Perón's enemies have done more for him than he has. His enemies: those "democrats" who are terrified of elections and turn over the chessboard every time they lose or suspect they might. There is the mythological image of a better time past and of a time of revenge to come: Perón left, but he stayed. Time, far from tarnishing the myth, polishes it. Distance, fatal for other leaders who in exile divorced the masses, helps him avoid direct responsibility for his acts. His image, idealized in the memories of his followers, is safe from the frequent inconsistent stands he takes. He supported Frondizi, but didn't Frondizi get knocked down by a Peronist victory? He encouraged Onganía's coup, and even applauded him when he took power: couldn't he take it for granted that Peronism would be outlawed anyway under the fragile legality of the Illia government? Perón's mistakes always get justified. The mistakes of his followers—the movement's local leaders who would like to act on their own—are always condemned as mistakes.

6

Perón believes that each of his decisions to support something lends greater weight to his future decision to reject it. He believes that this continual tactical zigzag—thumbs up, thumbs down—allows him to sustain his personal hegemony within the movement, and gives him great private satisfaction in his political confrontation with the other powers. The Peronist labor and party leaders are wise to this: a signed photo, a tape recording, a letter, supreme blessings, all may give notice of tomorrow's malediction.

I mentioned to Perón certain "tactical retreats" the Argentine labor movement took when faced with Onganía's first reactionary measures, and I asked him if these could be distinguished from unconditional surrender. Perón responded, "The people will move forward with their leaders at the head, or with the heads of their leaders, as I have said many times. What's the matter with Argentina's labor leaders? They're workers who leave the shop to have a fancy office with a secretary who at night doubles as a lover, a big car . . . they don't want to give that up. But they forget that behind them are others who want to take their place, and behind both are the masses, the workers who elected them to defend their rights. The ones who just signed a contract for a thirty percent raise when the people wanted forty or fifty, and on top of that signed a request for a five-billion-dollar credit for the bosses—they've forgotten.

Nevertheless, we have to recognize that they got the most they could, given the condition of the country. You're talking about leaders who get co-opted by the regime. But you have to keep one thing in mind: they get co-opted because I order them to get co-opted. I order them to let themselves be co-opted so they get all they can for the workers, while the government's demagoguery lasts. And we've already seen that the government doesn't have much to give. Then, when the government has the working class as its enemy, it will also have as its enemy the bosses, and that's what we want."

Since an open condemnation might point up the frequent crises of his authority, Perón tends to assume paternity for pacts and negotiations that go on in spite of him or behind his back. Yet when the conversation drifted toward certain concrete postures adopted by several Peronist leaders who were too sweet on the idyll of Onganía, Perón didn't try to disguise his low opinion of his own leading cadre: "Comrades from the movement come here often to denounce Tom who's a traitor, Dick who's subverting my orders, Harry who's spreading calumny, so-and-so who's not a good Peronist . . . and I tell them, Don't worry. . . . Do you know how the Chinese kill sparrows? They don't let them land. They harass them with sticks and don't let them light on branches, until they drop dead of a heart attack and fall to the ground. These people fly about like sparrows: just harass them, don't let them rest, and they'll end up falling to the ground as well. No, no . . ."

Raising one arm serenely over his eyes, he continued, "To handle men you have to fly like an eagle, not a sparrow. Handling men is a science, the science of leadership, an art, with military precision. I learned about it in Italy around 1940: those people truly knew how to give orders. I learned not to waste any strength, to strike a blow with all my energy focused on one decisive point. I learned to act with serenity. My victory in Mendoza was the liquidation of the so-called neo-Peronists. You have to let traitors and turncoats fly, but never let them rest.

And wait for Providence to act. . . ." And he emphasized with a wink, "Especially because Providence is quite often under my direction."

7

Such systematic Machiavellianism obliges Perón to live in a state of permanent contradiction. He writes one letter with the right hand and, at the same time, another with the left. He says yes, he says no, he deals with God and the Devil at once. He never bets on just one horse; he prefers to bet on them all without ever risking his capital. Running a mass movement from afar, by remote control, both requires and encourages such a foxy style, replete with the old tricks of politicking.

Perón's own contradictions reflect and worsen those of the Peronist movement, a heterogeneous conglomerate where you can find everything from the extreme right to the extreme left. Holding it all together is Perón himself, the cement of a mosaic; when the caudillo disappears, the mosaic will break into bits. But the caudillo, alternately obstacle and catalyst, is quite alive, younger than ever; he walks no less than five kilometers a day and works from morning to night without a break. He likes to feel the rhythm of the moment; he tells me, for example, "Many young members of the Falange come here seeking advice on certain political questions. They're nice enough to suppose that my opinions are still worth something. They're good boys . . . but what do you want me to say? When I talk to them, I feel like I'm talking to my grandmother."

I ask him if he's going back to Argentina. I ask him when. He smiles slyly, leaning back in his chair. He shakes his head and slaps his thighs. "I'm over seventy . . ." he says, and he lies, "My pins won't do what I want. . . ." At the same time, or very soon thereafter, he sends a letter to the Peronist paper in Buenos Aires, *Unica Solución*, in which for the thousandth time he announces his impending return. "I am in perfect health," he writes. "My legs don't tremble."

8

What must be done to get the country moving? asks *Unica Solución*. It answers with a brief seven-point program. Of the seven, three propose "liquidating Marxist influence" in cooperatives and certain industries. In the following issue, *Unica Solución* gives the greatest praise to the first conference of the notoriously Marxist Organization for Latin American Solidarity (OLAS). "Descartes" signs the editorial. "Descartes" is the pseudonym Perón has used for years ("He wrote under the name Perón, so I return the favor.") In the editorial, Perón adopts the banners of the OLAS conference held in Havana and concludes, "Today a pacifist revolutionary is something akin to a vegetarian lion."

The same Perón, who exalts violence as a right of the oppressed, earlier spoke to me at length about the possibilities of a pact with the United States to allow the legal return of Peronists to political life. Since the time of the contracts with the California Oil Company, Perón swings back and forth on the United States, between love and hate. During the Spanish summer of 1961, he made public a letter to President Kennedy: "In the Argentine Republic, if fraud and violence are not employed, Justicialismo [the Peronist party] will triumph. But if the reactionaries use trickery or force to block us from taking power, communism in one of its forms will be the winner." Perón has not stopped exploring the political uses of fear: "Imagine," he says, "if the Peronists see that the backwardness of the country is encouraged by the great Western powers who make common cause with the governments of the oligarchy. They may find the support offered by the other side attractive. Christian and Marxist philosophers are fighting over the world: you've got to hang yourself from one tree or the other."

9

Perón moved to front and center in Argentine history as a patriot who confronted imperialism: "Perón or Braden" was the slogan, nascent nationalist caudillo or U.S. ambassador. Against him conservatives and communists, radicals and socialists all closed ranks. "From the beginning the United States tried to stick a pole between our spokes," he said. "Think of a guy who has ants in his house. He'll get nowhere trying to kill them one by one, gathering them on a plate in his hand. No. He ought to go to the hole they're coming out of and put poison deep inside. That's what we did. We took substantive actions: we repatriated the foreign debt, we created the national merchant marine, we nationalized savings, we protected and encouraged industry that was genuinely Argentine. When I took power in 1946, I looked like a Christmas tree, my uniform covered with medals and ribbons. I told a million people in the Plaza de Mayo I'd cut off my right hand before I sign off on a loan. First the North Americans made us poor; then they discovered aid, which is nothing but speculation on ways to make us ever poorer. The ten years during which Argentina did without any U.S. aid was the only time the economy was in order. The United States was the center of the conspiracy against our government. Not only did they fail to help us, they did all they could to sink us."

Nevertheless, Perón tells me, "a few U.S. senators have come to see me, and we've talked a lot. Johnson is terribly worried about Argentina. He knows that Argentina is decisive in Latin America, and Johnson does not want another Vietnam. The war in Vietnam is costing them many dollars and many lives. They want peace in their rear guard. So we've talked quite a bit about this, and the senators have spoken about a possible agreement we might reach."

What agreement? I ask. "An agreement . . ." On what basis? "They would put the screws on Onganía to force him to hold free elections with our participation." In exchange for nothing? "The only condition is that I renounce any plan to return to office. But what do I care? At this stage of my life I'd rather be the patriarch of Peronism and nothing more. Let the young come forth."

And those senators, I ask, are they good friends? "Certainly," he says. "I have good friends all over the world. I'm also friendly with the Chinese. And with Fidel Castro, we have good relations with Fidel Castro. I'm a friend of Stroessner's and of the Brazilian nationalists and of all authentic revolutionaries everywhere."

(1967)

Guatemala in the
Barrels of Guns

We stop and I empty what's left in my canteen over my face. We've been walking, walking, and walking for several hours, up and down steep hills, cutting our way through the dense, humid forest with machetes. We are not far from the edge of a large lake. The first light announcing dawn reveals floating sails of mist that hang from the foliage like broad waving vines. I'm ashamed because I'm cold: even though the muscles in my legs are stiff, like fists, walking is better than trying to sleep with nothing to cover me and the sweat freezing on my body. My companions shed not a drop of sweat, and they feel neither sleepy nor cold.

Many times we've come down one mountain and climbed another. Finding this patrol would be no easy task; it's on a scouting mission far from its usual zone of operations. The guide, an Indian who never speaks, abandons us for a few moments: he climbs straight up to a summit, where the impenetrable brush closes around the tall trees, to get his bearings from the neighboring mountains. We light up cigarettes, my two companions, two guerrillas, and myself. We're sitting on fallen tree trunks in a small clearing. Someone tells a joke. I breathe out the smoke and discover that my eyelids will not close; perhaps because night has not yet left us and here, high up, the cold is still stronger than exhaustion.

The guide returns with good news. We have but an hour to go. We start walking again. At one point the Indian points vaguely to one side and says: "It's over there, close by." All I see is dense jungle. We continue walking in silence. Now we can see the sky in the east. It seems to be celebrating something. Something like its own sacrifice: it has opened its veins, it is morning.

Inside his tent, César Montes is reading Paul VI's encyclical *Populorum Progressio*. I glance at it: ". . . peasants are becoming aware of their unwarranted misery . . . the scandal of wounding disparities . . ." César winks at me: "The Pope is smarter than the Guatemalan right. Here he explains the causes of violence quite clearly."

Just a peek at the few official statistics will tell you. Those who accuse the guerrillas of firing the first shot not only conveniently forget that imperialism employed violence in 1954 to overthrow a peaceful nationalist and deeply popular revolution. They also forget—and this gross omission is hardly involuntary—how misery itself murders with impunity: of every ten thousand children born, twelve hundred die before they reach the age of four. Of those who live, nearly all are condemned to a life without schools or shoes or milk or Sundays or toys. Despite powerful military offensives in recent weeks, the guerrillas, far from being extinguished, have spread beyond their zones of control. Their loss of influence is only illusory; they are organizing new fronts elsewhere. Illiterate peasants and farm workers support their struggle not only because they can easily tune in Radio Havana on any receiver, but because of their own long experience of suffering and treason. A quart of milk costs the equivalent of two days' work for a peasant in Alta Verapaz; three days' work will buy a pound of meat.

Before he joined the guerrillas, Rocael was a soldier. He learned from experience, violently repressing student demonstrations. César Montes learned from experience too, but from the other side. Now the soldier and the student meet; they share common dangers and hopes; together they elude the clutch of death. Rocael is thirty-six, César twenty-five. "He's the oldest. He's even got rheumatism, right, Rocael?" Jokes are the inseparable companions of the guerrillas: they must take care of their joy, save it and renew it like the water in their canteens, like the necessary pinch of salt, or the bullets in their belts. As César says, "It's better to die happy, no?"

The commanders of the Rebel Armed Forces are all very young.

"Apple joined us in the mountains when he was seventeen."

"Apple?"

"Yes, we call him that because he's got rosy cheeks. Apple is now twenty, and he's the commander of the area north of the Sierra de las Minas, near Teculután. Camilo Sánchez is twenty-four, the same as Androcles. We call him that because he's just like a lion. They're also commanders in other zones."

"Are most of the guerrillas students?"

"No, no. In the mountains few of us are students. Most of the guerrillas are peasants from the zone of operations. In Apple's army there is not a single student."

César Montes is called El Chirís, a Guatemalan expression meaning "little boy." Short, skinny, with delicate features: "Don't ask me to put on a fearsome face for the photos, because no one would believe it," he says, smiling. A telegraphic history of a rebel: at thirteen, thrown out of a Catholic school, explodes with anger at the fall of the revolutionary government of Jacobo Arbenz; at eighteen, student demonstrations, unarmed school chums shot down, jail for the first time; at twenty, the die is cast, the challenge accepted, violence chosen, it's off to the mountains—walk with clenched teeth until you faint without letting out a complaint or asking for a break. At twenty-four, he was already a commander of one of America's most important guerrilla movements. Yon Sosa, then commander of another of the FAR's guerrilla fronts, says even the snakes respect El Chirís. He fools the soldiers by sleeping in the belly of an alligator. The previous chief of the guerrilla army FAR [Revolutionary Armed Forces], Luis Augusto Turcios, was also a legendary character to whom the peasants attributed the virtues of a phantom. (He was twenty-four and hot-blooded, and he learned guerrilla fighting from the Yankees, who taught him how to combat it at Fort Benning in Columbus, Georgia. The dictator Peralta Azurdia put a price on his head, and he put a price on the head of Peralta Azurdia. Since he rebelled in 1960, he had escaped death a thousand times; absurdly, death caught up to him when his car caught on fire on the highway.)

César Montes tells me, "The guerrillas are essentially struggling farmers. We raise one fundamental banner, with one principal demand: 'Land to the Tiller,' in one form or another. We seek different solutions for different regions, different problems. What's clear is that both the *minifundio* [small peasant land-holding] and the *latifundio* [large unproductive land-holding] have done a great deal of damage to Guatemala." Yon Sosa, known as "El Chino," believes that machine guns, rifles, and grenades are not the principal weapons in the mountains; they are but the means for securing contact with the peasants. The principal weapon is the word, and the best defense is the support of the people. "The peasants are the eyes and ears of the guerrillas," El Chino likes to say. "We are always aware of what the enemy is up to, and the enemy never knows what we're up to. They would have to destroy the entire population to defeat us. But before that happens, we'll have turned the enemy into dust."

"Armed propaganda" meetings play an important role in the struggle of both guerrilla fronts, the Rebel Armed Forces and the November 13 Movement: the guerrillas enter a village, they occupy it for a few hours, explain the reasons for the revolution, and organize clandestine resistance cells. The November 13

Movement also sets up peasant committees in each village, which operate almost above ground. The FAR does not, believing that makes the peasants an easy target. "Armed propaganda," says César Montes, "has achieved a lot in bringing the revolution to the peasants. When we took Panzós in the Kekchí Indian zone, for example, first we occupied the military post, where we got an MG34 machine gun. Then a Kekchí-speaking guerrilla began to speak over a loudspeaker at the town hall. Indians who had been frightened by the shooting and had hidden in the woods or in their homes heard the words of the revolution in their own language and began to come out."

"What did you promise them—land?"

"We didn't promise them anything. We only promised them struggle. We exhorted them to struggle for their rights, for their needs."

César Montes goes on talking while everyone shares the canned food we brought in our knapsacks. Every so often a cough interrupts the dialogue. César has quite a cold. He's got a fever, but we have to keep moving. The right to get sick is not the only right that guerrillas lose in the mountains: yesterday the men of this patrol ate nothing but wild greens boiled with salt. In a few days, who knows?

"Look at eastern Guatemala now," he says. "Despite fierce repression, Zacapa and Izabal are in the vanguard of the revolution. And take note that there is no agricultural proletariat there, just small property owners and middlemen who rent land. Nevertheless, right now they are resisting the largest military offensive yet. Why? Thanks to armed propaganda. It was thanks to armed propaganda that the peasants joined the struggle. We have militia who fight with us by night and till the soil by day."

In the minds of Guatemalans, nostalgia for their own revolution lives on, the burning memory of the achievements that the CIA quashed in 1954 with Castillo Armas and the other rented heroes. That defeat, the blood and tears, became a launching pad for new rebellions. The peasants haven't forgotten the agrarian reform destroyed by the invasion: César Montes tells them that his struggle is nothing more than the continuation by new means of the same revolutionary process. The guerrillas know they are not some exotic incident in the history of their country; rather, they're a chapter of a story that began before their arrival in the Sierra de las Minas. The reality that President Méndez Montenegro is a prisoner of the army, incapable of anything, helped convince many simple people of the simple truth that the guerrillas incarnate and spread: in Guatemala, only through violence can land and freedom be won. That is why most of the armed left is made up of peasants.

Méndez Montenegro promised agrarian reform. He did nothing but sign an authorization for landowners to bear arms—which they tend to use against peasants. He promised tax reform. In the end businessmen were the ones who decided who had to pay taxes and how much: no one and nothing, excepting the consumer. He promised that the rich would be less rich so that the poor could be less poor. But a congressman of his own party led the opposition to a ("communist!") bill for a 1 percent tax on landed property. The coffee oligarchy, owners of enormous plantations, is as untouchable as the coupon clippers of Wall Street who multiply the value of their investments in Guatemala in less time than it takes a cock to crow. On the other side of the same coin, the average Guatemalan is poorer today than he was a decade ago, when he was already *very* poor.

While twenty-two farms average 23,000 hectares each, 270,000 farms cover little more than *one* hectare each. Just outside the capital city on the way to the highlands, Indians chew away at the mountainsides and gulches with their rudimentary implements, digging among the rocks, pulling from the exhausted soil of their minuscule plots the grain of wheat or corn that they then grind by hand on a stone. There are a total of six agronomists and thirty-four mills for more than half a million Indian families who cultivate the weather-beaten lands of the western highlands. From among the men, women and children of these families come the cheap field hands for the cotton and coffee harvests in the great haciendas of the south. Each year Indians spend months there for the harvest; they return with a few cents and perhaps malaria or tuberculosis. *Latifundio* and *minifundio*, rich land, poor people: only 15 percent of the arable land is cultivated. There are no roads in Alta Verapaz where trucks or even carts can pass. The large landowners don't need them: it's cheaper to bring out the coffee on the backs of Indians.

This is the same country, without housing or drinking water or schools or hospitals, that occupies a "place of honor" in the State Department's rolls for having "joined the United States in helping South Vietnam, by sending medical supplies."

A dry whistle or a human voice imitating a birdsong. The conversation gets interrupted frequently by long minutes of silence and tension, fingers on triggers. "Was that a gunshot?" "No, a branch." The lookouts take note of the smallest strange movement, any suspicious sound and they may have to get going. Here, at the bottom of a deep cleft between two mountains, the far-off echo of a cypress punished by an ax could be confused with a gunshot; a little animal makes the foliage tremble in the same way a soldier would.

César Montes spreads out an Esso map. He shows me the Indian territories of the north and west where guerrillas are beginning to organize, using different methods from those employed in Zacapa. "It's not something you can do artificially, look at a map and say, 'Here or here we should start a guerrilla war.' No. An armed group must act where the situation is most explosive, where the people are living in a situation that may be politically unclear, but has reduced them to the level of animals struggling to survive, as is now the case in many parts of Guatemala."

Some guerrillas clean their rifles; others bury the cans and papers from the meal, and spread out the ashes of the fire; others converse in low voices. Someone comes back from the stream with several full canteens. César Montes keeps talking: "We know that the Indians, who make up half the population, will be the ones to decide the fate of the revolution in this country. But the work is slow, tedious, difficult. For four centuries the 'ladinos,' which is what we call mestizos and whites, have earned the distrust of the Indians. And U.S. intervention is also an obstacle, disguised as Peace Corps and religious missions parallel to U.S. military activities. As Turcios used to say, we know that the peasant question in Guatemala will only be resolved with the integration of Indians, through struggle, into the nation's political life. And that is where we must put our emphasis. The guerrilla army of the Sierra de las Minas is made up of Indians from the Verapaces, Alta and Baja Verapaz, and of peasants from other regions. We have Indian revolutionary leaders, like Emilio Román López, whom we called Pascual, killed by the army not long ago. He was a very influential leader in the Verapaces."

When Turcios died, Pascual became the second commanding general of the FAR. He was a Protestant, an evangelist. "All the peasant comrades you see here in this camp," says César, "are Indians and Catholics, fervent Catholics. The fact that a few communists like myself are part of the FAR does not mean that our movement is the armed wing of any party, especially of the PGT [Partido Guatemalteco del Trabajo, the orthodox Communist party]. We're not anybody's army. Ours is a broad patriotic movement with a simple program: that we Guatemalans rule ourselves without any foreign intervention, military, economic, or political. We organize people for revolutionary war: the guerrillas are the seed of the great people's army. We don't separate the political from the military; the military leadership is also the political leadership. Separating the two has led to serious errors in other countries. We want our men to be capable not only of defending their ideals and arguing in their favor, but also of taking to the trenches to make those ideals a reality."

Walking with César through the camp, I glance at the guerrillas' weapons: a couple of Thompson .45-caliber machine guns,
several Belgian Brownings and a few Swedish and German au-
tomatics, Garand rifles from World War II and a few M-1
carbines, the legendary Colt .45s. "The army claims frequently
that it captures our weapons and kills our people. But they've
never been able to show a single piece of our weaponry that is
Cuban or Czech or Chinese or Soviet. Neither have they been
able to exhibit the body of a single foreign soldier from our
ranks. Our arms don't come from Cuba as the army says, but
from the army itself. We take them during operations, or we
buy them with money we get from kidnappings or expropria-
tions of exploiters hated by the people. Both soldiers and officers
sell their weapons. If these officers are capable of selling out
their country, why shouldn't they be capable of selling their
arms?"

By night bombs shake the city, by the light of day right-wing
terrorists shoot up people and houses, more than five hundred
men have been threatened with death, and the papers supply
their readers with a daily quota of mutilated or burned bodies
that turn up at the roadside or floating in the waters of the Río
Motagua: most of these faces without features, disfigured by
torture, will never be identified. In the Gualán region, for example, no one fishes: too many bodies got caught in the *tapexco*
dikes they use to trap the fish. Hunting "communists" is practiced with a fury reminiscent of Indonesia, although of course
on a smaller scale. A presidential sash crosses Julio César Montenegro's chest, but behind the facade of a civilian regime rules
a military dictatorship. Often, members of the governing party
end up among the guerrillas that the army claims to have killed
in combat. Eleven leaders of Méndez Montenegro's party who
were captured by the military police in Sanarate turned up full
of bullets and with their faces burned. A wave of terror has

arisen from the right in this year officially designated "the year of peace": the peace of cemeteries, as we can see. The terrorist groups come from the army and operate with its protection. Their slogan: "A communist seen is a communist dead." And they fail to differentiate between communists and those members of the ruling party or right-wingers who have liberal scruples: union activism or democratic beliefs or youth itself may be enough to get one threatened and killed by the NOA (New Anticommunist Organization), a group of murderers who publicly announce that they will cut off the left hands and cut out the tongues of their enemies—and they do.

It's not poetic license that leads such terrorists to declare in their communiqués that they operate "together with the glorious army of Guatemala." Like the assassination teams that operate in Vietnam, these groups carry out part of what the U.S. Green Berets taught the Guatemalan military about exterminating guerrillas. The attacks and murders, the systematic terror, are synchronized with a military campaign to "circle and annihilate" launched at the end of last year against the FAR and the November 13 Movement. They've raised a "security perimeter" around the villages to isolate the revolutionary combatants and harass them until they perish in the mountains. The armed forces' "civic action" plans provide not only for the elimination of enemies and suspects, but for demagoguery as well: they hand out powdered milk, medicine, and promises to the peasants in the zones of guerrilla influence. "You've got to have the guerrillas close by to get drinking water," a peasant from Izabal told me with a sense of humor, or of reality.

One of the FAR guerrillas killed in the last military campaign was Otto René Castillo, considered Guatemala's finest young poet. His body was found burned in Zacapa. He had lived in exile ("exile is a very long avenue along which sadness walks"), and he returned to his country to fight. Prophet of his own sacrifice, he wrote:

> Come my people, let's go, I'll walk with you,
> I'll go down to the depths where you send me,
> I'll drink your bitter chalices,
> I'll go blind so that you may have eyes,
> I'll go mute so that you may sing,
> I'll have to die so that you never die.

But the guerrillas carry on. "The army and its Yankee advisers act mechanically," César Montes recounts. "They've read in Mao's books that the guerrillas are to the people as the fish to the sea. They know that on their weekend holidays, when they take fish out of water, the fish die. They think they can isolate the guerrillas the same way. You can fool some of the people all the time, or all of the people some of the time. But you can't fool all the people all the time. The peasants need land and they don't have it. They need housing, but the government builds it for the military. The fury that will let loose in Guatemala, that is letting loose, has been building for centuries."

The vice president himself, Don Clemente Marroquín Rojas, told me in an informal interview that once a squadron of U.S. planes, flown by U.S. pilots, left Panama, dropped napalm on a mountainside in Guatemala supposedly infected with guerrillas, and returned to Panama without even landing in the country. Rocael and another guerrilla now tell me of their own experience: they saw the napalm fall on a nearby mountain; groves of trees and grassy meadows burned for three or four days; the fiery gelatin burned trees to the roots, scorched the earth, left the stones black like charcoal. The bombs go off like fireworks and then spill over: a foamy red-hot flood flows down the mountainside or slips down the rivers setting fire to whatever it touches. "We were off to the west," Rocael says, "in Teculután, and we saw huge flames leaping up in the east. Did that meadow ever burn! We saw it all from a distance of about three hundred meters, in a well-protected gulch. An army plane dropped the bombs. The explosion was, you might say, softer than most bombs. A few days later in the woods by Alejandría near Río Hondo, eight of us guerrillas found five bodies totally charred in the middle of the blackened vegetation."

Thanks to napalm the authorities discovered the body of Ronald Hornberger at the edge of Teculután. The fire started downstream and burned its way up the banks. It left the humid rectangle of the grave clearly marked. "Hornberger was a Green Beret, a veteran of the Vietnam War," César Montes says. "He showed up claiming to be a journalist looking for material for a story. He was very sure of himself. We talked with him for several days in the mountains. As time went by, he mentioned names and addresses in the capital, which we checked out a day or two later. None of those people knew him or had even heard of him. He also lied about where he'd left his pack. He was only interested in the military aspects of our struggle, and not the political motivations behind it. All of his questions were quite specialized in military matters. His outfit had everything, and he was a star at handling all sorts of weaponry. He said his gear was a present for us. We executed him. Around his waist beneath his shirt he had a nylon cord, the ones the Green Berets use to strangle people."

A small number of Green Berets now operate in Guatemala. It's one of the many ways that imperialism intervenes in this country, many and visible, as in so many other places of the painful territory of Latin America. "In our tactics," explains César Montes, "we can't emphasize enough imperialism's current or future role. We know that sooner or later they will intervene massively with troops as they did years ago in Nicaragua against Sandino, and recently in the Dominican Republic, and as they are doing in Vietnam. We take U.S. intervention into account, and that gives our struggle a different character." In this context, contacts with other Latin American guerrilla

movements are decisive. Such contact began at the Tricontinental Congress held in Havana, and has successfully developed
since. "A large-scale imperialist intervention will come one day.
Then we cannot forget that Latin America is one. We will then
have the right to open our arms to revolutionaries of other
countries. Guatemala is not the Dominican Republic; we're not
surrounded by ocean. They can't isolate us: we have borders
with Mexico, El Salvador, and Honduras."

It's getting dark. Today the quetzal bird that has visited the
guerrillas at this hour for the past few days misses his appointment. Its white breast and beautiful plumage had glided through
the bit of sky visible from the camp. The quetzal is Guatemala's
national symbol. They say it lost its voice when the Maya were
defeated by the Spanish. They also say that it did not lose its
voice, that ever since that defeat it has refused to sing.

(1967)

Chronicle of Torture
and Victory

When the Peronist Youth held their convention in Montevideo at the beginning of 1967, unanimously elected to the post of honorary president was a member not present. Jorge Rulli was a prisoner at the time, suffering in a hospital bed. The police had torn him to pieces somewhere in the province of Buenos Aires during seventy hours of continuous torture. Rulli has just been released, and now he tells me what happened. It is the chronicle of a double victory.

This is the second time that Jorge Rulli has told his story. The first time, in the hospital, his lawyers heard it. Now his voice falters, he interrupts himself, he falls silent for minutes at a time, and he says: "It hurts to remember." The man I met a couple of years ago has lost thirty kilos in jail. Not only is he skinnier, his hands tremble when he serves me coffee, he bumps into me when he gets up, he can't bend over to pick up a fallen lighter, he has to watch what he eats and drinks. But he doesn't want to play the victim. He is aware that this is the price of his convictions.

He had been jailed before for three years, beginning in 1960. He had been fired from jobs again and again because of some accusation or a strike. He had decided it wasn't so bad that a long jail term annulled his exams, because he was no longer interested in studying to be a veterinarian anyway. To make a living once he'd gotten out of jail, he worked as a messenger and poll-taker, door to door, and as a journalist. One afternoon he received a call from the Buenos Aires provincial police. They wanted him to cover a "very special" procedure in Ramos Mejía for the magazine he was working for. Rulli went. It was an ambush. They were waiting for him across from a certain house on Pazo Street: federal police agents without epaulets or badges on their shirts, or uniformed coats or hats, or holsters. Rulli ran as soon as the first shots rang out. The bullets hit close by. The chase lasted fifteen blocks through a working-class neighbor-hood, a maze of streets and houses separated by empty lots. The residents came out to watch; a bunch of kids ran after Rulli, shouting. They came out of the woodwork, thrilled by the noise, and they made it easy for the police to follow his trail. He ran for a bus pulling out of a stop, but it almost hit him and he couldn't climb aboard. The kids wouldn't leave him, and un-intentionally they kept him from losing himself in a crowd or hiding in a house.

I'd been shot in one leg, but I hadn't noticed. You know, in combat there are cases of guys who lose an arm in an assault and only notice it twenty meters later. I think it was the heat of the chase that kept me from feeling it. The bullet had gone through my thigh and I didn't see or feel anything. I did feel terribly tired. To continue running was an unbearable sacrifice. My pace slowed by itself. The police were a block away, then half a block. Ex-hausted, I began to walk. They were after me in cars and on bicycles. They grabbed me behind a truck. The first to reach me was an officer. He tore my head open five times with the butt of his pistol. I sort of passed out, I was bathed in blood. They loaded me into the truck and I still hadn't noticed the hole in my leg.

Then they put him in a taxi and he starts to vomit. They take him to the hospital in Ramos Mejía and then to a clinic for surgery in Haedo. The police insult him and threaten to kill him. In Haedo, the doctors pinch him and beat the soles of his feet to see if he can still feel anything. In a flash of lucidity between vomiting and faints and pain and blood, Rulli screams out his name, pleads that they take down his name. That is perhaps what saves him. Felipe Vallese, kidnapped one night by the police, had disappeared without a trace.

The doctors promised to take care of me. But an orderly took me on a stretcher with two doctors, and told a bunch of policemen at the exit: "Here he is. If you like you can take him on the stretcher."

They put him in a police van. The seven policemen who ride with him are laughing about what awaits him: "You're going to the machine, kid. You are going to repent for a lot of things." They arrive at the Ramos Mejía police station. They go to the officers' clubhouse, a small room with a chair in the middle. Some twenty agents surround him there, nearly all of them without uniform. The "ball game" begins, question after question with no time to answer, threats, some blows. Where were you going, what were you doing, who are you, names, we want names, you killed a policeman, admit that you killed a policeman. They are all standing around him. They push the chair he is sitting in while they hit him. They don't let him speak. But Rulli has understood that the federal police have given him over to the provincial police, telling them that he killed an agent. It's an invention equivalent to an order to kill him: the esprit de corps demands it. The fallen comrade must be avenged.

I felt surrounded, depressed, very lost. That was it. Very lost. And nevertheless, at the same time, I felt very strong. I mean that I felt a lot of mysticism, some sort of political fanaticism, or religious fanaticism. Although at the same time physically I felt alone and lost and hopeless, certain that I was headed for the cattle prod.

Because I knew what the charge of killing a policeman means when you're alone with the police. I tell you, I felt very strong because I realized that I had to recover, to recover my dignity, to gain ground to be strong later on, for what was to come. I didn't think that I could stand it physically, you know? I had to put an end to that manhandling. So with the audacity of desperation I shouted: "Hold on!" And I told them that I would only speak to the chief. I told them that just as they belonged to an army of repression, I belonged to an army, the army of national liberation. It was crazy, but the "ball game" came to an end. One of them, who turned out to be the chief, jumped on me and started slapping my face. He was hysterical. He screamed: "Braggart! You'll see what that's going to cost you! So you are going to threaten me! Threaten us!" All of a sudden, he stopped. His face was all red. They left.

On the way out they give the order to begin "softening him up." It is already midnight. "Soften him up," the officer tells four agents, "because this one is going to the cattle prod. Don't leave any marks—that will come later." Rulli is in his underwear, with his shirt torn and his hands tied with bandages, barefoot. Blood flows from his bandaged head.

As always, there were "hard ones" and "soft ones." It was as if they were arguing among themselves. One told me: "How could you expect anything from Perón, fight for that monster." While the other one screamed that I was a son of a bitch for being a Peronist. "Don't be stupid," one said. "Don't let them use you. Perón is very comfortable over there, living well while you sacrifice yourself here." And the other insisted that all Peronists are sons of bitches, terrorist murderers of poor policemen who leave their families behind. "No, no," said a third, "not all Peronists are alike, no, I was once a Peronist too. But this guy, he's no Peronist, he's a terrorist, a murderer, that's what he is." And the first insisted, "If you are a Peronist, why do you expose yourself this way? Don't you see that you're being a useful idiot?" While they talked they were hitting me in the neck with the sides of their hands, in the kidneys, in the jaw, they hit me constantly, always catching me by surprise. When I expected a blow on one side, it came from the other, when I turned around I got it from behind. They never stopped talking for a second. Nor did they stop beating me. They tried all the angles to break my political will. All the torture was for that. They sought to break my morale. They didn't want information.

Rulli manages to tell them that they are not going to get anything out of him. "Do you know where we are going to take you?" "Yes, of course I know." "Why?" "Because I'm not the only one. This has happened to a lot of people, and I know what is going to happen to me. It'll be just like they did with Felipe Vallese. Because I'm not going to last either." They tell him not to worry, that he will handle all that they want him to handle: "That's why we have doctors on hand." Then an officer comes in. "Listen, chief," they tell him, "do you know what he is saying? That the only thing he asks of God is that he die to implicate us and get us all indicted." A new rain of insults falls on Rulli, a new rain of blows.

They blindfolded me and put me in a van. I was lying on the floor with their feet on me. I realized that we were going down 25 de Mayo Avenue because we went the length of the carnival parade. You could hear people laughing, the chorus of the street musicians, the sounds of noisemakers and horns. They told me: "Listen to the people having a good time. This is the last carnival you're going to hear in your life." This hurt. When they took me out of the car, I stepped on grass. I thought we were close to the train tracks. I prepared myself to be shot.

They go into a house. "Don't make any noise—you'll wake the kids," say the same voices. "What this one doesn't know is

that we're not the same ones as before," one comments loud
enough to hear. They drag him to a bed. It's like floating on
air. They lay him out on elastic and they tie down his arms and
legs, first covering his wrists and ankles with rubber bands. They
tear his shirt the rest of the way. Rulli feels them tie a string on
the second toe of his right foot; at the other end of the cable
is the cattle prod. They turn on a radio with the volume up full.
They spray water on his chest, near his heart, and then the doors
to hell open.

*I couldn't scream because they'd put a pillow or a rag, I don't
know which, in my mouth. They put the juice on my heart, in
my crotch, on my genitals. Those electric shocks are like bites,
they rip your skin, it seems like they're tearing out pieces of flesh.
I could distinguish their voices because at moments like that your
senses are so sharp. I kept track of the four of them constantly,
every moment, as if I were watching them. My nerves were raw.
The one giving me the shocks was crazed, a hyena. He laughed
the whole time. Before he began he said, "Too bad we have to
go right to the shocks. How I would have liked to bust your ass
first, the way you're tied up so nicely." He repeated it several
times in different ways. That is the worst humiliation you could
imagine. It was several months before I could tell anyone. It kept
coming back to me in nightmares afterward in the hospital, like
an obsession.*

One of the others works the radio and the electric generator.
A third is in constant touch by telephone with the police in the
capital, who are torturing someone else at the same time. The
fourth, the boss, sits on the edge of the bed and asks the questions, writes down the responses. Rulli refuses to answer. "Aren't
you ashamed to be doing this?" They give him the shock, wait
a few seconds for him to catch his breath and his voice, they
ask, give him another shock, and on it goes: Who killed the
policeman? Who stole the gun? Who stole the car? Take re-

sponsibility for it. Admit it. Give us names, a list of names. What were you doing? Who worked with you? Who are your contacts? Where do you meet? Where were you going? Where were you coming from? A white Peugeot, you had a white Peugeot, admit it. Who did this? Who did that? Who shot at the base? A red car, your comrade says there was a red car. Talk, you ought to. Talk, the other guy is talking. The other guy told us everything. Don't be stupid. Don't play the martyr. Son of a bitch, talk.

They were looking for a weak point with that made-up story about the dead policeman. If I showed any sign of weakness, it was going to go on and on and I wouldn't be able to hold on. If I admitted to any stupid little thing, it would lead to other questions to make me give them names and information about the movement. Now I can't believe how calm I was. Something incredibly calm deep inside me allowed me to think in the midst of all that craziness. When I was in jail, I spoke with many people who had been tortured. Some people try not to think about the possibility, they can't face it. But I knew it could happen to me at any moment. I learned that someone in the hands of the police can defend himself, he can make a plan and carry it out. It is possible to trick the enemy, to struggle with him, to fight against him even from a torture table. I felt the presence of those subhumans trying to break me, to break my consciousness, and I measured everything. I knew everything, I was more lucid than I had ever been. I knew that my relationship with my wife would be over. My relationship with my own daughter would be over. My relationship with my comrades. I wouldn't be able to look any of them in the face again. And as a man I would never again be good for anything. That offered me a lot of protection. I discovered that by keeping quiet I had a lot to gain. And that if I talked, I would lose everything.

Rulli speculates about how tired they might be. The interrogation can't go on forever. He tries to win a few precious

seconds. Several times he announces that he will talk. The torture stops. Then he hesitates: "Well . . . so, what do you want
me to talk about?" The torture begins again.

*I made up a list of names. Not one Pérez or González. I twisted
the last names of people I went to high school with, spelling one
with a double t, another with a t at the end, I made up strange
names to confuse them. Or I took people I knew who had nothing
to do with politics and I described them, switching names and
faces. I kept track of each one so that I wouldn't forget later on,
because I had to repeat the descriptions several times. You should
never describe a person without thinking of someone in particular.
Even so, at times I got mixed up, I got things incredibly confused.
I made up some other stories, I talked about being in the leadership
of a union where I had really been in the opposition. I interrupted
myself and said, "I can't talk anymore, I can't tell you anything
else, I'm a skunk." And I gained a bit of time. I would tell them,
"All this about confessing, I don't want you to write it down,
just listen, because otherwise everyone will hate me for squealing."
I'd mumble, "I won't sign anything." They'd give me more shocks.
"Okay, okay, I'll sign." And then I'd make up another story. I
was always thinking, they're going to get tired, they're going to
get tired. The electricity made me jump like crazy. The contortions
made my tied hands swell up to the bursting point, my torso
whacking down on the bed was more than my spine could stand:
I got a slipped disk.*

The contractions knock the wind out of the torture victim.
Rulli deliberately exaggerates their effects: every time they put
the shock on his heart, he stays stiff, without breathing, back
arched. "Take it away, take it away, he's not breathing." They
take off his mask and start pounding on his stomach. Rulli lets
out his breath as if he were just waking up. But soon this little
trick becomes impossible: they start giving him shocks on his
testicles every time, to see if he reacts. In the end, he doesn't

react. He isn't trying to lose his breath. The shocks don't make him jump anymore. They untie him, he falls, he grabs onto the bed as he falls. Then he notices it is an iron bed with V-shaped legs, like the ones the police use.

Afterward, I spent two nights and two days in a small room at the station, surrounded by a dozen agents who took turns beating me, insulting me, threatening me, humiliating me: "I don't know how these federal agents can be such imbeciles, capturing this one alive. Instead of a bullet in the leg, they should have put one in his head. I wish I'd been in on it." They'd spit on my chest and in my face. They'd pull out their guns in front of me and Click! they'd pull the trigger. "Oh, so you're afraid." They loaded and unloaded their guns all the time. One took a knife and jumped on me while another held my arms. He grabbed my balls and started playing with the knife, telling me he was going to slice them off. They didn't let me urinate. Nor did they give me anything to drink or eat. I was going crazy with thirst.

He gets out by chance. Led by a tip, his wife shows up at the station, takes the police by surprise. They don't manage to deny that he's there. They decide to take him to Buenos Aires, to hand him over to Federal Headquarters: "If you believe in God," the chief warns him, "pray, because the best that could happen to you is that you die before you get there." They force him to sign a confession dated three days previous. The judge intervenes in time; they take him out of Ramos Mejía.

In the San Martín hospital, the doctors were letting me die. I threw everything up, even mineral water. The burns from the cattle prod weren't noted on my clinical chart. Every day I vomited more bile, because I didn't have anything else. I'd regain consciousness every so often. One day I heard the doctor say, "This one's here for being a Peronist. He's a terrorist pretending to be sick to find a chance to escape. His family brings him things to

*make him vomit, some drug." On the tenth day, my comrades
were able to get a doctor friend to look at me. He did a urine
test and a blood test. Then he did it again, because he thought
he'd made a mistake. But the second result also showed my urea
level to be six, when the normal is point three, and eight grams
of potassium. "Get him out of there," he told my wife, "or he's
going to die." They took me to the Italian hospital, to a kidney
machine.*

He pees blood. His left eye gets infected; he loses it. The
infection moves into his right eye. Neuritis on the soles of his
feet makes walking impossible. The muscles from his waist down
are also completely atrophied. His kidney is worthless; he survives thanks to the kidney machine he's hooked up to for twelve
hours a day. Twenty-five comrades give him blood. Everything
in and out of tubes. He gets his nourishment through an IV;
he urinates through a catheter. He can't bend because of the
slipped disk. His entire abdomen is hard, like a board. From
the donated blood he gets hepatitis. Three times the police try
to take him from the hospital without the doctors' permission:
"Get dressed. Let's go." The members of the hospital workers'
union stop them. The fourth time the police drag him out half
dressed, to the Villa Devoto hospital.

*In the Italian hospital, members of the Peronist Youth had taken
turns guarding me. The different groups shared the shifts so that
each one was responsible for one day a week. They never left me
alone, day or night. It was growing pressure from the movement
that saved me. The solidarity of my comrades. Left behind were
all the confrontations we had had with each other, with other
groups in the movement, and with the comrades from other organizations. My experience taught me that we can't let small things
divide us. It was a rich experience.*

In a courtroom filled with his comrades, the appeals court decides to set Rulli free for lack of evidence. Rulli regains his freedom: the day he gets out of jail, his wife, her nerves shot, has to go into a sanatorium.

When they "softened me up" before taking me into the torture chamber, I told the police that we were struggling for the oppressed, for them, those poor men capable of torturing people for a miserable wage. I told them that history was on our side, the side of the oppressed. They laughed, and one of them said, "This time you got caught for being an idealist. But next time it'll be for being a thief." He was saying: We're going to break you; if we catch you in a robbery it will be because you're stealing for yourself. He was saying that my own comrades would reject me, that I would leave there turned into a delinquent or an informer. For the same reasons, the French in Algiers raped the wives of the guerrillas who were fighting in the mountains. I knew, definitively, that the police torture not for information, but to break you.

To choose dignity is like choosing death. When they pull him out of the van, Rulli realizes that he is not going to get out alive, and he swears he'll die with dignity. Paradoxically, that is what allows him to save his life with dignity.

(1968)

God and the Devil in the Favelas of Rio de Janeiro

At midnight the catacomb groaned, *a meianoite a catatumba gemeu: quem estava vivo morreu, quem estava morto nasceu.* This is the "great moment," the resurrection of the damned: "Rise up whoever is sitting, come alive whoever is dead." The damned sing, howl, dance, tremble, drink to the feverish rhythms and the thunder of drums; cane liquor runs and blood flows from the sacrificed roosters and goats.

Hours before, the gods and devils came down and possessed their devotees, entered into them, rode them hard; their passionate embrace brings howls of pain and pleasure from women who shake violently, faces rigid with ecstasy, and spin on the ground, or leap as if tossed in the air by the hand of an invisible giant. When the convulsions let up and a bell rings out from the altar, it means that the bodies have changed identities. The "horses" have been tamed. The crisis of possession has passed, because the woman who now receives a headdress of long colored feathers is no longer herself: she is Ogum Break-Bush, a Saint George of the jungle. She no longer suffers the violence of the trance; now she dances softly, smokes an immense cheroot, gives blessings and offers advice and prescriptions to the faithful in need of comfort, vengeance, immunity, and good luck. And this other is Jurema, the goddess of the jungle, and that one is Xangô, the young owner of thunder, and the one over there is the Caboclo of the Sun and Moon. Iemanjá, goddess of the waves of the sea, has also come down, and so have other divinities: the White Feather and the Black Mountains and the Spring, the Seven Arrows, the Seven Stars, the Seven Crossroads. Other Indian and peasant saints descend: Viramundo, Caboclo do Vento, Flor do Dia, and Boiadero, the herdsman who, with his rope, lassos all evil and draws it toward the desert where he lives. The spirits of the first owners of the land of Brazil wander about the air and sea. They are gods of nature, assimilated into African divinities from Angola and the Congo, which in turn have been fused with Catholic saints; or they are aboriginal versions of the inhabitants of hell.

Once possessed, the *filha do santo* becomes the divinity's instrument. The tone of her voice and the intensity of her gaze change: once sickened by tobacco, she smokes with relish; once satisfied by water, she drinks *cachaça*. Julia becomes Ogum, or rather his horse. *During* the trance, Ogum speaks: "I mount Julia and she trots." *After* the trance, Julia speaks: "When Ogum comes down, I lose consciousness. Ogum Break-Bush arrives and he's like a bell that covers me. I'm the clapper of the bell, he moves me, the music comes out."

This place is an open *terreiro* on the densely forested side of the Dois Irmâos Rock, between the jungle and one of the bluffs of Rio de Janeiro. The ceremony continues by the light of the moon and the surrounding campfires. Powerful echoes reach down to where lights blink at the edge of the sea: their rhythm habitually accompanies the city's sleep. Night after night, voices and drums vibrate from the weeds and the favelas, frequently lasting until daybreak.

EXU HAS TWO HEADS

Now Dona Maria, the principal priestess, a black woman with broad hips, large breasts, and embers in her eyes, dances around a small circle of stone in the center of the *terreiro*. With her

arms raised, she stops in front of a young man. The man falls
to his knees; disorderly and vigorous, the chorus chants:

> . . . *todo mundo bebeu,*
> *todo mundo comeu,*
> *só eu fiquei sem nada.*
> (. . . everyone drinks,
> everyone eats,
> only I have nothing.)

From up high she dumps a glass of cane liquor over the head
of the young man. She rubs it into his hair with her fingers.
Then she smashes the glass on the stone. He must take off his
shoes and dance on the shards of glass. And then she dances
on the broken glass herself:

> . . . open the door to hell,
> now I want to see
> seventy-seven devils . . .

The men dance with bare torsos wrapped in palm leaves;
green swords seem to be sprouting from their bodies. The glow
from the fires illuminates the vast skirts of the women and gleams
on black skin soaked in sweat. The smell of tobacco smoke and
cane liquor is stronger than the purifying aromas of the vegetation. Dona Maria lets out a scream, she roars like a bull, whines
like a dog, she howls. She throws herself back, and as she falls
they wrap her in a white sheet. Then she crosses the *terreiro*
slowly, dragging herself on her thighs and her fists. She holds
two lit candles, which burn her arms and her mouth as she
moves. She snorts like a wounded animal, but no one can see
her face. She is Omulú who crawls, covered by the sheet-shroud.
Omulú, San Roque in Bahia, San Lazaro in Rio de Janeiro, in
the north lord of wounds, sores, and diseases, and here king of
caves and cemeteries. Omulú neither drinks nor smokes; the

foam of his mouth smells of the dead, though no one sees it. His face is a skull: whoever sees it seals his own death sentence.

> *Omulú dêêê* . . .
> *Senhor da terra*
> *Atotô Abuluaitê* . . .

The rhythm of the drums grows more frenetic. Soon to arrive are Exús, the devils, and their women, the queens of hell, the Pomba-giras. This is the most violent ecstasy of all: arms, tense as boards, finally beat on the chest; hands become stiff, like claws. He is the only divinity who does not "come down": Exú comes from the earth, and enters through the soles of bare feet:

> *Pelo pé, pelo pé,*
> *Pelo pé, que êle veio.*
> *Pelo pé, pelo pé,*
> *pelo pé, que êle vai.*

> (By foot, by foot,
> By foot, he came.
> By foot, by foot,
> By foot, he goes.

In *candomblé* ceremonies in Bahia, Exú gets thrown out or tricked into leaving and not causing trouble. In the *umbanda*, a form of *macumba* ("black magic") relatively institutionalized by the middle class, the rhythm is devised as a battle against Exú, the demon, and the result looks like a Catholic mass with epileptics. The *quimbanda*, on the other hand, "black line" *macumba*, is a religion of the damned, a means for self-affirmation and vengeance for the poor who eke out an existence in the favelas and the slums. Exú is their principal guest: the ceremonies are performed in his honor, people clamor for his presence and his favors. A cult of the Devil, yes. But this is a curious Devil, who embodies both heaven and hell at once, who is the lord of evil but also does good, and who, bicephalous, is simultaneously God, in his own way:

> Exú has two heads
> to look at his flock filled with faith:
> one is Satan from hell,
> the other is Jesus of Nazareth.

Exú is hated and feared in the tile-floored "line of God" temples of the *umbanda*, where bleachers are sometimes installed for tourists. He is venerated by the *quimbanda*, "line of the Devil," in *terreiros* open to the storms of the bluffs, or in miserable huts made of tin and wood where tourists do not go. Exú uses two colors, red and black (the colors of the most popular soccer team of Rio de Janeiro), and those colors also define his wives, the Pomba-giras: red, for the blood of goats and roosters sacrificed to give life and strength to the sick and the weak; black, for caves and cemeteries, indicating Exú's capacity to kill or "tie" a life to eternal misfortune.

Exú lives at the crossroads; the fig tree, condemned by Christ to bear no more fruit, is his favorite tree. There are numerous Exús, just as there are many Pomba-giras: Skull Exú, Ember Exú, Exú of the Seven Crossroads, Exú of the Shore, Pepper Exú, Velvet Exú, Seven Mountains Exú, Roadblock Exú:

> At the crossroads stands a King,
> a King who is Lord Roadblock.
> In the fig tree sits another,
> Mr. Lucifer and his Queen Pomba-gira.

On the street corners of Rio de Janeiro, at the point where paths cross, on the beach, or at the foot of certain dead fig trees, Exú has his "offices." Usually, you find flour, *dendê* oil, and rooster blood mixed in a clay bowl, cane liquor (*marafo*) poured out in the form of a cross, boxes of matches with crossed cheroots, and the head, feet, and wings of a black rooster with red feathers whose blood has been offered: everything for him to eat, drink, and smoke. But the offerings vary as much as the motives. For example, squares of black cloth and white candles are used to ask Exú to open a path that has been closed. A candle broken in two and pointing away from the crossroads is lit to derail enemy thoughts. At a feminine crossroad, marked with a +, Exú receives praise, support, promises, and requests. At a closed masculine crossroad, marked with a T, the offerings are to the queens of hell.

THE HOWL OF FORBIDDEN VOICES

Appeals to hell have become more and more frequent on the populous margins of Rio de Janeiro. Officially, nearly every Brazilian is a Catholic, and in fact even the most fervently devoted follower of Exú claims to be one, without a trace of insincerity. The cult of the *quimbanda*, very often hidden behind a "legal" *umbanda*, spreads everywhere and wins new converts every day. In innumerable small *terreiros* in the slums, the Devil is invoked and offered sacrifices, and the pagan cult of Afro-Brazilian gods escapes all the disciplinary straitjackets imposed in order to "domesticate" these dangerous blind forces. It is not by chance that after long periods of police persecution the *umbanda* has won a certain respectability that the *quimbanda* will not get and does not need. Some of the most important *umbanda* temples are run by retired generals and a vast array of middle-class professionals. In those temples the trances are controlled, no alcohol is drunk, no drums are heard, and the generals preach against witches, sin, immorality, and the contemporary world: "In Paris," I heard one say, "women go completely naked, wearing only a belt. A belt and hair and nothing else. This perverse world is condemned. Only one hundred and forty-four thousand people will survive, and the rest will be annihilated within thirty-one years. But it could happen today, or it could happen tomorrow. Sinners will be liquidated by fire;

they will all melt, as in Hiroshima. There is a planet coming toward the earth. There will be no escape for the perverse who call themselves 'modern,' like those husbands today who allowed their wives to leave the house because others came by and took them." This is the textual version of part of a sermon given by the retired general who is head of the *umbanda* temple in Meier, in Rio.

The characteristics of the poorest *terreiros* are very different. People belong to the "white line" or the "black line." They practice the *caboclo* cult of indigenous deities or the *pretos velhos* cult of the slaves of Bahia. There is no moral terrorism, and the work of Nature's forces is celebrated with joy. From the heights of heaven or from the depths of hell, gods come to *this* land to dance, eat, drink, smoke, make love, take vengeance, and perform miracles for those who need them. The "white line" and the "black line" of the *macumba* are practiced side by side without major problems; God and the Devil are of this earth, they understand that they are mutually necessary: "He who rules in the world is God . . .", a sagacious *pai de santo* (priest) told me, "but he who rules on earth is Exú."

THE BEAUTIFUL FIRES OF HELL

The immense majority of the poor have black skin. Black is the voice of this populous underworld of the damned that cries out in the *terreiros*:

> Power from Africa
> Power from Bahia
> power so divine
> come here.
> Come and help us.

African roots flower throughout Bahia in the land of Brazil. The original rites and gods are transformed, they become Brazilian: without a doubt, all or nearly all of these divinities of good and evil emerged on the coast of West Africa. But they moved through the centuries of Brazil and its successive realities and became the vengeful ghosts of bloodied slaves, exterminated Indians, peasants persecuted by drought and hunger, and all the innumerable humiliated, dispossessed and forgotten poor:

> . . . in the street of Bitterness
> that gave light to Cipriano
> because he worked all day,
> worked all day,
> all night,
> all year.

These are savage services, popular fiestas, acts of collective catharsis, exasperated expressions of freedom in which dance, song and drink are embraced ferociously:

> I'm dressed in feathers, my brother,
> but I don't ever pip.
> Whoever has *cachaça*, please,
> give me a little sip.

Not without self-compassion:

> Oh, Sandpiper,
> what a life, eh?
> Either drinking *cachaça*
> or falling by the way.

The gods are spoken to, the music calls them, the voices call them, and the gods invade women and men. They dance *inside* them, they *become* them, in a violent communication that tosses the children of the divinities about the earth. Appeals to Jesus Christ:

> Oxalá, my father,
> have pity on us,
> have pain.
> The trip around the world is long . . .

and to the forbidden forces:

> At the crossroad there are seven swords.
> One cuts the wind in the air,
> another cuts the waves in the sea,
> another is for those who have faith
> and the other four belong to Lord Lucifer.

Because:

> Oh, God is good
> and the Devil is not evil.
> Save us, God.
> Save us, Devil.
> And save this worthless black bum,
> standing on this cold earth.

In the rites of the Rio suburbs, Exú is the synthesis of all the invocations. Only Ogum, Saint George, the warrior saint, is said to have the power to control Exú's behavior, but he lets Exú do what he wants. He helps him, even sends him women:

> The bell of the little church
> goes ding-ding-dong.
> It rang out midnight
> and the rooster already crowed.
> The Lord Seven Crossroads
> is the owner of the Pomba-gira,
> a steady Gira sent him by Ogum.

God is reinvented, created in the image of a wicked reality and of innumerable inherited curses, by the wretched of this earth, generation after generation. What signs do they read in the sky of the favelas? These signs are earthly, and so they often belong to hell—hell as reality and as a destiny to be embraced:

> Oh, what a lovely fire,
> that which lights up hell . . .
> Oh, my lord of arms.
> Oh, they say that Exú is worth nothing
> but he is king,
> king of the seven crossroads,
> my lord.

The God of the pariahs is not the same God as the God of the system that makes them pariahs. At least, He is not *always* the same one. He is often a little bit the Devil, and sometimes He is nothing but the Devil:

> I am Exú! I am Exú!
> No one can beat me,
> but I can beat all.
> At my crossroads
> I am king.

They call on the arms of hell, the heaven of the excluded. For vengeance: put the name of the enemy in the mouth of a frog sewed shut with red and black thread. For protection and to transmit the potencies of life: use the spilled blood of animals sacrificed to Exú.

THE STRANGE CULT OF MARIA PADILHA

Pomba-gira, the dove that turns, the queen of hell, has several identities. One of them is Maria Padilha, born in the lower

depths of Rio. The cult spread so widely that life-size wax man-
nequins representing Maria Padilha are now commonly found
in the poor barrios of the north: high heels, silk stockings, a
short skirt slit open at the side to reveal her thigh, breasts
jumping from her blouse, necklaces and bracelets, heavy makeup
on her eyes and mouth, long doll's hair, grotesque smile, and a
filtered cigarette between two fingers sporting long red nails.
Of course, this is the deification of the prostitute, elevated to
the highest rank among the gods of the damned. Significantly,
the priestesses possessed by the spirit of Maria Padilha in the
terreiros are usually prostitutes in "real life." Her roars of laugh-
ter split the night; as soon as the trance is over, the queen of
hell demands expensive drinks and cigarettes. Like other divinities, during the ceremony she tends to requests, gives advice,
resolves problems; she also uses her particular charms to in-
tercede with the Devil to benefit those in need.

A curious vengeance of bodies on sale. Prostitution, as we
know, is a by-product of virtue. This society, in which everything
is bought and sold, hypocritically condemns the services of those
it uses to maintain its taboos intact and its moral code in force.
Prostitutes are produced like clothes: they are consumer goods,
used and discarded. These illiterate women, their lives so bitten
by humiliation and misery, know nothing of any rebellion that
could vindicate them as human beings in a different kind of
society, one that has no price for love. Instead, in a sort of
reverse exorcism, they project their own flesh onto a religious
plane. They make her in their own image, the same image that
the system made of them in order to use them and scorn them.
But note: this self-portrait is printed like a negative; the object
of scorn becomes an object of adoration; abomination turns into
devotion. The prostitute decides she is sacred. You thought I
was a bitch? I'm a goddess. Invulnerable:

> At midnight the cemetery caught fire.
> The Devil's wife did not die.

A strange shortcut to dignity? Roles get reversed. The last shall be first, and this is their catharsis. Voices rise, drums boom: "The living died, the dead were born . . ."

THE DEVIL IN PERSON

The sick man knocks three times on the sole of his left foot:

> Recognize me, Vovô Catarino,
> for the love of God and the Devil,
> at this time,
> on this day,
> from the depths of hell,
> with its seven soldiers
> at the gate of the cemetery.

Vovô Catarino is coming. He who receives him, a *pai de santo* in a humble *terreiro* on the side of Corcovado hill, is dressed in red and black rags and has a steel trident in his hand. The convulsions of his body make his cloth horns tremble and fall over his eyes. Only candles light up this room with its floor of dirt and walls of tin. The sickly light projects gigantic shadows of the saints, the talismans and fetishes on the two altars: the altar of heaven, where Jesus Christ stands surrounded by Saint George, indigenous divinities and the "old blacks," and the altar of hell, upon which the Exús and Pomba-giras raise their red horns and their seven-toothed *garfos* (spears). The *terreiro* is called Our Lady of Conception, but this heretical Virgin Mary is the mother of both Jesus Christ and Exú.

There is a little pile of broken glass from a bottle; one hand pours alcohol over it; a fire is lit. Vovô Catarino is already on earth. He sits on the flaming glass, jumps and laughs with glee. The priestesses, dressed in red, sing:

The sun is coming,
it's coming, Bahian.
The sun is going,
Bahian, it's going.
The waves of the sea were stirring.
There he comes,
Lord Catarino,
warlock of Bahia.

The ceremony begins:

Whence has Catarino come?
Where does Catarino live?
He lives at the edge of the beach,
where the rooster does not crow,
the chick does not peep,
the child does not cry.

When at dawn Vovô Catarino abandons the earth, the same voices sing:

Open the door to hell.
Lord Catarino wants to enter.

Vovô Catarino belongs to the line of the *pretos velhos*, slaves of Bahia, and it is through him that the *pai de santo* of this *terreiro* receives Exú. With his raspy voice, from a throat that has given up, Vovô tells me he has lived six centuries in this world; he invites me to his birthday: "I can't stand up anymore. That's why I work like this, sitting down, and I move with the aid of my trusty trident. I've been working on this earth five hundred and ninety-seven years, to fulfill the orders of the Nation of Hells. No, I don't remember anything about when I was a servant. Because back then I was already maaaaany million years old." The language is untranslatable: not only does his voice seem to come from the depth of time, but also Vovô entertains himself by switching syllables and undoing words. "Sanctufry? I give charity, but sanctufry, no I do not sanctufry. They can take me anywhere, and I'll drag myself and go, but to the door of the church, never. Never. For what purpose would I want salvation?"

He prepares the *obrigação* to pull the fever from the body of the sick man: seven black candles, seven red candles, seven jars of *dendê* oil, a rooster of black-and-red plumage, yellow flour (*fubá*), cruel jokes. With his trident, he pokes anyone who gets distracted throughout the incredibly slow ceremony. A giant frog keeps watch over the progress of the sacrifice:

"Confirme meu serivço, meu sapo."

The rooster shrieks, desperate, as if it knows it is awaiting its own sacrifice. The frog swells up like a balloon: the service is going well.

"E socé, minha filha?"

"Yes, Vovô. Better, Vovô. Today makes a week since my husband last beat me."

THE DEVIL IS A POOR DEVIL

Suddenly the frog jumps from its box and the man grabs it, but the frog is cold and slippery and it gets away. Someone screams. Everyone laughs. The Devil's ceremony is the fiesta of the bluff. After all, in the favela fraternity is not an abstract idea:

"Is he your brother?"

"No."

"And is she your sister?"

"No."

"How can this be? Nobody can . . ." Vovô insists. "You might not be brothers of the same mother. But the same father . . ."

Vovô Catarino rubs the rooster on the body of the sick man,

up and down, back and forth. The sick man is shaking with fever:

"This poor guy could get eaten just the same, fever and all. Anybody'd eat him. Rich people get fevers too. But nobody will eat a rich guy."

Once the rooster's neck is plucked, the knife is raised to cut:

"Save the crossroads."

"Save."

"Save my fig tree."

"Save."

"Save the cemetery."

"Save."

Catarino drinks the blood with pleasure, slowly. The sick man concentrates. He must think of his sickness, of the curse which made him sick, of his certain salvation. His body has been sprayed with blood.

> Seven gatekeepers, seven crossroads,
> Catarino is from the heavy band.
> From the heavy band,
> from the heavy band.
> Seven gatekeepers, seven crossroads.

Each small *terreiro* makes up the music and words of the many *pontos* sung during the ceremony. And the *pontos* are innumerable, following upon one another while the sacrifices, commentaries, rituals all take place to knock down the doors of love or death, to win hearts, avenge offenses, regain lost health, or achieve the happiness to be found fleetingly among the misfortunes of each day.

This man who at night is the Devil incarnate during the day earns a living as a janitor at the airport. With his trident in hand and wearing his cap with cloth horns, he is the source of encouragement and consolation, the adviser for matters of the heart, the confessor, the doctor who takes the place of the nonexistent physician, the prophet and the avenger of the favela. "For what purpose would I want salvation?" he says. "I don't want salvation. I want to stay here in my hell, which is pleasurable, *meu filho*. Hell is my home. And there I am the boss. No one gives me orders."

With red and black chalk (*pemba*), Vovô draws a complicated design of crossed tridents on the dirt floor. Then he carefully spreads gunpowder on the lines. The powder explodes; the Pomba-giras come to life in the *filhas do santo*:

"There in the *umbanda* of the rich, they call them mediums. They dress in white and the floor is tiled, you can't spit. Ah, how sad!"

Between long drinks, he continues working. He tells me of a great killing for Good Friday. Several goats will be sacrificed, roasted, and eaten on the day of obligatory fasting. Not just to challenge God, although Vovô insists that a man's disgrace begins the day that God remembers he exists in this world He made for men to suffer. No, not only for that. On Good Friday the goats will be sacrificed, and the faithful will drink the hot blood out of the palms of their hands. That way the black goats will suffer the suffering reserved for men, and the men, all of them, will be relieved.

And thus it occurred. On Good Friday the great killing took place. The rain beat down all night long on the favela.

(1969)

All Bolivia in a Railroad Car

The tracks are washed out. It's the rainy season, and for several kilometers a pudding of clay and rocks that came loose from the mountains blocks the way. The tracks are washed out: we don't know how long we will be stuck here in the middle of the deserted cordillera. "A day?" "Maybe." "Two weeks?" "Maybe."

A pin wouldn't fit in this second-class coach, filled as it is with smugglers and contraband, granite-faced Indian women with children on their backs, children of all sizes, chickens, half-fleeced sheep, bags of merchandise that form solid unmovable fortresses the entire length of the aisle. People come and go by way of the windows; nobody can get near the doors. The stuffiness and the heavy smell have become unbearable after such a long trip.

So I, too, prefer to shiver, and I slip outside like a snake through the tiny hole. To ward off the cold, I walk briskly along with two Bolivians and a Peruvian. The train has yet to arrive at the brutal desolation of the Oruro plateau; the scenery is dry but still beautiful. The mountains seem to be divided into perfectly drawn waves, and in the pink, ocher, greenish, and violet strips you can see the different geological ages of the living rock. A mountain chain of blue granite rises up farther on against the horizon. A cold breeze strikes my face, and I think that this country could be the Canaan of America: it has iron and manganese, tin and antimony, copper and zinc and radioactive minerals, gas and oil. It still has silver, even though the Spaniards didn't leave even a speck in Potosí. "No other country has more right to smokestacks," Adolfo Perelman will tell me a few days later in La Paz. But there are no factories in Bolivia. Bolivia is one of the poorest countries of poor Latin America.

"YOU'LL LEAVE ME IN THE STREET . . ."

A fifth of Bolivia's economically active population is jobless. But how can underemployment and all the other hidden forms of unemployment be measured? Each year, forty thousand young people reach working age: the country denies them a steady job. At least a quarter of a million Bolivians live in northern Argentina. Of a recent graduating class of thirty physicians at San Simón University, twenty-six are working in the United States. Street vendors, carriers and bootblacks, "merchants" who sell three apples or a couple of carrots or loose cigarettes are everywhere. The blossoming bureaucracy hides unemployment as well, albeit poorly and clumsily.

Smuggling is a national habit. An infinite number of Bolivians live off bringing foreign merchandise into the country under and over the customs barriers. This is another form of unemployment without the name. And after all, in the same boat are the dozens of customs officials who climbed aboard the train in which I was riding, with cans of cooking oil nearly hanging from my ears, to wage a long war of shouts, tears, and offers of bribes with the smugglers. Bolivia has a series of domestic customs offices, as it had when it was a colony, and the customs agents multiplied endlessly station after station. Railroad inspectors appeared with much the same frequency, as if they had come out of the dunes, the rocks, or the clumps of *pajabrava* grass. An enormous number of mountain climbers in blue uniforms clambered over the towers of Babel made of packages and bags and cans and bottles and human beings to perforate the train tickets pitilessly with a thousand little holes. The poor little piece of cardboard got filled with stars, moons, triangles, dots, and all sorts of fantasies of control.

The tough inspection for contraband took place just before we got to Oruro. It was the third invasion since crossing the Argentine frontier. Panic spread. Someone warned that the customs agents were waiting at the next station like ants. The reddish splendor in the west glowed over the vast frozen steppe, gray-green and limitless, and the sparkling light broke the terrible monotony of the puna. We were passing through the kingdom of anguishing empty spaces, but inside the coach there was no place to hide anything. Someone put an immense package on my knees and said: "Don't get upset . . . it's nothing, nothing." An elderly teacher who was traveling in the other end of the car suffered an attack of hysteria: "Excuse us, señora," they had said, then they buried her under a cargo of Buenos Aires liquor. She screamed, and the smugglers explained: "We are protecting your comfort, señora."

The shifting sands of people and merchandise devoured all legs, then faces and soon the arms and hands of anyone who dared to enter. But the customs agents climbed and managed to make it through. "Just this little thing. The only thing I have is this little candy, nothing else." The agents were implacable. The women cried, the children wailed, the men pleaded, the agents mumbled: "You're not paying us what you ought to, nope." They took away a poor old woman's boxes of powdered milk. The dense air smelled of fried food and children's pee. "But I already paid for mine." "You always want to get by without paying anything." "But I've already paid, don't you understand that I've already paid. . . ."

On the other side of the window, the remains of abandoned

mining towns looked like prehistoric ruins. Only cooking fires, ruminating in the distance, were alive. The customs inspectors fought among themselves. Some wanted to accept the bribe of two hundred Bolivian pesos, but another was tough, intransigent. He wore the sort of green beret they use in the war against the guerrillas, and his price was much higher: "Forget it, get away from me, the orders are strict."

An Indian woman carrying an immense basket of peanuts under her arm flew past me. Later on I found out that under the peanuts she was carrying contraband from the cars in the train that had not yet been checked to those that had. "He's just ambitious," cried a woman holding her head. "A soulless Tartar, that Gómez." Another shouted at them not to be so mean, that it was only a pittance, just enough for their daily bread. A man hung on to the shirt of the inspector with the green beret, placing himself between the inspector and a large wooden box: "Not this one, not this one, little brother, for the love of God." And the inspector kept pushing him on his chest, and he kept repeating: "Not this one, you'll leave me in the street, in the street you'll leave me. . . ."

A RICH COUNTRY IN RAGS

After the heroic struggles of April 1952, Bolivia lived through a cycle of revolutionary change. This was a very important period in the nation's history, but many of the tasks were left incomplete, and others, no less important, were betrayed as the revolution itself fell apart. Of every ten Bolivians, six still cannot read. Half of the children do not go to school. Without a doubt, the Nationalist Revolutionary Movement (MNR) repaired the Indians' broken sense of dignity. On the Bolivian side of Lake Titicaca, no Indian falls to his knees to speak to a white man, nor are serfs, family and all, given away, rented or sold for life. But I have seen Aymara Indians in the highlands carrying loads up to their teeth in exchange for a crust of bread, and Quechua Indian beggars fighting with dogs for the edibles from garbage dumps.

Thanks to the agrarian reform, food intake has improved considerably in vast areas of the countryside, so much so that the average height of peasants has increased measurably. Nevertheless, the Bolivian people as a whole consume only 60 percent of the protein and a fifth of the calcium required for a minimally healthy diet. And in the countryside the deprivation is much more pronounced than these averages show. The agrarian reform has by no means failed, although one-fifth of Bolivia's foreign exchange goes to pay for imported food.

The revolution of 1952 nationalized the tin mines, taking them away from the "ring" of the great mining oligarchy. But tin boss Patiño not only demanded a large indemnification for the nearly exhausted mines his father had squeezed dry, he maintained control over the price and market of Bolivia's expropriated tin through his Williams Harvey smelter in Liverpool. Only in mid-1970 did Bolivia manage to set up its own national tin smelter.

This country, which can't even produce its own ingots, enjoys the luxury of having eight different law schools to produce vampires in industrial quantities. In place of the traditional "ring," the revolution engendered a new "ring" of technocrats and bureaucrats who earn secret salaries in dollars and sabotage the country under the auspices of the Inter-American Development Bank and the Agency for International Development. They earn up to a hundred times more than the miners. Wasted away by silicosis and malnutrition, the workers don't live even thirty-five years. Of every two children born in the mines, one dies before he learns to walk. According to the Health Ministry, 120,000 Bolivians have tuberculosis, of whom less than 1,000 get medical attention, and 400,000 Bolivians have parasitical Chagas' disease. For every 4,600 inhabitants there is only one doctor, and of the 720 doctors graduated from the medical school in Cochabamba, 600 are working outside the country.

Since time immemorial, Bolivia has produced raw minerals and refined speeches. Rhetoric and misery abound. Doctors in frock coats and mediocre writers have worked forever to absolve the guilty of all guilt. But from their shipwrecked existence, an immense crowd of outcasts accuses the entire system. Bolivia's plight is the result of its station in the world capitalist system. It is poor because its poverty has always fed the wealth of others. The silver from Cerro Rico in Potosí nourished the first thrusting kicks of European capitalism, and in Potosí only holes and ghosts remained. Four centuries later, during World War II, the "democratic prices" of tin, wolfram, and rubber gave Bolivia misery and the honor of having fulfilled its duty, and gave U.S. Steel, U.S. Rubber, and General Motors fabulous profits. In its short life cycle, the MNR's revolution sought to create a national capitalism: in place of a creative bourgeoisie, it gave birth to a caravan of merchants and traffickers in currency. For Bolivians, free enterprise has meant nothing more than free delivery.

In this sense, the Barrientos regime, which grew out of the 1964 coup d'état, broke the sound barrier. In one of his books, Sergio Almaraz Paz tells the story of the tin tailings concession given to the International Mining Processing Company. With a declared capital of $5,000, this pompously named company won a contract that allowed it to earn over $900 million.

WHITEN YOUR SKIN!

"Let's save a little bit. The night is going to be tough, comrade," one of them said. But there was enough *singani* in the bottles for everyone, and now with the first light in the sky and sufficient warmth in the body we are approaching the station in La Paz. Divine Providence hands me a newspaper. It is the first I've seen in a week, a right-wing daily, an old edition. I read a violent editorial against the Ovando government: "Bolivian Oil for Cuba's Lamps." I imagine that this is a good approximation of what awaits me in the capital.

I turn the pages, reading carefully out of simple boredom, even the ads. I'm struck by the face of a woman in a rather large advertisement: "Whiten your skin! In four short weeks, with Beautiful Dawn cream. Why let your dark skin be a barrier to romance and an impediment to your happiness? Put Beautiful Dawn cream on every night. You'll be astonished by the glorious change. . . ."

I look up, and sure enough: I'm the only white person on the train. I recognize the faces, one by one, of the people with whom I've shared during the long trip food and drink, few but sufficient words, hours of cards and stories, old blankets. I tear up the newspaper, set it on fire. And with the little paper torch, I light a cigarette.

(1970)

The Civilization
of Black Gold

Venezuela is one of the richest countries on the planet. It's also one of the poorest and the most violent. I know a businessman who has twelve automobiles, among them a Chrysler Imperial exclusively for the servants to go to market to buy vegetables. Three hundred thousand automobiles circulate in Caracas, an astonishing city. They travel on highways that cross over and under each other amid skyscrapers and bridges and tunnels. I've seen kitchens here that look like the offices of cabinet ministers.

THE KINGDOM OF WASTE

Oil pumps have nodded their heads without respite for half a century. Their birdlike beaks extract profits so fabulous that they now come to double the amount spent on rebuilding Europe under the Marshall Plan. Since the first well gushed up in torrents, the national budget has grown a hundredfold. Yet the majority of the population remains as poor as in the era of cacao and coffee. Social contradictions, regional contradictions: the privileged minority live in Caracas, which could just as well be the capital of Texas. In contrast, the oil towns on the shores of

Lake Maracaibo, which produce all the country's opulence, produce misery for themselves.

Is there another city in the world with such a capacity for
waste? In Caracas, enormous and expensive machines abound
for producing pleasure or speed or sound or light. Like poor
frightened ants we face these machines and wonder: "Jesus, is
each of these really worth more than me?" The homes of the
middle and upper classes are like furniture-store windows: os-
tentatious scenes of plastic and stereophonic sound, untouched
by human hand. Caracas chews gum and prefers synthetic products and canned food. Caracas has trouble sleeping because it
can't turn off the urge to buy, to consume, to obtain, to spend,
to take control of everything. In Caracas you can get Indian
rings from Carnaby Street and fresh salmon from the Baltic,
pâté from Strasbourg, Irish jams, California dates, chestnuts and
snails from France, cheese from Holland, herring from Scotland,
oil from Portugal, butter from Australia, Chanel perfumes.
Handkerchiefs are called *foulards* and are by Pierre Cardin,
Dior, Givenchy, or Yves Saint-Laurent. If a boutique doesn't
carry them all, it goes under. Venezuelan rum is stupendous,
but it has no status: people drink scotch with water from Scotland, which, believe it or not, Venezuela imports in plastic bags
from across the sea. The entire population of Germany or England could fit in the vast virgin territories of this underpopu-
lated country. Yet Venezuela imports lettuce and corn from the
United States, and buys beans from Mexico. Venezuelan farmers
are threatening to invade the capital aboard their tractors: in
ten years they have been unable to raise the price of most of
their products, while they pay five times as much for fertilizers
and machinery.

In a massive exodus, peasants leave the countryside for Caracas. Foreigners from the four cardinal points of the globe also
join the flow to Caracas, hoping to make it in America. They
use the city, but do not love it. In three decades its population
has increased sevenfold. When World War II began, Caracas

reached only as far as the Anauco ravine, a few steps from the old downtown; everything else was sugar and coffee up to the edge of the valley. Overnight, skyscrapers sprouted from the soil of the haciendas. From oil's top hat, the dictator Pérez Jiménez pulled out the longest network of highways in Latin America. The city extends its enormous asphalt tentacles, making a thing of ridicule of the small towns it incorporates with dizzying speed. Not long ago, in certain Caracas neighborhoods people still moved about slowly and tied their burros up to poles. Caracas grows as if by magic, with its elevated avenues and car cemeteries; the city is ruled by Mercedes-Benzes and Mustangs. The economy of waste: spending on automobiles devours a tenth of the national income. Anguished, the poet Aquiles Nazoa protests: "This is a vast garage surrounded by horror and hopelessness on all sides." The hit song that all *caraqueños* hum all the time calls on the Lord. "Jesus Christ, Jesus Christ," it prays, "Jesus Christ, I'm here." Rebellious young people from a group called Youth Power write an open letter to the Founding Father: "Bolívar, we're fucked!"

FORGOTTEN AND VIOLENT

In consumer civilization, not all consume everything. While the latest models flash like lightning down Caracas's golden avenues, more than half a million people contemplate the wasteful extravagance of others from huts made of garbage. These *ranchos* climb up the steep sides of hills and down the steep sides of ravines; they lie under bridges and at the edges of the valley where the city sits. The government announces that it will bulldoze the *ranchos* at La Charneca so they can't be seen from the windows of the four-star Caracas Hilton.

The vast poor zones of Caracas are called "barrios"; the rich ones are called "urbanizations." The poor heights are called "hills"; the rich ones, "knolls." The barrios have ugly names: the Mastic Tree, Last Shot, the Guarataro Tree, Yellow Sewer, Pawnshop, Black Cat, Last Resort. The urbanizations, on the other hand, have been delicately baptized: Beautiful Mountain, the Delicacies, Country Clearing, Country Club, the Marquis, Lawns of the East, Beautiful Fields. The wealthy race to the eastern part of the city, as the rabble invade the streets once blocked off by urbanizations. The excluded number more and more; the included fewer and fewer. This is an invasion: the poor masses move like an avalanche. Of the 135,000 young people who reach working age each year in Venezuela, barely 50,000 find work. By the end of the century, experts estimate, three-fourths of Caracas will be occupied by *ranchos*.

Youth make up the majority of the country. Half of all Venezuelans are under eighteen; over half the children and adolescents receive no education at all. In the *ranchos*, prolific beds of the poor, the youth make up an even greater portion of the total population. Every Sunday afternoon at sunset, the poor barrios hold their breath: horses' hoofs are flying at La Rinconada Downs, and the races are broadcast on radio and TV. The "five-and-six" is a betting system that has achieved the status of a national rite. People bet desperately, in order to "get out from under." Everyone bets, but those who actually get out from under can be counted on one hand. The *ranchos* are violent. What remains, except for anger?

All of Caracas is violent. The city itself has become a repressive structure: the minority must be protected from the growing majority's blind urge to attack. The penal code forbids carrying arms, but an estimated 300,000 people own revolvers or pistols. Personal quarrels are no longer settled with fists.

The *ranchos* rose up against the dictatorship of Pérez Jiménez. Then they continued in open insurrection. Each poor barrio became an arms bazaar: under Rómulo Betancourt, the police didn't dare go near the daily shower of stones and bullets. In the barrios El Guarataro and January 23, you can still see holes in the walls made by machine-gun fire from the forces of order. Day and night people fought, continually: 1961, 1962, 1963. Today the defeat of the left can also be measured in the rancorous silence of the slums. No longer vented collectively, fury explodes in private conflicts. Neighbors kill each other; rebels become common delinquents. The barrios overthrew Pérez Jiménez over twelve years ago; today they adore him. People no longer believe in politicians, nor in politics. To escape the present and lacking alternatives for the future, the poor take refuge in the past.

A curious mixture of the cultures of oil and poverty. The poor youth of the barrios dance to pop music and wear psychedelic T-shirts, and the *ranchos* have TV antennas. Advertising bombards them from twenty-one-inch screens. Smiling faces sell love for mother and love for Oscar Meyer hot dogs: "Happiness is giving my mother a flower. Happiness is having a million hot dogs, eating twenty, and selling the rest." The Celanese Corporation makes pants out of oil, blue jeans from synthetic fibers. And its advertising eggs on the fury of youth, including the thousands and thousands of poor kids whom society condemns to unemployment and crime. "Rebel," it advises on television. "Buy your rebellion. Buy Lois jeans." A hand falls like an ax and splits the enemy's neck. The camera zooms in on the killer's wrist: "Real men use Tissot watches."

CHIMERA AND REALITY OF OIL

Lake Maracaibo is a forest of oil wells. The pumps, black birds of prey, dig their beaks down to the bottom of the wells. The pumps are not only inside the crossed-iron towers that pepper the lake, they are in backyards and on street corners in the cities that gush forth like oil around the lake and its fabled riches. To provide labor for Shell or Standard Oil, and at the whim of the companies, oil towns have been born and died on these shores for half a century. The oil workers ride in flashy Mustangs, but there are ever fewer of them. In a little more than ten years, the number of oil workers and oil company employees fell by half: from forty thousand to twenty thousand in all Venezuela. Just twenty thousand people keep Latin America's greatest source of prosperity functioning.

Neocolonial dependency is not only reflected in social contradictions, and not only subjects a country's fate to the will of others. It reproduces the international structure of plunder within the subjected country. The oil companies have taken $10 billion out of Venezuela, free of dust and straw in net profits confessed to in their balance sheets. And they've taken another fortune, in secret, under the table. At the same time, Caracas exploits the rest of Venezuela, especially Lake Maracaibo. From there come the luxuries of the capital's nouveau riches: ostentation always has roots in poverty.

No city in Venezuela has generated so much wealth as Cabimas. But Cabimas doesn't even have sewers, only a couple of paved streets. Cabimas is a vast swamp filled with big-bellied barefoot kids. After squeezing Cabimas for half a century, Rockefeller abandoned it and even had the company buildings razed. All he left was the iron-and-reinforced-concrete skeletons hovering over the dead wells. The story of Cabimas is that of many other oil towns, and it presages the future of all the others, miserable, dark, shining with oil, born to die. The millions in profits they generate mostly vanish into the distance, or disappear into the ever-open jaws of Caracas.

The national government, which resides in Caracas, outlawed the songs that sprang up angrily during New Year's celebrations in Maracaibo, in the state of Zulia. The voices were praying to the town's patron Virgin, La Chinita:

> And that's why this sovereign man,
> sings to you ceaselessly,

implores you, Mother of me,
for God's sake give a hand.
Come save our Zulia land
from centralism and the bourgeoisie.

(1971)

Chronicle of Diamond Fever

They come from all directions. With machetes flying, the miners open up paths into the jungle. Each carries on his back a shovel, a sieve, a crowbar, and a pail. They come from Gran Sabana, from Caroní, from Río Claro, from Playa Blanca. In one fell swoop, the Guaniamo jungle becomes Venezuela's principal source of diamonds. Not only Venezuelans come. Colombians, Brazilians, Trinidadians too: hard-faced men, without documents or last names or any interest in talking about the past.

In a toss of the dice, camps spring up. This is a combination of the first day of Creation and the last day of Civilization: snakes sleep under the hammocks, while in them the miners smoke Lucky Strikes. This is a scene from the discovery and conquest of America, Diego de Ordaz resurrected with sword and shield, but with garish neon lights and pop music from Wurlitzer jukeboxes.

Towns are born and die before they make it onto the map. In the jungle, they jump from one spot to another, to a rhythm set by the successive diamond "bombs." "Another rush blows and we don't stop to think about having settled into a house or anything. We grab the essentials and off we go. We never think about failing." Malavé is an old miner. For many years he's made his way about the state of Bolívar, searching for the shiny hard rocks. Malavé respects diamonds. He believes they are mysterious and very powerful. To find diamonds, the miners follow the songs of certain birds, or trace favorable signs in the river sands or in the depths of the earth. Sometimes they follow sounds and images from dreams. Diamonds appear, they disappear, they reappear. Some miners, like Malavé, say that diamonds grow like plants.

An army of whores, gamblers, and merchants accompanies the miners' pilgrimage. The "red zone" is set up when the first wood-tin-and-palm-leaf huts appear and a clearing is made for the helicopters to land. Diamond towns have no cemetery, nor any pharmacy, church, hospital, or school. They are called, for example, Chilblain, Crazy Shot, Devil's Chute, the Governor's Moustache. One of the camps was baptized the Twenty-Four, in homage to a giant ant whose bite makes you crazy for twenty-four hours. Another is called Runback, because a lot of miners got only that far, then stole burros or horses and turned back, unable to stand any longer the march through hostile hills. The Snail was born in July 1970 and lasted until April 1971. It grew to five thousand inhabitants at the peak of the euphoria. Now it lies abandoned. Salvation sprouted up in October of last year. Right now it is Venezuela's most important diamond mine. It is also the prime source of malaria for the entire country. A miner named it Salvation because before diamonds were discovered in these ravines and riverbeds the miners weren't finding enough even to eat.

THE DELIRIUM OF PRICES

They say there are diamonds even in the gravel they use to pave the runway. Salvation's minuscule airport is a cemetery for the planes that don't make it on takeoff or landing. One crashed during Easter, they say, because the pilot forgot the fuel; it ended up nose-down amid the trees. The wind does what it pleases with these toylike Cessnas, but the airlines set the fares as if the planes were made of gold. After all, they provide the only way to come and go.

On the other hand, thanks to the planes, prices in Salvation have come down. Before, when food and drink had to be carried in over the mountains, an aspirin cost half a dollar. When a helicopter landed for the first time at the Padlock mine, the miners assaulted it like buzzards: it had two steer. In less than a hundred days, a merchant earned the equivalent of $150,000. Now prices are low in Salvation; that means that a week-old newspaper or a can of beer costs four times as much as in Caracas. Milk is six times as expensive; rice or coffee ten times. The price of rum is twelve times higher than in the capital city, and gasoline forty times.

The only things that go for free are the abundant diseases. One sip of river water will infect your intestine, and the bites of certain mosquitoes are enough to give you malaria, the chill-and-fever sickness that miners accept as if it were God's will. There is only one doctor in Salvation. He looks like a fugitive from Sing Sing and many doubt his degree. Nobody knows how he came here, or why. But he charges forty dollars for a shot of streptomycin. He has plenty of patients. The garbage and the flies help him out.

The miners complain about the merchants and the merchants complain about the soldiers. There are no legal permits for selling drinks, but Salvation is one bar after another. On their own, the soldiers charge a tax that they themselves set and that never leaves their pockets. The miners drink rivers of beer and rum; brandy and scotch, too, at fairy-tale prices. The bars are a tin or wooden counter. They have no walls, because a mine has no walls. A nylon curtain provides intimacy for lovemaking. When the women fight, knife blows bring the curtains down. The miners are men without women, and love is also expensive. For a few minutes, the specialists charge them the equivalent of forty dollars.

TO BE ROCKEFELLER FOR A NIGHT

Black Barrabas started Venezuela's diamond rush thirty years ago. He found a pure diamond the size of a pigeon egg. Some versions claim that Barrabas's diamond was sold for $500,000 in the United States. He was paid much less. The morning he found the diamond, Barrabas had not been able to have breakfast: he couldn't find anyone to give him credit. Later, Barrabas became the stuff of legend, not only in the mine known as the Pole, but in all of Venezuela. In Caracas, in the times of General Medina, Barrabas was a grand figure of ephemeral glory. Money melted in his hands. Now he's very poor and very old and lives in Icabarú, a far-off mine near the border.

It's the norm. For the miner, fortune has wings. In Abequí mine in the Great Savannah, a miner named Pariaguán left the diamond buyer's office with a hat filled with 106,000 bolívares (some $24,000). He went into the Tibiritábara Bar in Ciudad Bolívar, and out he came twenty-eight days later with his pockets empty. In Black Water mine, a miner named Paleta got 160,000 bolívares for a jelly jar filled to the brim with pure diamonds. Ninety days later he had to beg for his fare home. More recently, here in the zone of Guaniamo, a miner got 200,000 bolívares for a pile of good diamonds he found at the Snail. In the end he didn't have enough to buy a rope to hang himself.

The man who has a nice pile of diamonds in his hands is said to be "enchanted." He pays for everything, for everyone, and he doesn't regret a thing. "A miner's life is a bitch," explained one who had been diving in the Caroní River for eighteen years. "But a miner's life has a lot of camaraderie. If I find a diamond worth two or three hundred thousand bolívares, and all of us here are destitute, well, you've got to let everyone in on the party. And the next morning we wake up broke. But we've had a good time. That is the life of the miner. It's the buyers who really win. They drink too, but when they drink up a thousand bolívares, the buyers, it's because they've stolen two thousand." This man no longer dives for diamonds. He says he's too old: "My body's worn out." He was born thirty-three years ago.

The diamond buyers operate next to the "red zone." They wear .38-caliber revolvers in their belts and permanent furrows in their brows from looking through the powerful magnifying glass that reveals the black graphite dots of imperfect diamonds; they use tiny scales that look like toys. At the buyers' little counters, set up one beside the other, the miners' dreams either come true or are dashed to pieces. The people who discovered the Guaniamo mines knew nothing about mining. They had never seen a sieve, the three-filtered sifter that washes the silt and separates out diamonds by their own weight. They were peasants, peons who lived the life of slaves picking tonka beans for three months in the mountains and spending the rest of the year working on the haciendas unable to ever pay off their debts for food. They found many diamonds at first by chance, then searching for them frantically, and the buyers paid them in small bills, notes of five or ten bolívares, to impress them with the wad.

HELL AND GLORY

The arena is a circle of poles. In the center lies the cockpit. A black cock is fighting a speckled one: they peck out each other's eyes, tear each other to pieces with their spurs. The miners throw money on the sand while the cocks leap, flutter, corner each other, fall and rise and fall again and rise once more. "Twenty-to-one on the black one!" "I'm with the speckled one! I'm with him!" The shouting increases, as do the bets. The judge bets too, a lot. And the soldier as well, shouting and waving his fist. The miners are crazy about cocks. Of course, cockfights always end up as human fights, and many times the party ends poorly.

I'm sitting next to the Girl, who is nineteen and gorgeous. She came from near La Guayra a few months ago, and already she's got a sizable bank account in Caracas. While the speckled cock agonizes with its head bathed in blood and an enemy feather in its beak, the Girl, laughing uproariously, tells me the tragedy of her life. In just one night of love, without overdoing it, the Girl earns more than a government employee does in a month.

Cocks, women, and drink: these are the miners' compensation. They are also the open mouths that devour whatever the miners earn. You'd also have to mention cards and dice, which the professional gamblers manipulate with hands of magic. Sometimes the miners bet money, sometimes diamonds; once, they say, someone bet his life and paid it off. "Those who win the most are those who lose the most: the ones who are truly ruined."

Diamonds are found in alluvial streams or in veins. The miners stand in water for hours, days, years; or they crawl underground, digging like moles. Sometimes, down in the depths, the candles give out for lack of oxygen. And sometimes the miners also give out, and there they stay. Or they get hit in the head with pieces of rock or earth that fall from the roof of the tunnel they're digging: in the Guaniamo mines there is Hennessy cognac, but there are no hard hats.

There are holes everywhere. At the edges of the little streets that the lines of huts create, or amid the weeds; four yards from the counters of the bars, or far from the camps. The diamond sometimes rests in inhospitable places, amid plagues and wild animals: it must be pursued during scorching days and freezing nights. "It doesn't need a pretty place to be." The miner spends his life scratching in the dirt with his fingers. For many, the years go by with no luck. "The diamond is powerful. In all of history, nothing more powerful has been found," says Malavé the miner. "They've tried to make synthetic ones, but they can't. There is no way to imitate it. And it's a mysterious rock. Some people have diamonds in their blood, others don't. In fact, I'm one who doesn't. And there must be some mystery to that. The diamond is a stone that's very . . ." And he sums up: "I've got a lot of respect for it."

Often the implacable glass will reveal a fraud: what seemed to be a diamond, that compact transparent brilliance, is no diamond after all. It's an "almost almost," as the miners call these deceptive stones. And what about those who are lucky? Those who have "blood" for pure diamonds? Barrabas's lineage found no better destiny for the unfortunate than fruitless digging in the mines. Bejeweled rings shine on the fingers of the merchants, but the miners are naked. The vengeance of the poor does not last long: their delirious dream of becoming millionaires is gone before morning. One night when a torrential downpour trapped us in a shed, a wise old woman said slowly: "Next to glory lies hell. You take one step and in you fall."

"Miners have radar," say the miners. They claim to know the secrets of the language of the birds. But they also lose easily. Money moves here like nowhere else. What is it worth? All these men come thinking they will not stay. Peasants and unemployed workers take on this life as a penance or as time off. Later on they get used to it. The mines devour them, take them over, tie their legs. After all, the cities are no less hostile than the jungle even if they are free of malaria. And the countryside offers only the routine of misery. In contrast, this is another world.

(1971)

Fascism in Latin America:
A Letter to a Mexican Editor

Dear Javier,

Thank you very much for your invitation.

No, I can't write about fascism in Latin America. It's a serious subject and I couldn't just dash it off. Here in Buenos Aires I don't have my books, nor my sources of information and consultation. Besides, it's been a while since I last worked on articles or essays. I'm attempting a more intimate, but no less dangerous, penetration into the reality that surrounds me and pains me. And I sincerely believe that there are much more capable people than I to write about subjects like this one you propose, which requires long years of reflection and research. Sometimes I'm afraid of getting it wrong. I'm not a sociologist, nor a historian, nor an economist, nor anything. My work as a journalist and columnist has always been limited to publicizing other people's ideas, and facts that the system hides from the nonspecialist. To do the activist's work of denunciation and counterinformation, I've fashioned a certain ability for story-telling, learned by the campfires of Paysandú and at the tables of the old cafés of Montevideo. But nothing more.

Sometimes I wonder, looking at what is occurring around me, if the dictatorships now burdening Uruguay, Chile, or Bo-

livia, for example, should be called "fascist" or "Nazi." Aren't
they worthy of Hitler or Mussolini, these machines for grinding
up human flesh? Don't they imitate Goebbels, these machines
for proscribing and lying? The death squads, machines for ha-
rassing and murdering from the shadows, don't they operate in
Argentina today as if they were the "white bands" of Italy or
Germany of the thirties?

I'm a man of the south, and that's what I write about.

Impotent, I watch my country sink, and I wonder: Could
someone compare Uruguay, which is an empty ranch—an empty
hacienda as you Mexicans say it—with those European centers
of industry that brewed fascism and Nazism?

Uruguay is a dependent country, which is what those in the
know call colonies today. It depends on the central capitalist
powers; from them it receives prices, loans, technicians, arms,
automobiles, and ideology. This certainly was not the case of
Germany or Italy in those times. Nazism and fascism were the
expression of an aggressive nationalism, but nationalism none-
theless, born from the entrails of two unsatisfied imperialist
forces anxious for revenge. The capitalism that gave rise to
Hitler's craziness, and the delirium of the multitude that followed him into horror and conquest, was highly developed and
arrived late to the carving up of the world, as has been said so
often. In the slaughterhouses of human flesh, the hangmen
hummed patriotic songs.

In countries like Chile, Uruguay, or Bolivia, the dictatorships
don't have the least capacity to mobilize people. The "mystique"
of superpatriotism burns only in the hearts of policemen and
soldiers, and they're paid for it. These are solitary regimes,
condemned to end sadly and without grandeur. They don't
inspire the youth; they just hate them, as they hate happiness
and everything that grows. They rely on the force of arms and
are incapable of transmitting any conviction, not even a rotten
one like the superiority of their race or the imperial destiny of
their nations. Our dictators are, at most, patriots of a homeland

that is not theirs, satellites of a far-off empire: echoes and not voices.

The monopoly capitalism of Germany or Italy in those black years generated corporatism and "labor fronts" and transformed the state into an omnipotent god. Among us, the state is only powerful in crushing, killing or deporting men who think or rebel or doubt, but it has less and less economic power. It is the repressive arm of power, and it uses techniques worthy of the fascist nightmare, but it is never *the* power. A curious mix of Adam Smith and Mussolini, or of their respective caricatures: the state is dismantled by de-nationalizing its most profitable productive activities, and turning them over to private and foreign hands. At the same time, it grows stronger as a structure of oppression. Among us, the state prefers jails to factories; soldiers and prisoners multiply as under fascism, but the sources of employment do not.

In a small and sparsely populated country like mine, the militarization of society does not correspond to any expansionist plans; neither is it meant to defend the borders, which are threatened by no one. Will we have a "war economy in peacetime?" The arms come from without and the enemies from within. Who are the enemies? How many of them are left? In Uruguay there are between four and five thousand political prisoners. In proportion to the population of Mexico, for example, the equivalent would be ninety thousand people behind bars for political motives. It is not a few. First, it was the guerrillas. Then the members of leftist parties. Then union members. Then intellectuals. Then some traditional politicians. Then anyone. The machine does not stop, it demands fuel, it goes crazy, it devours its inventor: the parties of the right gave special powers and extraordinary resources to the armed forces to get the Tupamaros guerrillas off their backs, and in short order the military were in power and the parties were dissolved. Twenty thousand persons passed through the jails and the barracks in 1973 and 1974; torture became the habitual "system of interrogation." In the chambers of torment, many men lost their lives. Some were kicked until their livers burst. Others had heart failure when their heads were submerged in buckets of dirty water and shit. Some died from being forced to stand several days and nights, others from electric shock. And there was one girl who suffocated, a plastic bag tied around her head.

Union and political activity have become forms of delinquency; the illiterate have assaulted the university with knives between their teeth; freedom of expression and the right of assembly do not exist. Liberal bourgeois institutions have been blown to bits; the Switzerland of America is now a concentration camp. Thinking is outlawed; the regime suspects—and it is right—that he who thinks conspires. In the streets all you see is poverty and rancor.

There are no longer any political intermediaries to exercise power on behalf of the ruling classes. Buffeted by their own crisis and by the threat of accelerated political awakening among the youth, the regime turned to blood and fire. It is the hour of the armed bureaucracy. Military spending and salaries multiply, and at the same time school buildings crack and collapse. Teachers and professors, persecuted by both misery and the holy fury of the Inquisition, have to be magicians to put food on the table.

If all this is not fascism, let's agree that it looks a lot like it. The fascist machinery of threat and repression is in gear, and sure enough it works. Not for conquering the world, but for crushing the internal forces of change, for decapitating the working class and annihilating intelligence. The petit bourgeois ideology of history is adapted to the necessities of the regime, and it fits like a glove. The scapegoats aren't the Jews, but the entire working class. The regime employs the characteristic big words—Fatherland, Family, Tradition, Property—to mask the oppression and horror of the dictatorship. They snuff out the life or liberty of anyone who disagrees or rebels; or at the least they take his documents and condemn him to wander about the world like a pariah, without a country or a legal identity.

We are living our own "time of scorn." The hangmen are in charge, and informers prosper. For the owners of power, who dream of a quiet world, history is subversive because it always changes. And in that they are right.

Forgive me for bending your ear, Javier. I didn't write you the article, but you see, I did get it off my chest.

Cordially,
Eduardo Galeano

(1974)

In Defense of the Word

LEAVING BUENOS AIRES, JUNE 1976

1

One writes out of a need to communicate and to commune with others, to denounce that which gives pain and to share that which gives happiness. One writes against one's solitude and against the solitude of others. One assumes that literature transmits knowledge and affects the behavior and language of those who read, thus helping us to know ourselves better and to save ourselves collectively. But "others" is too vague; and in times of crisis, times of definition, ambiguities may too closely resemble lies. One writes, in reality, for the people whose luck or misfortune one identifies with—the hungry, the sleepless, the rebels, and the wretched of this earth—and the majority of them are illiterate. Among the literate minority, how many can afford to buy books? Is this contradiction resolved by proclaiming that one writes for that facile abstraction known as "the masses"?

2

We were not born on the moon, we don't live in seventh heaven. We have the good fortune and the misfortune to belong to a tormented region of the world, Latin America, and to live in a historic period that is relentlessly oppressive. The contradictions of class society are sharper here than in the rich countries. Massive misery is the price paid by the poor countries so that 6 percent of the world's population may consume with impunity half the wealth generated by the entire world. The abyss, the distance between the well-being of some and the misery of others, is greater in Latin America; and the methods necessary to maintain this distance are more savage.

The development of a restrictive and dependent industry, which was superimposed on the old agrarian and mining structures without changing the latter's essential distortions, has sharpened social contradictions rather than alleviating them. The skills of the traditional politicians—experts in the arts of seduction and swindling—are today inadequate, antiquated, useless. The populist game which granted concessions—the better to manipulate—is no longer possible in some cases, and in others it reveals its dangerous double edge. Thus the dominant classes and countries resort to their repressive apparatuses. How else could a social system survive which more and more resembles a concentration camp? How, without barbed-wire fences, keep within bounds the growing legion of the damned? To the extent that the system finds itself threatened by the relentless growth of unemployment, poverty, and the resultant social and political tensions, room for pretense and good manners shrinks: in the outskirts of the world the system reveals its true face.

Why not recognize a certain sincerity in the dictatorships that today oppress the majority of our countries? Freedom of enterprise means, in times of crisis, the deprivation of freedom for people. Latin American scientists emigrate, laboratories and universities have no funds, industrial "know-how" is always foreign and exorbitantly expensive; but why not recognize a certain creativity in the development of a technology of terror? Latin America is making inspired universal contributions to the development of methods of torture, techniques for assassinating people and ideas, for the cultivation of silence, the extension of impotence, and the sowing of fear.

How can those of us who want to work for a literature that helps to make audible the voice of the voiceless function in the context of this reality? Can we make ourselves heard in the midst of a deaf-mute culture? The small freedom conceded to writers, is it not at times a proof of our failure? How far can we go? Whom can we reach?

A noble task, that of heralding the world of the just and the free; a noble function, that of rejecting a system of hunger and of cages—visible and invisible. But how many yards to the border? How long will those in power continue to give us their permission?

3

There has been much discussion of direct forms of censorship imposed by diverse sociopolitical regimes, of the prohibition of books or newspapers that are embarrassing or dangerous to them, and the exile, imprisonment, or murder of writers and journalists. But indirect censorship functions more subtly; it is no less real for being less apparent. Little is said about it, yet it is what most profoundly defines the oppressive and excluding character of the system to which most Latin American countries are subjected. What is the nature of this censorship which does not declare itself? It resides in the fact that the boat does not sail because there is no water in the sea; if only 5 percent of the Latin American population can buy refrigerators, what percentage can buy books? And what percentage can read them, feel a need for them, absorb their influence?

Latin American writers, wage workers in a cultural industry which serves the consumption needs of an enlightened elite, come from, and write for, a minority. This is the objective situation of both those writers whose work condones social inequity and the dominant ideology and those who attempt to break with it. We are, to a large extent, blocked by the game rules of the reality in which we function.

The prevailing social order perverts or annihilates the creative capacity of the immense majority of people and reduces the possibility of creation—an age-old response to human anguish and the certainty of death—to its professional exercise by a handful of specialists. How many "specialists" are we in Latin America? For whom do we write, whom do we reach? Where is our real public? (Let us mistrust applause. At times we are congratulated by those who consider us innocuous.)

4

One writes in order to deflect death and strangle the specters that haunt us; but what one writes can be historically useful only when in some way it coincides with the need of the collectivity to achieve its identity. This, I think, is what one wants. In saying "This is who I am," in revealing oneself, the writer can help others to become aware of who they are. As a means of revealing collective identity, art should be considered an article of prime necessity, not a luxury. But in Latin America access to the products of art and culture is forbidden to the immense majority.

For the peoples whose identity has been shattered by the successive cultures of conquest, and whose merciless exploitation contributes to the functioning of the machinery of world capitalism, the system generates a "mass culture." Culture *for* the masses is a more precise description of this degraded art of the mass media, which manipulates consciousness, conceals reality, and stifles the creative imagination. Naturally it does not lead to a revelation of identity but is rather a means of erasing or distorting it in order to impose ways of life and patterns of consumption which are widely disseminated through the mass media. The culture of the dominant class is called "national culture"; it lives an imported life and limits itself to imitating, stupidly and vulgarly, so-called universal culture—or that which passes for such among those who confuse it with the culture of the dominant countries. In our time, an era of multiple markets and multinational corporations, both economics and culture (that is, "mass culture") have been internationalized, thanks to accelerated development and the mass media. The centers of power export not only machinery and patents to us, but also ideology. If in Latin America the enjoyment of worldly goods is limited to the few, it then follows that the majority must resign itself to the consumption of fantasy. Illusions of wealth are sold to the poor, illusions of freedom to the oppressed, dreams of victory to the defeated and of power to the weak. One need not be literate to consume the inviting symbols presented by television, radio, and films in their effort to justify the unequal organization of the world.

In order to maintain the status quo in these lands, where each minute a child dies of disease or hunger, we must look at ourselves through the eyes of those who oppress us. People are trained to accept *this* order as *natural*, therefore eternal; and the system is identified with the fatherland, so that an enemy of the regime is by extension a traitor or a foreign agent. The law of the jungle, which is the law of the system, is sanctified, so that the defeated peoples will accept their condition as destiny; by falsifying the past, the true causes of Latin America's historical failure are passed over—Latin America, whose poverty has always fed alien wealth. On the small television screen and on the large, the best man wins, the best being the strongest. The waste, the exhibitionism, and the unscrupulousness produce not revulsion but admiration; everything can be bought, sold, rented, consumed, including the soul. Magical properties are attributed to a cigarette, a car, a bottle of whiskey, or a wristwatch: they can provide us with personalities, they can guide us toward success and happiness. The proliferation of foreign heroes and role models parallels the fetishism of brand names and fashions of the rich countries. The local *fotonovelas* and soap operas take place in a limbo of pretentiousness, peripheral to the real social and political problems of each country; and the imported serials sell Western, Christian democracy together with violence and tomato sauce.

5

In these lands of young people—young people whose numbers grow incessantly and who find no employment—the tick-tock of the time bomb obliges those who rule to sleep with one eye open. The multiple methods of cultural alienation—mechanisms used to drug and to castrate—take on increasing importance. The formulas for the sterilization of consciousness are put into practice with greater success than those for birth control.

The best way to colonize consciousness is to suppress it. In this sense also, the importation, whether deliberate or not, of a false counterculture, which finds a growing echo in the rising generations of some Latin American countries, plays a role. Those countries which do not offer the option of political participation—because of the fossilization of their structures or because of their stifling mechanisms of repression—offer the most fertile ground for the proliferation of a so-called culture of protest, originating outside the country, a sub-product of the leisure and waste which is focused on all social classes and originates in the spurious anticonventionalism of the parasite classes.

The customs and symbols of the resurgent youth of the sixties in the United States and Europe, born of a reaction against the uniformity of consumption, have become objects of assembly-line production in Latin America. Clothing with psychedelic

designs is sold, accompanied by exhortations to "free yourself";
music, posters, hair styles, and clothing that reproduce the aesthetic models of drug hallucination become mass-market items
for the Third World. Together with the symbols, colorful and
appealing as they are, tickets to limbo are offered to young
people who are attempting to flee the inferno. The new generations are invited to abandon a history which is painful for a
trip to Nirvana. By joining this "drug culture" certain young
Latin Americans achieve the illusion of reproducing the life-
style of their metropolitan counterparts.

Originating in the lack of conformity of marginal groups in
industrial alienated society, this false counterculture has nothing
to do with our real needs of identity and destiny; it provides
adventures for the immobilized; it generates resignation, egotism, noncommunication; it leaves reality intact but changes its
image; it promises painless love and warless peace. Furthermore,
by converting sensations into consumer goods, it dovetails perfectly with the "supermarket ideology" disseminated by the mass
media. If the fetishism of cars and refrigerators is not sufficient
to mute anguish and to calm anxieties, it is at least possible
to buy peace, intensity, and happiness in the underground
supermarket.

6

To awaken consciousness, to reveal reality—can literature claim
a better function in these times and in these lands of ours? The
culture of the system, the culture of reality-substitutes, disguises
reality and anesthetizes consciousness. But what can a writer
do—however much his or her flame burns—against the ideological mechanisms of lies and conformism?

If society tends to organize itself in such a way that contact
between humans is precluded, and human relations are reduced
to a sinister game of competition and consumption—of isolated
individuals using and abusing each other—what role can be

played by a literature of fraternal ties and collective solidarity? We have reached a point where to name things is to denounce them: but, to whom and for whom?

7

Our own fate as Latin American writers is linked to the need for profound social transformations. To narrate is to give oneself: it seems obvious that literature, as an effort to communicate fully, will continue to be blocked from the start, so long as misery and illiteracy exist, and so long as the possessors of power continue to carry out with impunity their policy of collective imbecilization, through the instruments of the mass media.

I don't share the attitude of those who demand special freedom for writers, independently of freedom for other workers. Great changes, deep structural changes, will be necessary in our countries if we writers are to go beyond the citadels of the elites, if we are to express ourselves, free of visible and invisible restraints. In an incarcerated society, free literature can exist only as denunciation and hope.

At the same time, I think that it would be a midsummer night's dream to imagine that the creative potential of the people could be realized through cultural means alone—the people, who were lulled to sleep long ago by harsh conditions of existence and the exigencies of life. How many talents have been extinguished in Latin America before they could reveal themselves? How many writers and artists have never had the opportunity to recognize themselves as such?

8

Furthermore, can a national culture be achieved completely in countries where the material bases of power are not indigenous but are dependent on foreign metropoli?

This being the case, does it make sense to write? There is no "degree zero" of culture, just as there is no "degree zero" of history. If we recognize an inevitable continuity between the stage of domination and the stage of liberation in any process of social development, why negate the importance of literature and its possible revolutionary role in the exploration, revelation, and diffusion of our real and potential identity? The oppressor does not want the mirror to reflect anything to the oppressed but its quicksilver surface. What process of change can activate a people that doesn't know who it is, nor from whence it comes? If it doesn't know who it is, how can it know what it deserves to become? Cannot literature aid, directly or indirectly, in this revelation?

It seems to me that the possibility of contribution depends to a large extent on the level of intensity of the writer's responsiveness to his or her people—their roots, their vicissitudes, their destiny—and the ability to perceive the heartbeat, the sound and rhythm, of the authentic counterculture, which is on the rise. That which is considered "uncultured" often contains the seeds or fruits of *another* culture, which confronts the dominant one and does not share its values or its rhetoric. It is frequently and erroneously dismissed as a mere degraded imitation of the "culture products" of the elite or of the cultural models turned out by the system on an assembly-line basis. But a popular narrative is oftentimes more revealing and more meaningful than a "professional" novel, and the pulse of life is conveyed more forcefully in certain anonymous folksong couplets than in many volumes of poetry written in the code of the initiated. The testimonies of the people as they express in a thousand ways their tribulations and their hopes are more eloquent and beautiful than the books written "in the name of the people."

Our authentic collective identity is born out of the past and is nourished by it—our feet tread where others trod before us; the steps we take were prefigured—but this identity is not frozen into nostalgia. We are not, to be sure, going to discover our hidden countenance in the artificial perpetuation of customs, clothing, and curios which tourists demand of conquered peoples. *We are what we do, especially what we do to change what we are*: our identity resides in action and in struggle. Therefore, the revelation of what we are implies the denunciation of those who stop us from being what we can become. In defining ourselves our point of departure is challenge, and struggle against obstacles.

A literature born in the process of crisis and change, and deeply immersed in the risks and events of its time, can indeed help to create the symbols of the new reality, and perhaps—if talent and courage are not lacking—throw light on the signs along the road. It is not futile to sing the pain and the beauty of having been born in America.

9

Neither press runs nor sales figures necessarily provide a valid measure of the impact of a book. At times the written work radiates an influence much greater than is apparent; at times, it answers—years in advance—the questions and needs of the collectivity, if the writer has known how to experience them first, through inner doubts and agonies. Writing springs from the wounded consciousness of the writer and is projected onto the world; the act of creation is an act of solidarity which does not always fulfill its destiny during the lifetime of its creator.

10

I do not share the attitude of those writers who claim for themselves divine privileges not granted to ordinary mortals, nor of those who beat their breasts and rend their clothes as they clamor for public pardon for having lived a life devoted to serving a useless vocation. Neither so godly, nor so contemptible. Awareness of our limitations does not imply impotence:

literature, a form of action, is not invested with supernatural powers, but the writer may become something of a magician if he or she procures, through a literary work, the survival of significant experiences and individuals.

If what is written is read seriously and to some extent changes or nourishes the consciousness of the reader, a writer has justified his or her role in the process of change: with neither arrogance nor false humility, but with the recognition of being a small part of something vast.

It seems to me appropriate that those who reject the word are the ones who cultivate monologues with their own shadows and with their endless labyrinths; but the word has significance for those of us who wish to celebrate and share the certainty that the human condition is not a cesspool. We seek interlocutors, not admirers; we offer dialogue, not spectacle. Our writing is informed by a desire to make contact, so that readers may become involved with words that came to us from them, and that return to them as hope and prophecy.

11

To claim that literature on its own is going to change reality would be an act of madness or arrogance. It seems to me no less foolish to deny that it can aid in making this change. The awareness of our limitations is undoubtedly an awareness of our reality. Amid the fog of desperation and doubt, it is possible to face it and wrestle with it—with our limitations, but at the same time in opposition to them.

In this respect a "revolutionary" literature written for the convinced is just as much an abandonment as is a conservative literature devoted to the ecstatic contemplation of one's own navel. There are those who cultivate an "ultra" literature of apocalyptic tone, addressed to a limited public, convinced beforehand of what it proposes and transmits. What risk do these writers run, however revolutionary they claim to be, if they write for the minority that thinks and feels as they do, and if they give that minority what it expects? In such cases there is no possibility of failure; neither is there a possibility of success. What is the use of writing, if not to challenge the blockade imposed by the system on the dissenting message?

Our effectiveness depends on our capacity to be audacious and astute, clear and appealing. I would hope that we can create a language more fearless and beautiful than that used by conformist writers to greet the twilight.

12

But it is not only a problem of language; it is also one of media. The culture of resistance employs all the means available to it, and does not grant itself the luxury of wasting any vehicle or opportunity of expression. Time is short, the challenge a burning one, the task enormous; for a Latin American writer, enlisted in the cause of social change, the production of books constitutes one sector on a front of multiple efforts. We do not share the sanctification of literature as a frozen institution of bourgeois culture. Mass-market narrative and reportage, television, film, and radio scripts, popular songs are not always minor "genres" of inferior character, as is claimed by certain lords of specialized literary discourse, who look down on them. The fissures opened by Latin American rebel journalism in the alienating mechanisms of the mass media have frequently been the result of dedicated and creative works, which need no apology for their esthetic level or their efficacy when compared with good novels and short stories.

13

I believe in my vocation; I believe in my instrument. I cannot understand why those writers write who declare airily that writing makes no sense in a world where people are dying of hunger. Nor can I understand those who convert the word into the target of their rage and into a fetish. Words are weapons, and they can be used for good or for evil; the crime can never be blamed on the knife.

I think that a primordial function of Latin American literature today is the rescue of the word, frequently used and abused with impunity for the purpose of hampering and betraying communication.

"Freedom" in my country is the name of a jail for political prisoners, and "democracy" forms part of the title of various regimes of terror; the word "love" defines the relationship of a man with his automobile, and "revolution" is understood to describe what a new detergent can do in your kitchen; "glory" is something that a certain smooth soap produces in its user, and "happiness" is a sensation experienced while eating hot dogs. "A peaceful country" means, in many countries of Latin America, "a well-kept cemetery," and sometimes "healthy man" must be read as "impotent man."

By writing it is possible to offer, in spite of persecution and censorship, the testimony of our time and our people—for now and for later. One may write as if to say: "We are here, we were here; we are thus, we were thus." In Latin America a literature is taking shape and acquiring strength, a literature that does not lull its readers to sleep, but rather awakens them; that does not propose to bury our dead, but to immortalize them; that refuses to stir the ashes but rather attempts to light the fire. This literature perpetuates and enriches a powerful tradition of combative words. If, as we believe, hope is preferable to nostalgia, perhaps that nascent literature may come to deserve the beauty of the social forces which, sooner or later, by hook or by crook, will radically alter the course of our history. And perhaps it may help to preserve for the generations to come—in the words of the poet—"the true name of all things."

(1976)
Translated by Bobbye S. Ortiz

Exile, Somewhere Between
Nostalgia and Creativity

1

Crisis of identity, anxieties born of expulsion, ghosts that haunt
and accuse: exile sows doubts and raises issues not necessarily
faced by those who live far away *by choice*. The outcast *cannot*
return to his country or to one he had taken as his own. When
you're washed up on foreign shores, your soul is bared to the
storms and you lose your habitual frames of reference and shelter. *The distance is greater when there is no alternative.*

2

For writers, banishment confirms the fact that literature is not
benign. Most of the Chilean, Argentine, and Uruguayan writers
forced into exile in recent years are paying the consequences of
using words freely. As everyone knows, the dictatorships of the
South have erected a machinery of silence. They hope to hide
reality, to erase memory, to empty consciences. From the vantage
point of this plan for collective castration, the dictatorships are
right to send books and newspapers that smell of gunpowder
to the bonfires, and to condemn their authors to exile, prison,
or the grave. *Some literature is incompatible with the military's
pedagogy of amnesia and lies.*

3

But be careful, don't get confused. It's not an occupational hazard. The victims of the prohibition and persecution of the living word are not just a few writers. The dictatorships expose the essential contradiction in Latin America between freedom for business and freedom for people. Who is not gagged? Those giving the orders. Books are outlawed and so are meetings: is any space for communication and meeting not potentially dangerous?

A couple of examples from Argentina that I found revealing: one decree forbids the publication of any story about what happens in the street, as well as "the opinions of nonspecialists" on any subject; another policy mandates six-year jail terms for anyone who fails to wipe out any graffiti painted on his house the same day it appears.

According to the doctrine of national security, the people are the enemy.

4

Neither is exile the dramatic privilege of a few intellectuals and political activists. I think, for example, of the multitude of Uruguayan emigrants sent overseas by the economic crisis during the last decade. The most conservative estimates put at half a million the number of Uruguayans obliged to seek under other skies the daily bread that their own land, paradoxically fertile and empty, denies them. They too are exiles, suffering a fate they did not choose. And it's no bed of roses to have to earn a living fighting like hell in countries that have a different history and different ways of speaking and living.

The general truth does not contradict the specific one. The former simply helps to place the latter in context. *In exile are writers and also masons and lathe mechanics.*

5

The price we pay is not that high in comparison. Especially compared to the fate some of our comrades have suffered in our countries. To de-dramatize the plight of writers in exile, you needn't search far. A few examples from Argentina and Uruguay that recently scarred my soul: poet Paco Urondo, shot dead; authors Haroldo Conti and Rodolfo Walsh and journalist Julio Castro, lost in the sinister fog of kidnapping; playwright Mauricio Rosencof, broken by torture and now rotting behind bars.

In the best of cases, if you could escape the torture, jail, or cemetery, what would be the alternative to exile, at least in the River Plate today? *To survive we would have to become mute, banished in our own countries, and internal exile is always harder and more futile than any exile outside.*

6

Not to mention another exile that nearly all Latin American writers are condemned to suffer, an invisible one yet perhaps more serious. I'm referring to the fact that we will always be exiled from the great majority of our countrymen until the economic and social structures that block or restrict access to the printed word are profoundly altered. *Even when we can enjoy total freedom of expression in our countries, we are only read by the educated minority who can afford the books and are interested in them.*

7

Given what I've seen and heard, and given my own experience, I believe people often confuse a sense of belonging with geography.

National identity would be very fragile if simple physical distance were enough to break it. The most Latin American of recent novels were written off the borders of our map. After all, I know quite a few writers born in Montevideo or Buenos Aires who live in the River Plate and wish they were French, or so it appears. They anxiously await the latest literary fashions, which arrive late and outdated from Europe. They peer at Uruguayan or Argentinean reality from far above, as if they were forgiving it for being so alien and "far away from everything." Inversely, in the mythological city of Paris, which so seductively invites dizziness and confusion, many Latin American artists live and create without losing their identity or scribbling it away. In Paris, Julio Cortázar writes a literature that is very Argentine. Years ago Pedro Figari painted there the most Uruguayan paintings of all time. And César Vallejo, who spent a quarter of his life there, never stopped being a Peruvian poet.

Go where I may, I will never forget the land I belong to, because I wear her, I walk with her, I am her.

8

I cover my ears and think: There is nothing worth writing. I cover my eyes and conclude: There is nothing worth seeing.

You are far from your land and your people. Yes, but other lands appear, you discover other peoples, other fountains at which to drink, new publics with whom to converse. Every consciousness won over to indifference and selfish defeatism is a victory for the enemy. Doesn't the enemy repeat day and night that the dictatorships act in the name of their victims? That the oppressed deserve their fate? And that misfortune is predestined? What alternative could we offer by crying and complaining?

In no way does the new reality I've encountered in exile offend me for being what it is. On the contrary, even though I don't see myself in it and I continue feeling like a foreigner, it can be enriching and, thus, it can enrich my people, as long as I enter it without fear. Without a doubt the experience of exile makes writers question the language they employ. And not only language: somehow it obliges us to be "born again" in many ways, to make the creative dialogue possible. But at the same time doesn't it broaden the potential for communication and coming together? *Hard as it might be, doesn't the challenge confirm that we are alive? That the word lives and flies? That there is no customs office that can stop it, or cage that can hold it?*

9

No dictatorship falls without being pushed. And the decisive blows are not dealt from overseas. *But in a thousand and one ways, with our solitary and sympathetic craft, we can help denounce what is occurring, find out what happened, and encourage what will happen when these evil winds change.*

10

I look at myself in the mirror and I see a glowing god. I say: "What would the world do without me? We writers are the salt of the earth." But then in rotten exile, I look at myself in the mirror and I see myself as I am, nude, just a little person, and then I say: "Writing makes no sense; I'm being punished by mistake; the writer is not a man of action." Perfect symmetry of arrogance and repentance, two extremes of the same negation of reality: the writer who believes he is one of the chosen can at any moment reach the conclusion that the world is not worth saving. It is just a tiny step from pedantic messianism to the dense soup of self-pity. Little or no distance separates "disappointment" from literary creativity done as a favor for others. In this sense, some writers suffer in exile a crisis like that which occurs in the conscience of certain members of the self-proclaimed political vanguards: if reality doesn't change at the pace I wish, I won't wait: from this moment on, I "pass" on politics. The "popular masses" rapidly become "those shitty people" when they fail to follow the path that intellectuals have cut out "for" them. *If the world doesn't act like me, neither does it deserve me: exile undresses the contradiction between the importance that intellectuals tend to attribute to themselves, and the real measure of their influence on reality.*

11

Exile involves the risk of forgetting. But sometimes memory, which changes along with me, sets traps. Is it not comfortable to take refuge in the past, when reality scares me or angers me because it does not obey my desires? Do I take refuge in the past that really occurred, or in one I invent, unwittingly, to fit my current necessities? The present, which is alive, sulks. The past, being quiet, is more tame, it contradicts me less, and in that bag I can find whatever I put in it. Sometimes, it seems, forgetting disguises itself as an homage to memory. Alibis of fear: to freeze myself in nostalgia could be a way to negate not only the reality in which I live, or the current reality of my country, but also the reality of my past experience.

Paradoxically, however, exile opens up a distance in time and in space that can help you recapture the true dimensions of everything, of how much of you is in others, and of the task of writers in the great collective work of which we form a part. *With neither omnipotence nor humiliation, we have to wash out our eyes. To help change reality, first we have to see it.*

12

In a recent work, Angel Rama emphasized how productive were the exiles of certain Brazilian intellectuals after the 1964 coup d'état. Mario Pedroza in Chile, Ferreira Gullar in Argentina, Darcy Ribeiro in Uruguay, and Francisco Juliao in Mexico, says

Rama, not only became ambassadors of Brazilian culture, unknown in Spanish America, but at the same time took advantage of the contact with Spanish American cultures unknown in Brazil. Exile developed this exchange to a degree that would be improbable in "normal" situations, when in Latin America "normal" is reciprocal ignorance.

The possibilities for Latin American writers who are in exile far from the *patria grande*, in countries that speak other languages and in superindustrialized societies that have little or nothing in common with our own, are much less bountiful. However, I think that even there positive examples could multiply. The waves of Latin American exiles in Europe in the past few years have at least contributed to a more realistic mutual understanding, slowly surpassing the easy folkloric stereotypes, the tourists' amazement, the demagoguery. In addition, denunciations and polemics have led to a more "totalizing" vision of reality itself. In the era of multinational corporations, when automobiles and ideologies are built worldwide, contentious meetings between opposite realities can better illuminate the contradictions of this one world of ours, to which the outskirts have as much a birthright as the centers, in which prosperity and freedom for a few countries is not unconnected to the poverty and oppression of many others.

The revelation of identities that universalize man is not the only nourishment that obligatory contact with foreign realities can bestow: I get nourished by what I choose, but also by what I reject. The voices of these traditional metropolitan cultures have a lot to tell us; but they are *also* eloquent in their weariness. We have a lot to learn from societies with a high standard of living, but they *also* teach us, for example, that economic development should not become an end in itself, that it does not always make people freer or happier, and that sometimes it ends up putting people at the service of things.

In this way I widen my perspective and find keys to creation and orientation that could be of some help, sooner or later, when the hour to return arrives and the lands now being razed by the dictatorships must be sown anew. *Exile, always born of a defeat, offers us more than painful experiences. It closes some doors, but it opens others. This is a penance, and at the same time a freedom and a responsibility. It has a black face and it has a red face.*

(1979)

Ten Frequent Lies or Mistakes about Latin American Literature and Culture

1. "LITERATURE" IS WRITING BOOKS.

A writer is one who writes books, says bourgeois thought, which splinters everything it touches. The compartmentalization of creative activity has ideologues specialized in raising walls and digging ditches. Up to here, they tell us, we have the novel; this is the dividing line of the essay; there poetry begins. And above all, make no mistake about it: here is the border that separates literature from its lesser forms, the minor genres of journalism, song, movie scripts, television, and radio.

Literature, however, embraces the sum of written messages that make up a given culture, apart from the value judgments their quality deserves. An article, a verse, a film script are also literature—mediocre or brilliant, alienating or liberating—as good or bad, indeed, as any book can be.

These meat grinders of the soul would leave no place for many of Latin America's most effective and beautiful literary creations. The work of the Cuban José Martí, for example, was above all written for publication in periodicals, and the passage of time showed that it belonged to an instant and yet also belonged to history. The Argentinian Rodolfo Walsh, one of the finest writers of his generation, developed most of his work in the journalistic medium and through his reports gave a timeless testimony to the infamy and hope of his country. The open letter Walsh wrote to the Argentine dictatorship on its first anniversary is a great document of the Latin American history of our time. It was the last he ever wrote. On the following day the dictatorship kidnapped and "disappeared" him.

I wonder, as I cite examples, whether the work of Chico Buarque de Holanda lacks literary value because it is written to be sung. Is popularity a crime against literature? The poems of Chico Buarque, perhaps Brazil's best young poet, go from mouth to mouth, hummed in the streets; does this diminish their value and debase their category? Is poetry only worthwhile when it is published, even if only in editions of a thousand copies? The best Uruguayan poetry of the last century—the *cielitos* of Bartolomé Hidalgo—was written to be accompanied by guitars and remains alive in the repertoires of popular troubadours. I am sure that Mario Benedetti does not regard his poems to be sung as less "literary" than his poems to be read. The poems of Juan Gelman, which do not imitate the tango because they contain it, lose none of their beauty when they become tangos. The same with Nicolás Guillén. Doesn't the *son*, his most characteristic poetic form, derive from popular Afro-Cuban music?

In a social system as exclusory as that which prevails in most Latin American countries, we writers have to use all possible media of expression. With imagination and skill, it is always possible to open cracks in the walls of the citadel that condemns us to noncommunication and makes access to the multitudes difficult or impossible. In the years of World War II, Alejo Carpentier wrote radio plays that were very popular all over Cuba, and one of today's best Venezuelan narrators, Salvador Garmendia, writes soap operas in Caracas. Julio Cortázar based one of his latest books, *Phantoms Against the Multinationals*, on a comic strip, and it was sold in comic-strip form at Mexican newsstands.

I am far from denying the value of the book as a medium of literary expression. I simply believe that it would be appropriate to begin to question its monopoly. And this leads us to another concept that I believe is wrong and that is no less common.

2. "CULTURE" MEANS THE PRODUCTION AND CONSUMPTION OF BOOKS AND OTHER WORKS OF ART.

As a general rule no one dares formulate this definition, but implicitly is exists everywhere. I think it is very limited. In the first place because it excludes science, the immense body of scientific knowledge that is part of culture and is systematically put down by intellectuals dedicated to the arts. Also because it reduces culture to the terminology of industry, an industry of luxury articles, while overlooking the so-called mass culture that is the cultural industry *par excellence*. And finally, but no less important: this definition of culture does not take into account the spontaneous and valuable expressions of popular culture.

The first omission, the nonrecognition of science as cultural work, seems inexplicable in the light of most recent Latin American history. The floodtide of military dictatorships in the seventies swept before it not only dangerous writers, subversive theater people, protest musicians, disobedient artists, and teachers for whom education meant the creation of free men. The dictatorships also attacked liberating scientific projects. And understandably, from their viewpoint: such projects may confuse the victims of the system; the masters, never.

The monopoly of technology is a key to domination in the contemporary world, and the Latin American dictatorship—the political party of multinational corporations—carry out their function: they destroy the few scientific research centers with a national vocation, so that our countries may remain condemned to the consumption of foreign technology, controlled by the master. Like the writers, the scientists are never innocent: there is a way of practicing science which by its mere existence accuses the owners of a system contrary to the interests of the country and the people.

As for the second omission, who could deny the influence of "mass culture" on the Latin American multitudes, who need not be able to read to listen to the radio or watch television? This mass culture is churned out in the great power centers of the capitalist world, above all in the United States, and is exported to diffuse life-styles on a universal scale. Cultural imperialism functions through the educational apparatus, but above all through the mass-communication media—television channels, radios, large-circulation newspapers and magazines. The TV set is king. This familiar totem of our time immobilizes its devotees for more hours than any preacher and transmits ideology with an astounding power of diffusion and persuasion.

Most Latin American countries are undergoing a reformulation of the power of the state. In the era of "national security," people live imprisoned so that business may live free, and the cultural industry consolidates an alliance with the military apparatus. With few exceptions, the mass media spread a colonialist and alienating culture, designed to justify the unequal organization of the world as the result of a legitimate triumph by the best—that is, the strongest. They falsify the past and lie about reality; they propose a model of life that postulates consumerism as an alternative to communism and that exalts crime as a heroic feat, lack of scruple as a virtue, and egotism as an inherent need. They teach competition, not sharing. In the world that they set forth, people belong to automobiles and culture is consumed, like a drug, but is not created. This is also a culture, a culture of resignation, that generates artificial needs to obscure real ones. No one could, I believe, deny the breadth of its influence. One must ask, however: Are the media that transmit it to blame? Is television bad and are books good? Is the knife to blame for the crime? Aren't there plenty of books that teach us to despise ourselves and to accept history instead of making it?

Regarding the third omission, some recent examples from the River Plate region seem striking to me. When the Argentine military retook power, they promptly made new rules for communication media. The new censorship code banned, among much else, the broadcasting of man-in-the-street reports and nonspecialized opinions on any issue. This monopoly of power implied the monopoly of the word, which in turn condemned the "common man" to silence. It was the apotheosis of private property: not only factories and land, houses, animals and even persons have owners, but issues, too. Popular culture, which resides in the fields and the streets, is always a "nonspecialized opinion." Some intellectuals look down on it, but dictatorships make no mistake when they forbid it.

In Uruguay, for example, cultural repression was not limited in these recent years to shutting down almost all the newspapers and magazines, burning books in autos-da-fé or shredding them to sell as confetti, and condemning many scientists and artists to exile, jail, or the ditch. The dictatorship also banned gatherings and all opportunities of encounter, dialogue, or debate; and in primary and secondary schools students could not contact their teachers outside of class hours. And more: they banned some lyrics of carnival tunes, fearful of the power of protest and mischief, and those who sang them ended up in jail. It's no accident that carnival—a time of truce and vengeance, when night becomes day and the beggar a king—worries repressive regimes. Nor that dictatorships keep up with the cleaning of walls. In countries that operate as jails, walls have no inscriptions or drawings. The wall is the poor man's press: a communication medium of which, riskily, furtively, fleetingly, the forgotten and condemned of the earth can avail themselves. It is no wonder that in Buenos Aires, whoever failed to erase within twenty-four hours anything written on the front of his house went to prison.

3. POPULAR CULTURE LIES IN FOLKLORIC TRADITIONS.

From the standpoint of the dominant ideology, folklore is a pleasant and minor thing, but this paternalism is exposed as pure and simple contempt when "handicrafts" invade the sacred sphere of "art." In 1977, the Peruvian painter Fernando Szyszlo resigned from the National Culture Commission because a sample of artisanship had been sent to the São Paulo Bienale representing Peru. A year before, there was a scandal when an altarpiece by Joaquín López Antay won the national prize. The Association of Plastic Arts raised a heated protest and split apart over this episode. I remember the frowns on the faces of more than one easel painter in Panama when it occurred to me to suggest that certain colored appliqué fabrics of the Cuna Indians of the San Blas Islands deserved inclusion among the best *present-day* examples of fine arts in that country.

In this system, it is clear that no one denies, at least in theory, the right of the people to *consume* the culture *created* by specialized professionals, although this consumption is in fact limited to the vulgar products of so-called mass culture. As for the creative capacity of the people, it's acceptable as long as it stays in its place. A few more or less exotic archetypes, colorful clothing, a language that repeats itself and means nothing: what is "popular" is "picturesque." The revenues from tourism more than suffice for any guilty-conscience tax. An embalmed memory and a cardboard identity provide adornment and offend no one.

But why does the *Popol Vuh*, for example, the sacred book of the Mayas, outlive the libraries of historians and anthropologists? Constructed through ancient times by the Maya Quiché people, this great anonymous collective work not only continues to soar among the peaks of Latin American literature; for the indigenous majority of Guatemalan society, it is also a beautiful sharp-edged tool, because the myths it contains remain alive in the memory and on the tongues of those who created them. After four and a half centuries of humiliation, these people continue to endure the life of beasts of burden. The sacred myths, which announce the time of battle and punishment of the high and mighty, remind the Indians of Guatemala that they are human beings and that they have a much longer history than the society that uses and despises them; that is why they are reborn each day.

In reality, the culture of the dominant class, imposed as the culture of the entire society, contains its own negation. It carries in its belly embryos of another possible culture that is, at the same time, the memory of a long-accumulated inheritance and the prophecy of a different reality.

That authentic national culture, which in some regions of Latin America has very ancient popular roots, does not function as a debased replica of the dominant culture. Indeed, the almost total lack of creative imagination is an essential characteristic of our ruling classes. Rarely have they shown themselves able to conceive of any cultural project that went beyond a translation of a model conceived by the metropolitan powers. If the material bases of a country belong to foreigners and its society is organized along concentration-camp lines, what national culture can flourish and breathe freely, shared by all? The dominant culture functions as a dominated culture, because the class that produces it is dominated from afar—a copycat, impotent bourgeoisie of managers, whose popularity doesn't reach beyond its demagogy. If in Venezuela the national dish, the black bean, is imported from the United States in sacks with the word "beans" printed in English, should one be surprised that Venezuelan children are ignorant of their country's history? A recent survey shows that an overwhelming number of Venezuelan children think Guaicaipuro is a television award and don't know it was the name of the native hero who resisted the Spanish conquest.

But at the same time that the dominant culture *distributes* knowledge—or rather, distributes ignorance—another insurgent culture *unchains* the capacity for understanding and creativity of the vast majority condemned to silence. This liberating culture nourishes itself on the past but does not stop there. From afar come some of the symbols of collective identity capable of opening, to Latin Americans of our time, new spheres of participation, communication, and encounter; but they are alive only to the extent that the winds of history keep them moving.

Popular culture does not consist *only* of folkloric traditions, which sometimes have dubious vernacular roots. The rescue of the River Plate peoples' cultural identity does not consist of blue jeans being replaced by baggy gaucho pants, which actually come from surplus production by the British in the Crimean War. And, as Carlos Monsiváis has noted in a recent work, the singer Jorge Negrete, symbol of official Mexico, was an adaptation of the "cowboy singer" in the style of Gene Autry and Roy Rogers. At the heart of the matter, it is value systems and not formalities that are in conflict. What is genuine popular culture if not a complex system of identity symbols that preserves *and creates* the people? By denying it this creative dimension, you send it off to the museum.

4. THE WRITER PERFORMS A CIVILIZING MISSION.

The messianism of the writer, who attributes to his craft a religious prestige and claims the attendant privileges, evolves in Latin America in a direct line from the romantic tradition and liberal ideology that sanctify the book as a treasure of civilization. Anyone who writes, publishes and, finds a reader who is not in the family considers himself or herself among the chosen. It is also a reflection of cultural colonialism and the result of a Eurocentrist vision of the world: "We are Europe, although we may have been born in barbarous lands." "The cultured are those who resemble us." "Being developed means being like us." Culture is identified with academic apprenticeship or inborn talent and poses "civilization" as coming from above or outside against "barbarism," which is below and within.

An effective Argentinian writer of the last century, Domingo Faustino Sarmiento, blessed with the slogan "civilization or barbarism" the exterminating wars that the port of Buenos Aires waged against the rebellious provinces. The dilemma still lives and still wreaks havoc: civilization, imported culture, against barbarism, national culture. Civilization, culture of the few, against barbarism, the ignorance of all the rest.

This cultural pedantry rounds out the system of alibis invented by the dominant classes and rich countries to justify the exploitation of some classes by others and of some countries by others. It is, furthermore, a result of the social division of labor. In reality, both the *intellectuals*, an expression that reduces people to heads, and the *manuals*, people reduced to hands, are the result of the same fracturing of the human condition. Capitalist development generates mutilated people.

Most Latin American countries are far from being societies in which creation is no longer a privilege but a collective right. "Art," said Marx, "is the highest joy of man." A necessity for all, but a luxury for few. We writers come from and write for a minority, although we are spurred by the intention and the hope of communicating with all the others.

Meanwhile, there are those who believe they are heirs to a certain illumination that comes in a direct line from the Parthenon: the writer "grants" culture; he doesn't converse with the others, giving back what he receives every day from them, but rather transmits truth to the others as a favor, usually inadequately compensated by collective ingratitude. Deep down, these talent aristocrats share the philosophy implicit in so-called mass culture, which could be summed up thus: "The people eat shit because they like it."

The same attitude, I believe, although a guilty conscience would prevent me from admitting it, underlies some petit-bourgeois intellectuals who write a literature "for workers," schematic and simplistic, as if workers were a pack of mental midgets. Lenin scoffed at "literature for workers." He admired and enjoyed Tolstoy, Dostoyevsky, and Pushkin and advocated access by the workers to "literature for all," as he put it, as a means to enrich their understanding of reality and their critical conscience. Lenin made fun of pious intellectuals "who think it's enough to speak to the workers about life in the factory and chew over what they have known for a long time." This pater-nalistic tone, repetitive and foolish, not only abounds in certain epic novels of "social realism" but is also customary in many political documents, newspapers, and pamphlets of the Latin American left—and from what I have seen, it is fairly common among leftists of other areas too, whether they speak from a position of power or of abjection.

The polemic between the monopolizers of beauty, who refuse to "stoop" to the level of the people, and the well-intentioned who seek to "descend" to that level to communicate with the masses is false, I believe. Both are on the same tack: they operate from the heights and scorn what they don't know.

5. A TRUE DEMOCRACY IS ONE THAT GUARANTEES FREEDOM OF EXPRESSION TO WRITERS AND ARTISTS.

This notion, typical of liberal thought, places writers and artists on the fringe of the trials and tribulations of the world. It stands guard over the fate of poets, but ignores the fate of machinists, typists, bricklayers, or ranch hands. Thus one often hears furious protests against *textual censorship*, with Olympian ignoring of the existence of *structural censorship*. The banning, murder, imprisonment, or exile of writers, the looting of libraries, the closing of newspapers and burning of books are condemned as if they were simply "abuses," "excesses," "arbitrary acts," and not the dramatic consequences of the functioning of a system that can resort only to violence to keep at bay the growing legions of the jobless, the hopeless, and the damned.

A report of the International Labor Organization a few years ago indicated that there exist in Latin America 110 million persons "in conditions of abject poverty." Isn't *structural censorship* being applied to a huge number, denying them access to books and magazines which "circulate freely"? How can these multitudes read if they don't know how to read, or have money to buy what they would need to read? Isn't it *structural censorship* that reserves the right of expression and creation, in our societies, to a privileged minority, while closing the eyes and mouths of everyone else?

In these last years, the militarization of power in several Latin American countries has implied an accelerated militarization of culture. The "irrational" violence of the dictatorships has not one iota of irrationality: the dictatorship is not the dictator, but rather the system which makes dictatorship necessary in order to keep political and social tensions from exploding. In this framework, some writers, artists, and scientists share the misfortunes of the immense majority. Literature is not innocent, art is not innocent, science is not innocent. There are also intellectuals who bless the executioners, or maintain, in their presence, a conspiratorial silence. They are those who dream of a free art, although the society is imprisoned.

There is an abundance of writers and artists who claim the privilege of irresponsibility. For them the cultural function is metaphysical, detached from history and the social struggle: books and paintings emerge "through" the elect one, blown into his ear by elves, demons, and private phantoms. Hence, the artist is born with impunity insurance.

It is said, for example: "Jorge Luis Borges believes that Argentinians are imbeciles, blacks are inferior and smell bad, Indians, gauchos and Vietnamese deserved to be slaughtered, and the swords of Pinochet and Videla have not been long enough. Ah—but Borges's literature is *something else*." However, contempt for the people, the idea that everything in the past was better—the past of his ancestors—and the fatalistic concept of life are present both in the books and in the declarations of this man who said, for example, in August of 1976: "Free will and liberty are necessary illusions," and "Democracy is a statistical abuse." An inexplicable and immutable universal order toys capriciously with human will in the work of this writer, brilliant without a doubt; and in it, life is a labyrinth—the labyrinth of an endless library, which leads us nowhere. We are left with, at most, nostalgia: hope, never. In what way does his conception of the human condition contradict a system that seeks to confuse itself with eternity and empty man, precisely, of freedom and history?

6. ONE CANNOT SPEAK OF LATIN AMERICAN CULTURE, BECAUSE LATIN AMERICA IS NOTHING MORE THAN A GEOGRAPHICAL REALITY.

Nothing more than a geographical reality? And yet it moves. In actions, unimportant at times, Latin America reveals each day its fellowship as well as its contradictions; we Latin Americans share a common space, and not only on the map. They were well aware of it, at the beginning of the last century, those heroes who tried vainly to unite it, and the efficient empire that in successive fracturings divided it in order to rule it. They are well aware of it today, those multinational corporations that plan their business on a Latin American scale and manipulate at their whim the mechanisms of integration.

True, in Latin America there coexist societies of diverse origins, differing characteristics, and sharp unevenness of development. And one cannot speak of "Latin American culture" in the same sense in which one also could not speak of "culture" without stating an empty abstraction. But a common framework encompasses the infinite cultures, adverse or complementary, that stir in our lands. Realm of contradiction and encounter, Latin America offers a common field of battle between the cultures of fear and the cultures of freedom, between those that deny us and those that give us life. This common framework, this common space, this common battlefield, is historic. It originates in the past, is nurtured by the present, and is projected as a necessity and a hope toward the times to come. Obstinately it has survived, although it has several times been injured or broken by the same interests that underline our differences in order to mask our identities.

The Spanish experience since the death of Franco can help us understand better, strange as it may seem, our contradictory Latin American identity. These last years have made it clear that the unity of the Spanish state conceals very intense national contradictions. Those contradictions, which have a long history and have been suffocated in blood and fire, are now in full explosion. Spain is going through the period of autonomies and fertile debate about basic restructuring of the state. No legitimate supranational unity can rest on the humiliation of some nationalities by others, on the oppression of some cultures by others. Now then: there is little resemblance, at first glance, between a Brazilian and a Bolivian, a Mexican and a Uruguayan. But the new Spanish political reality has brought to light differences no less profound—differences of origin, of tradition, and even of language—that really do exist between a Catalonian and a Castilian, between a Basque and an Andalusian or a Galician.

Beginning with that which unites us, and based on respect of the numerous national identities that compose us, Latin America is above all a task to be performed. Our economies have been oriented outward, in function of servitude, and also our cultures still have their vertices in European capitals, where the literary customs officers, for example, still give their okay for a Paraguayan novel to be considered worthwhile in Venezuela.

Our most genuine disconnected cultures make contact, when they are permitted to, with eloquent facility. Many things, some understood and others a mystery, make all of us feel like little bits of a great homeland, where beings from all over the world and all cultures have made an appointment, throughout the centuries, to mix and exist together. Beyond the diversity of races, roots, and statistics, the cultural patrimony of Mexico or Ecuador also belongs to Uruguay and Argentina, and vice versa, to the extent that one or the other can offer keys to the challenges of present-day reality. The black culture of Haiti is not foreign to the indigenous culture of Guatemala, because in both, people who join in a common space, time, and historical drama can find clear water to drink. What Hispano-American cannot feel his own heartbeat in Guimarães Rosa, Drummond de Andrade, or Ferreira Gullar? What Brazilian doesn't feel in some way that Carpentier, Cortázar, or Rulfo are his? The revolutions of Cuba and Nicaragua are not foreign for any Latin American. The tragedy of Chile opened a gash in the breast of all Latin Americans. Whatever our skin color or language, aren't we all made of assorted clays from the same multiple earth?

7. THE GREAT TASK OF THE NEW LATIN AMERICAN LITERATURE CONSISTS OF THE INVENTION OF A LANGUAGE.

The long romantic novel, the paternalism of the "indigenist" writer, and the false "nativism" written in and for the cities, have fortunately been left behind. In the last twenty or thirty years Latin American literature has reflected a new awareness of reality, which was incubated in certain youthful middle-class circles and was projected, on the cultural level, with as much energy as on the political level.

Those who specialize in confusing the peel with the fruit tell us: "It's the language revolution. Language is the true protagonist of the new Latin American novel." Voices or echoes? The styles of cultural *haute couture* arrive in our lands with the usual delay, when no one is paying them much more attention in their centers of origin. The Pierre Cardins of letters have invented the theory—or resuscitated it, because it is ancient—in Paris; and the copycats have applied it to emerging Latin American literature in order to kidnap its critical content. But language is the instrument, not the melody: and the true protagonists of the new Latin American narrative are not pronouns and adjectives, but men and women of flesh and blood.

It will certainly not be through a revolution in syntax that the word will be restored its lost dignity. The system empties language of content, not for the pleasure of a technical pirouette, but because it needs to isolate men in order the better to control them. Language implies communication and therefore becomes dangerous in a system that reduces human relations to fear, mistrust, competition, and consumption. The same mechanism that plunges new generations into despair and the police files is the one that names a jail Liberty, as in Uruguay, and a concentration camp Colony of Dignity, as in Chile.

The reduction of literature to pure pyrotechnics reveals, on the aesthetic plane, a cult of form equivalent to the one manifested in the political field by those who confuse democracy with elections, and in the field of economics, a confusion of means and ends similar to that of the technocrats who believe development is the ultimate goal of all societies.

8. LATIN AMERICA HAS AN EXUBERANT NATURE; HENCE ITS LITERATURE IS BAROQUE.

My point here is not to discuss the thousand and one theories that exist about the baroque. The label is applied to painters as opposite as Rembrandt and Rubens, and to writers who have in common only the fact of being born in the same country, like Alejo Carpentier and Severo Sarduy.

A common denominator would be impossible. Everyone understands the baroque in his own way; for some, the term defines specific styles; for others, a period in art history. Indeed, every theoretician finds behind the word what he previously put there.

In an essay published a few years ago, the Cuban Leonardo Acosta protested, and rightly so, against this "stylistic fatalism," as unacceptable as any other fatalism, in which the baroque style corresponds to the exuberant nature of Latin America. He noted that the baroque arrived on American soil as a product of colonial importation, from the arid lands of Castile, which know nothing of exuberance.

Latin American literature, we are told, is baroque because it speaks the language of the jungle—as if jungle language were the only one possible in an area of the world that has large cities, vast deserts, steppes, mountain ranges, and plains; and as if there really existed "a" language of the jungle. Didn't the sparse tales of Horacio Quiroga speak the jungle language of the Upper Paraná? And what of the stylized masks, that have nothing baroque about them, created in the villages of the African jungle?

The notion of the baroque style is a cliché as false as all clichés, which alludes to flowery language and fits into the widespread belief that a Latin American novel, to be good, must unfold over many pages and use quantities of words. Such an arbitrary criterion would exclude from Latin American literature many of its best writers, such as Juan Rulfo, a man of naked and sparse prose; the complete works of Rulfo, one of the world's best storytellers, cover less than three hundred pages.

Another great Latin American novelist, Alejo Carpentier, uses the expression "baroque" in a sense that has nothing to do with the rococo discourse, pompous and empty, of other writers. For Carpentier, the baroque comes from the mixture of styles and cultures that generate, in our lands, "magical realism," and has an original and vital feeling, completely foreign to the colonial view that from the outside petrifies us in exotic scenery and tourist picture postcards. In the work of Carpentier, the style that he calls baroque "names" reality and rediscovers it; in others, such as Severo Sarduy, the baroque masks it. Reading Carpentier, Lezama Lima, Guimarães Rosa, Jorge Enrique Adoum, one has the sensation and the certainty that the complexity of style corresponds exactly to the complexity of the world it is expressing; it could not be said any other way. There are many inverse cases, where complexity of style, poor in images but pretentious in arabesques, hides the fear of clarity; if the prose were stripped naked, it would expose its irreparable stupidity.

The fatalists of style want to convince us that baroque is "the" language of Latin America, as if there were only one language possible for a world that contains so many worlds. In the end, they are only attempting to claim a high aesthetic level for the tediousness of their works, written in the traditional pompous style of frock-coated doctors. The wordiness does not act in the service of nature, but in the service of the system, by providing it with disguises. That must be why the poorer a country is, the showier and hollower its literature—as if the smaller quantity of calories in the people's diet corresponded to a larger number of words in the work of intellectuals who have turned their backs on reality.

9. POLITICAL LITERATURE TREATS POLITICAL THEMES; SOCIAL LITERATURE, SOCIAL THEMES.

But does there exist any literary work that is not political and social? All are social, because they belong to human society; and all are also political, inasmuch as the printed word always implies—whether the author likes it or not, or knows it or not—a participation in public life.

The written message "chooses," by the simple fact of existing; by addressing itself to others, it inevitably occupies a space and takes part in the relationships between society and power. Its content, liberating or alienating, is in no way determined by the subject. The most political literature, or most deeply committed to political processes of change, can be that which least needs to *name* politics, in the same sense that the crudest social violence is not necessarily manifested through bombings and shootings.

Often books, articles, songs, and manifestos about "political and social themes," written with the most revolutionary motives in the world, do not produce results resembling the good intentions which inspire them. Sometimes they approve, without meaning to, the very system they want to challenge. Those who address the people as if they were dull-witted and incapable of imagination confirm the image cultivated by the oppressors. Those who use a language of boring ready-made phrases and create one-dimensional characters, cardboard characters, lacking fear or doubts or contradictions, mechanically executing the orders of the story's or novel's author, bless the system they purport to oppose. Doesn't the system specialize in disintegrations? A literature that shrinks the soul instead of multiplying it, no matter how militant it calls itself, objectively serves a social order which each day cuts away at the multiplicity and richness of the human condition. In other cases, no less frequent, the attempt at communication and contagion fails in advance if it addresses an already-convinced audience, in the parochial language that this audience expects to hear: however revolutionary it may claim to be, this riskless literature comes out, in fact, conformist. It induces sleep although it aspires to zeal. It says it is for the multitudes, but it merely chats with the mirror.

Literature can, I believe, claim a liberating political role whenever it contributes to revealing reality in its multiple dimensions and, whatever its subjects may be, in some way nourishes the collective identity or rescues the memory of the community that generates it. A love poem may end up, from this point of view, politically more fruitful than a novel about the exploitation of tin miners or banana-plantation workers.

One can find many examples in Latin American literature of the highest level. In a work published not long ago, Pedro Orgambide said he suspected that Pablo Neruda's *Canto General* is most political in the seemingly least political passages of the text. It seems to me his suspicion was well-founded. The poems of Neruda have more vigor and political depth in "Heights of Macchu Pichu" than in some pages devoted to denunciation of certain dictators or the outrages of the United Fruit Company. In my judgment, the book *Weekend in Guatemala* by Miguel Angel Asturias, written in the heat of fury over the invasion and slaughter of 1954, is, of all his books, the one with the most explicit political content, but is politically the least effective. I don't share the almost unanimous opinion that *A Manual for Manuel* is the most committed work of Julio Cortázar, and I think that Gabriel García Márquez's *Autumn of the Patriarch* is less rich, in the political sense, than *One Hundred Years of Solitude*, although political denunciation does not appear as a major theme in this great novel.

10. IN THE BEST OF CIRCUMSTANCES, LITERATURE CAN INTERPRET REALITY; BUT IT IS INCAPABLE OF TRANSFORMING IT.

In interpreting reality, in rediscovering it, literature can help to know it. And knowing it is the first necessary step toward beginning to change it: there is no experience of social or political change that does not develop out of a deepening of the awareness of reality.

Works of "fiction," as they are called, usually reveal more effectively than "nonfiction" the hidden dimensions of reality. In a famous letter, Engels wrote that in Balzac's novels he had learned more about certain aspects of the economy than in all the books by economists of his time. No sociological study teaches us more about the violence in Colombia than García Márquez's short novel *No One Writes to the Colonel*, in which, if I remember correctly, not a shot is heard, and *The City and the Dogs* by Mario Vargas Llosa X-rays the violence in Peru more deeply than any treatise on the subject. The best work of political economy on the Argentina of the last century is the poem of a surly gaucho named Martín Fierro. The novels and stories of José María Arguedas bear the most eloquent witness to the wrecking of native cultures in Latin America. Augusto Roa Bastos's novel *I the Supreme* opens broader channels than any history book for anyone who seeks deep understanding of Paraguay in the times of Gaspar Rodríguez de Francia. The disintegration of present-day Uruguay was masterfully forseen by Juan Carlos Onetti in *El Astillero*. Is there a better key for entering Guatemala than the books of Asturias? Isn't it the breath of life and death in present-day Argentina that blows the tenderness and fury into Juan Gelman's poems? And El Salvador and Nicaragua, those small, untamed countries, don't they speak to us through the mouths of Roque Dalton and Ernesto Cardenal?

Revealing reality does not mean copying it. Copying it would be betraying it, especially in countries like ours, where reality is masked by a system that forces it to lie in order to survive, and that daily forbids calling things by their names. Reality is given life by those who are capable of penetrating it. Picasso's *Guernica* offers our eyes more reality than all the photographs of the bombing of the small Basque city. A fantastic tale may reflect reality better than a naturalistic story respectful of what reality seems to be. Mario Benedetti, in a recent work, very correctly said that a story such as "The Occupied House" by

Julio Cortázar is more connected to reality, although a fantasy, than the tedious inventories of more than one author of the French *nouveau roman*. By means of the right symbols, "The Occupied House" represents the Dunkirk of a social class that is gradually being dislodged by a presence it lacks the courage to face.

Often writers politcally identified with the revolutionary cause suffer pangs of guilty conscience; wouldn't fantasy be a cowardly escape, a misrepresentation of the world? They feel then, or rather, we feel, because it can happen to me anytime, guilty of writing, guilty of flying. We forget, sometimes, that hope will die of thirst without the hallucinations and chimeras that nurture human creation.

As with a two-way mirror, literature can show what is visible, and what is not but still is there. And since nothing exists that does not contain its own negation, it often works as revenge and prophecy. The imagination opens new doors to the understanding of reality and foresees its transformation: it anticipates, through dream, the world to be conquered, at the same time that it challenges the immobility of the bourgeois order. In the system of silence and fear, the power to create and invent strikes at the routines of obedience. This social order, say its masters, is the natural order: a static world, front view and profile like a mug shot in the police files. The creative imagination reveals that its presumed immortality is fleeting and that there is no face without a mirror image.

The value of a text could well be measured by what it unleashes in the reader. The best books, the best essays and articles, the most effective poems and songs, cannot be read or listened to with impunity. Literature, which addresses the conscience, acts upon it, and when accompanied by intention, talent, and luck, it triggers the imagination and will to change. In the social structure of the lie, revealing reality implies denouncing it; and the process goes beyond that when the reader undergoes a small change through reading. It is said that a book doesn't change the world, and it is true. But what does change it? A process, fast or slow, as the case may be; always continual and of a thousand simultaneous dimensions. The written word is one of those dimensions, not just a spare wheel. To deny all literature that is not urgent constitutes, I believe, an error as serious as the scorn for forms of literary expression that escape the boundaries of the book, or that find no place on the altars of academic culture.

Haroldo Conti, an Argentinian storyteller I knew well in Buenos Aires, spent his final years tormented by the suspicion that his literature was politically useless. He was a man of revolutionary political ideas who felt that he wrote perfectly innocuous stories and novels, because he didn't employ explicit denunciation. In long nights over cigarettes and wine, on an island in the Tigre delta, we talked about this; and I never knew how to tell him that his work as a writer had a profoundly vital, renewing, and liberating feel. He was, or perhaps is, a humble magician capable of telling stories of much beauty. Like all worthwhile literature, his stories tell about life and make it happen. Fleetingly they pull us out of time in order to return us better than we were. By telling us what we are, they help us to be—because how can a people who do not know their identity become protagonists in history, making history instead of suffering it?

Later, toward the end of April 1976, Haroldo was kidnapped. Someone saw him, destroyed by torture in a barracks; and then nothing more was ever known. As was the case with many thousands of Argentinians, Chileans, Guatemalans, and Uruguayans, the earth swallowed him up. The Argentine newspapers did not print one line about the disappearance of one of the country's best writers; and he, who had an inquisitive conscience, became lost in terror and fog, anguished by the idea that his literary work was not consistent with his political ideals. In this sense, Haroldo was a victim of the schematism that at one extreme sings the praises of literature as the work of the gods and at the other scorns it as a harmless pastime.

I had looked for the words and had not found them. I tried to help him believe in what he was doing, and I didn't succeed. I wanted to tell him that by lighting small fires of identity, memory, and hope, works like his make up the forces of change in a system organized to erase our faces, disintegrate our souls, and empty our memory, and that in that way his works provided shelter to many people who are naked in the storm.

Because I wanted to help and couldn't, I now write these pages by way of expiation and affirmation.

(1980)
Translated by Cedric Belfrage
with Monica Weiss

Notes for a Self-Portrait

VOCATION

First comes the image. Then the word. I'm incapable of communicating a situation, an emotion, or an idea if I don't *see* it first with my eyes closed. And I always have difficulty finding words to communicate that image that seem worthy of its splendor. I believe that because I lack the talent for painting with paints, I paint when I write. Since I couldn't be a painter, I had no other choice but to become a writer. The woman you love ignores you, so you marry her cousin.

EVOCATION

I got published for the first time when I had just turned fourteen. It was a drawing, a political cartoon in the socialist weekly of Montevideo. And since then I have published many more drawings, signed "Gius," the Spanish pronunciation of my father's surname, which I got from a great-grandfather who came to Uruguay from Wales a century and a half ago.

Until I was seventeen I alternated between drawings and a few attempts at written journalism. I published essays on art, driven more by audacity than knowledge—adolescent brazenness—and essays on the labor movement, which I knew well from my early life as a "gofer" in factories and offices. At eighteen I felt my first panic facing a blank page, the same panic that still, today for example, I feel often: I wanted to write from the heart, with everything, I wanted to give myself to it—and I couldn't. I had tried it with brushes, and it didn't work either.

At nineteen I was dead, but I was born again.

At twenty I wrote a bad novel. I signed it Galeano, my mother's last name, which came to me from a great-grandfather from Genoa.

Later I died and was born again several times. Hokusai, that amazing Japanese artist, chose sixty different names for each of his sixty rebirths. I don't have either the audacity or the shadow of his talent.

REVELATION

Grandparents from Great Britain, Italy, Spain, and Germany; the face of the Swedish consul in Honduras. Nevertheless, I always knew that I was as Latin American as the stones of Machu Picchu, or the most humble pebble of my country. I came to know this, I know it, the way you really get to know things: traveling my insides from my guts to my head, and not the other way around.

I belong to a land that is still unknown to herself. I write to help her reveal herself—to reveal, to rebel—and seeking her out I seek out myself, and finding her I find myself, and with her, in her, I lose myself.

OBSESSION

I was a terrible history student. They taught me history as if it were a visit to a wax museum or to the land of the dead. I was over twenty before I discovered that the past was neither quiet nor mute. I discovered it reading novels by Carpentier and poems by Neruda. I discovered it listening to stories over coffee about some old, very old, warrior on the Uruguayan plains who kept his tired eyelids open with orangewood twigs while he speared enemy horsemen on the point of his lance. Asking and wondering, from where did this planet that we inhabit come? This planet that spends a million dollars on arms every minute, so that every minute thirty children can die of disease or hunger and no one is accused. Asking and wondering: This world, this slaughterhouse, this nuthouse, is this the work of God or man? What past time gave birth to this present? Why have some countries become owners of other countries, and some men owners of other men, and men owners of women, and women of children, and things owners of people?

I am not a historian. I am a writer obsessed with remembering, with remembering the past of America above all, and above all that of Latin America, intimate land condemned to amnesia.

EXPLORATION

In three months, in ninety nights, I wrote *The Open Veins of Latin America*. It was the result of much reading and many trips, angers, loves, stupors. And, above all, it was the result of many doubts: the fertile doubt, always pregnant.

Thirteen years have passed, and I do not repent. *The Open Veins* publicizes facts that show that Latin America's present reality does not stem from some indecipherable curse. I wanted to explore history in order to encourage people to make it, to help open up spaces of freedom in which the victims of the past can become protagonists of the present. I am told that the book has been very useful, as useful as a book can be in the land of illiteracy, misery, and dictatorship: useful for those whose gold and silver and copper and oil have been stolen, and whose voice and memory have been stolen as well.

SONG

I do not repent; and yet I am afraid that *The Open Veins* may reduce history to a single economic dimension. And if by history I mean reality—a living memory of reality—I mean a living life, life that sings with multiple voices; and in America, the land where all the cultures and all the human ages mix, that diversity of voices seems infinite. I don't know if my mouth will be worthy of them; and on the contrary I do know that no literary work could take them all in. But they resound so intensely that they are an irresistible temptation.

I'm trapped for good in this effort to converse with America, and above all with Latin America, as if she were a person, as if she were a woman, wishing to share her secrets. From what clays was she born? From what acts of love and how many rapes does she come?

It's called *Memory of Fire* and it will be a trilogy. I have just finished writing the second volume. I'm happy as a dog with two tails, although my body protests. In the four years that I have spent in this adventure, I have lost the few hairs that adorned my once-bushy head and I have gained a duodenal ulcer and a herniated disk.

CONCLUSION

Now, in these lines I'm supposed to be writing something like a self-portrait. I could get back to my very Catholic infancy, everyone guilty in the eyes of God, God Universal Police Chief, the soul and the body like beauty and the beast. Or I could talk of my later conflicts with the dogmatic versions of Marxism that proclaim the Only Truth and that divorce man from nature and reason from emotion. Or I could tell that I have ridden through a number of misadventures and several times been thrown from the horse; that I have known the machinery of terror from the inside and that exile has not always been easy. I could celebrate that at the end of so much sorrow and so much death I still keep alive my capacity for astonishment at marvelous things, and my capacity for indignation at infamy, and that I continue to believe the advice of the poet who told me not to take seriously anything that does not make me laugh.

A self-portrait. I could say that I detest opera and plastic tablecloths and computers, that I am incapable of living far from the sea, that I write by hand and I cross out almost everything, that I have married three times, that . . . But so much talk bores me. It bores me: I understand it, I confess it, and I celebrate it.

Some time ago, I saw a chicken pecking at a mirror. The chicken was kissing its own reflection. In a little while, it fell asleep.

(1983)

The Discovery of America
Yet to Come

1. THE CRIME OF BEING

Four years after Christopher Columbus first set foot on the beaches of America, his brother Bartholomew inaugurated a crematorium in Haiti. Six Indians, found guilty of sacrilege, were burned at the stake. The Indians had buried a few little drawings of Jesus Christ and the Virgin Mary. But they had buried them so that these new gods would make their plot of corn more fruitful, and they felt not the slightest twinge of guilt for such a mortal offense.

DISCOVERY OR COVER-UP

It's already been said that in 1492 America was invaded, not discovered, since thousands of years previous it had been discovered by the Indians who lived there. But it could also be said that America was not discovered in 1492 because those who invaded it did not know *how to see it*, or simply could not do so.

Gonzalo Guerrero saw it. He was the conquered conquistador, and for having seen it he was slain. Certain prophets saw it, like Bartolomé de Las Casas, Vasco de Quiroga, and Bernardino de Sahagún. And for having seen it they were loved and condemned to solitude. But America was not seen by the warriors and the monks, the notaries and the merchants who came in search of quick fortune and who imposed their religion and culture as the only and obligatory ones. Christianity, born among the oppressed of one empire, became an instrument of oppression in the hands of another, one which was taking history by storm. There weren't any other religions, there couldn't be, only superstitions and idolatries; other cultures were nothing but ignorance. God and Man lived in Europe; the New World was inhabited by demons and monkeys. The first Columbus Day, known in Latin America as the Day of the Race, began a cycle of racism from which America has yet to free itself. Many are still ignorant of the fact that back in 1537 the Pope decided Indians had souls and minds.

No imperial undertaking, neither the old kind nor today's, has the capacity to discover. An adventure of usurpation and plunder does not discover: it covers up. It doesn't reveal: it hides. To be successful it needs ideological alibis that turn arbitrariness into law.

In a recent essay, Miguel Rojas-Mix ventured that Atahualpa was condemned by Pizarro because he was guilty of the crime of *being another*, or simply being. The voracity for gold and silver needed a mask to hide behind; so Atahualpa was accused of idolatry, polygamy, and incest, which was equivalent to condemning him for practicing a *different* culture.

ON EQUAL FOOTING

The Spanish conquest reproduced in America what had occurred and was still occurring in Spain during those same years. In 1562, Fray Diego de Landa burned the Mayan codices in a gigantic bonfire in the Yucatán. In 1499 in Granada, Archbishop Cisneros threw Islamic books on the flames and turned them into ashes. The Spain that conquered America was not the sum total of its parts. On the contrary, it was suffering the most ferocious amputation of its history: Catholic Spain was imposing itself as the only Spain, annihilating with blood and fire both Muslim Spain and Jewish Spain. Intolerance and haciendas, the Inquisition and land grants—these sealed the fate of a multi-faceted Spain open to the winds of progress, the Spain that could have been and never was.

Some time after compulsory conversion to Christianity, under the Bourbon dynasty, came compulsory conversion to the Castilian language. Castilian centralism, bane of Spain's national and cultural pluralism, reached its paroxysm under the dictatorship of Franco. Now, after centuries of repression, Spain is discovering itself, it is rediscovering itself. With new eyes, in the awakening of democracy, Spain begins *to see itself* in its own diversity, and to recognize its true identity, a contradictory identity, because it is alive and it manifests itself in contradictory ways. Nation of nations, with many peoples and ideas, cultures and languages, Spain enjoys a fruitful pluralism that makes it unique. In this difficult, threatening and threatened process, Castilians, Catalonians, Andalusians, Basques, and Galicians recover their own profiles and see them reflected in the space they share.

By *seeing itself*, Spain can *see us*. On equal footing. Not from below, as some Spaniards still view the rest of Europe and the United States. Nor from above, as some Spaniards still view the countries of Latin America and the rest of the pejoratively named "Third World." Seen from below, everyone looks like a giant. Seen from above, everyone looks like a dwarf.

On equal footing. That is the way to discover.

2. THE AREA OF THE DAMNED

Last year in Barcelona, in a beautiful and painful speech, Tomás Borge said: "Columbus found America, but Europe has yet to discover her."

Tomás Borge, a founder of the Sandinista Front and a leader

of the Nicaraguan revolution, had come to Spain a few days before. He had come to denounce the giant bully that threatens his small country, but from the moment he arrived, he could do nothing but defend himself. As soon as he left the plane, the storm hit: Spain's newspapers, radio stations, and television channels began preaching that Nicaragua was responsible for terrorism in the Basque country. No one had exhibited, nor will anyone ever, a single element of proof; but *well-informed sources* knew that Nicaragua offered training and safe haven to Basque separatist terrorists.

A TOPIC FOR FREUD?

It was not surprising that such a grotesque story would be fabricated for Spanish consumption. Nor is it surprising that the most reactionary media would broadcast it with such enthusiasm. But it was indeed astonishing, revealing, and painful that many democratic and progressive media gave ample space and time to that dirty lie.

Why couldn't the Mother Country be more supportive when one of her most unfortunate daughters undertook a process of serious transformation? The voluble and at times intolerant and arbitrary attitude of many of Spain's and Europe's democratic politicians and intellectuals regarding Latin American revolutions is striking. The case of Spain hurts the most, for reasons that the mind knows and the gut knows better. And because, in the end, common history implies shared responsibility. To give only one example, we could cite the problems homosexuals have had in Cuba, a favorite topic in the Spanish press. Homosexuality was practiced freely in pre-Columbian times throughout the Caribbean. And it is no folly to assume that Cuban prejudices against homosexuality come not from their Soviet advisers, but from the conquistadores who at the dawning of the sixteenth century threw homosexual Indians to the dogs. In the same way, one could underline the obvious fact that the poverty and violence of many Spanish-American countries do not come from their exotic nature, but have deep roots in history: from the times in which colonial America was made to serve Europe's accumulation of capital.

REGARDING DIFFERENCES

Neither does slapping European labels on processes that develop in different realities contribute to the necessary *discovery* of America. Latin America's reality is *another* reality. Spain is one of her historic and cultural mothers, and is fundamental for those of us who speak Castilian. But she is not the only mother. And from Spain, from Europe, it is not always possible to have an exact picture of the urgent tragedies being played out in our lands.

Does Latin America only make copies? That seems to be believed by those who reduce Peronism to tango fascism, and those who dismiss the Cuban revolution as Stalinism with palm trees. The spectators of history, always ready to feel betrayed by her, speak of Nicaragua as if she were nothing but the newest ballerina brought into the vast company of the Bolshoi.

Nicaragua, an incredibly poor country, wants to be born. An empire much more powerful than that of Charles V wants to keep it from happening. It wants to oblige Nicaragua to become a barracks filled with hungry people, to prove to the world once more that poor countries are only capable of changing one dictator for another. In this tiny piece of the vast community of Spanish-speakers, an essential question is being addressed. Is democracy a luxury only rich countries can afford? Is democracy part of the booty that rich countries steal through the international structure of piracy? Does democracy eat misery?

Latin American countries, which make up the suburbs of the capitalist system, fall in the area of the damned. The veto wielded by the powerful both inside and outside the country impedes the very deep changes needed if democracy is to be more than a fragile mask: a real face. Spain, on the other hand, which is part of Europe—delayed but still Europe—and which has achieved a fairly high degree of capitalist development, is not being strangled by the world market, nor is it under siege from its creditors. In the past few years, Spain has managed to consolidate, within the capitalist free-market economy, a democratic process that enjoys broad national consensus, and it now seems safe from putsches.

This process is very encouraging. But even if we wanted to copy it, we could not.

3. THE TWO HISPANIC IDENTITIES

My generation of Latin Americans, born while Franco erected his dictatorship on the ashes of the Republic, learned as children the songs of the vanquished. We felt and we still feel that those Republican tunes are very much our own, and we sang them at the top of our lungs while in Spain the survivors whispered them in obligatory silence.

The writers of my generation were marked for life by our early readings of Antonio Machado, Pedro Salinas, León Felipe, Miguel Hernández, Lorca, Alberti, and other prolific poets banned or mutilated by censorship in Spain. We had the privilege of inheriting the words of those exiled or murdered creators, long before their voices could fully resonate in Spain.

BACKING IN

For Latin America, those songs and poems still symbolize a way of understanding and of living as Hispanics that has nothing to do with the rhetorical and somber "Spanishness" traditionally used as a battle mount by the enemies of democracy. One form of "Spanishness" is reflected, for example, in Fray Luis de León; the other in the inquisitors who condemned him for translating the Song of Songs into the language of Castile.

This latter "Spanishness" has been used as a shield and an alibi by the most reactionary sectors of Spanish and Latin American societies. They hope to back their way into history—as if the solution to the problems of the twentieth century lay in a return to the sixteenth. This "Spanishness" is the nostalgia for empire, invoked with great frequency by the inquisitors of our days. In its name, the forces of change have been condemned and punished for smelling of sulfur and having tails. And in its name, the blood of the just has flowed. There are still those who long for the conquering legions who imposed in Spain and America one religion, one culture, one language, and one truth. Messianic swords get raised in attempts to repeat the feat of redemption.

Some years back, Dominican butcher Rafael Leónidas Trujillo, who liked to pose for statues dressed up as El Cid, received the Great Necklace of the Order of Isabel the Catholic for being a champion of Hispanic culture, of "Spanishness," in the crusade against atheistic communism. More recently, the Uruguayan dictatorship imposed new official textbooks for "Civic and Moral Education," which teach certain maxims of "Spanishness" coined by Francisco Franco. Among them, for example: "The Fatherland is one with universal destiny, and each individual has a special mission in the harmony of the State. The Fatherland is order. . . ." The thuggish catechisms of a dictatorship near its end tried in vain to convince students that the function of a people consists in obeying and working, and that women's equality "encourages their sexuality and their intelligence at the expense of their roles as mother and wife."

ENTERING FACE-FIRST

The other "Spanishness," that of the democratic trenches, that of persecuted poets, finds new channels for realization in the Spain of today.

These new channels take up the legacy of Gonzalo Guerrero, who died fighting on the side of the Indians, in place of the legacy of Hernán Cortés. They come from Bartolomé de Las Casas, a fanatic of human dignity, and not from Juan Ginés de Sepúlveda, the ideologue of racist humanism. They invoke the memory of the communities led by Vasco de Quiroga, who believed that America was the land of Utopia, in place of the memory of the court sages who mocked him. And they continue down the trail blazed by Bernardino de Sahagún, the man who spent half a century of his life searching for and compiling the lost voices of the America demolished by the Conquest, instead of getting lost on the path of the lugubrious King Philip II, who buried Sahagún's books because they were suspected of spreading idolatry.

This other "Spanishness" could open up myriad opportunities for encounter and reencounter, for discovery and rediscovery, between Spain and America, so that they might speak and walk together.

GOODBYE

I have lived in Spain for eight years of exile. As if a Spaniard, I have shared in the resurrection of democracy and the pure air of freedom that this nation of nations now breathes. Being Latin American, I have celebrated the solidarity of many Spaniards, those who *see* without cobwebs in their eyes, and I have lamented the indifference, ambiguity, and scorn that often keep such solidarity from coming to full flower.

Now that my exile is ending, I write these lines to say goodbye to Spain; they are also my say of saying sincerely: thank you.

(1984)

The Dictatorship and
Its Aftermath:
The Secret Wounds

THE SYMBOLS

A lot of ash has fallen on this purple land. During the twelve years of military dictatorship, Liberty was only the name of a plaza and a prison. In that prison—the principal cage for political prisoners—it was against the rules to draw pregnant women, birds, butterflies, or stars; the prisoners could not speak, whistle, laugh, sing, jog, nor greet one another without permission. But then everyone was a prisoner, except for the jailers and the exiles: three million prisoners, even if the jails seemed to hold only a few thousand. One out of every eighty Uruguayans had a hood tied over his head; but invisible hoods covered the rest as well, condemned to isolation and incommunication, even if they were spared the torture. Fear and silence became a mandatory way of life. The dictatorship, enemy of all that grows and moves, paved over the grass it could capture in the plazas, and cut down or painted white all trees within range.

THE MODEL

With slight variations, a similar model of repression and inoculation against the forces of social change was applied in several

Latin American countries during the 1970s. To enforce the Pan-American doctrine of national security, the military acted as occupying armies in their own countries, as the armed wing of the International Monetary Fund and the system of privilege that the fund embodies and perpetuates. The guerrilla threat provided the alibi for state terrorism, which then moved into high gear to cut workers' salaries in half, crush unions, and suppress critical thinking. By spreading mass terror and uncertainty, they hoped to impose a reign of the deaf-mute. The computer at the Joint Chiefs of Staff of the Armed Forces placed all Uruguayan citizens into one of three categories, A, B, or C, according to the threat they posed to the proposed military kingdom of the sterile. Without the Certificate of Democratic Faith, spit out by that computer and delivered by the police—specialists in Democracy, having taken courses from Dan Mitrione, U.S. Professor of Torture Techniques—one could neither obtain employment nor keep it. Even to have a birthday party, police authorization was required. Every house was a cell; every factory, every office, every school became a concentration camp.

THE AGGRESSION

The dictatorship demolished the system of education and in its place imposed a system of ignorance. By the brutal substitution of professors and programs, it sought to domesticate students and oblige them to accept both the barracks morality that calls sex a "hygienic outlet" or "marital duty" and a mummified culture that considers "natural" the right of property over things and people, as well as the duty of women to obey men, children to obey their parents, the poor to obey the rich, blacks to obey whites, and civilians to obey the military.

The order was given to dismember and detongue the country.

All ties of solidarity and creativity that brought Uruguayans into contact with one another were a crime; a conspiracy, all that brought them into contact with the world; and subversive, any word that did not lie. All who took part were punished—political and union activists *and* whoever did not denounce them.

THE RESPONSE

And nevertheless, Uruguayan culture managed to keep breathing, inside the country and out. In all its history it never received higher praise than the ferocious persecution it suffered during those years. Uruguayan culture remained alive, and was able to respond with life against the machinery of silence and death. It breathed in those who remained and in those of us who had to leave, in the words that passed from hand to hand, from mouth to mouth, like contraband, hidden or disguised; in the actors who spoke today's truth through Greek theater, and in those who were forced to wander about the world like errant jesters; in the troubadours who sang defiantly in exile and at home; in the scientists and artists who did not sell their souls; in the insolent carnival musicians and in the newspapers that died and were reborn; in the pleas scrawled on the streets and in the poems scrawled in the jails on cigarette papers.

But if by culture we mean a way of being and of communicating, if culture is all the symbols of collective identity we express in everyday life, then the resistance was not limited to these outward signs. It was much broader and deeper.

In the final days of the dictatorship, Obdulio Varela, a popular soccer player who knows well the people and the land, offered a bitter summation: "We have grown selfish," Obdulio said at the beginning of 1985. "We no longer see ourselves in others. Democracy is going to be difficult."

And yet, the Uruguayan people knew how to respond with

solidarity to the system of dismemberment. There were many ways of finding each other and of sharing—though it be little, though it be nothing—that also formed part, a shining part, of Uruguay's cultural resistance during those years, and that flowered above all among the poorest of the working class. And I am not referring only to the great street demonstrations, but also to less spectacular events like soup kitchens and housing cooperatives and other works of imagination and anger that confirmed that solidarity is inversely proportional to income level. Or to put it à la Martín Fierro, the fire that really heats comes from below.

THE DAMAGE

There are no statistics of the soul. There is no way to measure the depth of the cultural wound. We know that Uruguay exports shoes to the United States, and that nevertheless Uruguayans now buy five times fewer shoes than twenty years ago. But we cannot know to what point they have poisoned our insides, to what point we have been mutilated in our consciousness, our identity, and our memory.

There are a few facts, it's true, that are plain to see—circumstances caused, or at least worsened, by the dictatorship and by the economic policies in whose service it turned Uruguay into a vast torture chamber. For example, there are books that can help us to know and to understand ourselves, and that could contribute a great deal toward the recuperation of the country's culture. But if the price of just one of those books is equivalent to one-seventh or one-eighth of the monthly salary earned by many Uruguayans, then *censorship by price is functioning just as efficiently as censorship by the police did before.* The circulation of Uruguayan books has fallen by five or six times; people do not read, not because they don't want to, but because they can't afford to.

The impossibility of return is another fact. There is no damage comparable to the drain of human resources that the country has been suffering for years and that the dictatorship multiplied. Of those of us who went into exile for having, as one commissary put it, "ideological ideas," some have been able to return. Some, I say, not all, nor even close to all. Of the hundreds of thousands whom the system has condemned—and continues condemning—to seek beyond the borders their daily bread, how many can return? *Sick with sterility, the system performs a curious alchemy: it converts the keys of progress into a national malady.* The high cultural level of Uruguayan workers, which could and should be a factor that encourages development, is turned against the country insofar as it facilitates the departure of the population. Now we have a democracy, a civilian government instead of a military dictatorship; but the system is the same and economic policy remains essentially unchanged.

Business freedom—enemy of human freedom—usurpation of wealth, usurpation of life: this economic policy has had cultural consequences that are quite evident. *The encouragement of consumption, the consumers' squandering that reached paroxysm during the dictatorship, not only led to an asphyxiating sixfold increase in the foreign debt, it also discouraged creativity. The speculative urge not only empties us of material wealth, it empties us of moral values and, therefore, of cultural values, because it derides productivity and confirms the old suspicion that he who works is a fool.* In addition, the avalanche of foreign merchandise that destroys local industry and pulverizes wages, the readjustment of the economy to adapt to the foreign market, and the abandonment of the domestic market *imply, culturally speaking, self-hate*: The country spits in the mirror and adopts the ideology of impotency as its own.

"Sorry. It's made here," a shopkeeper told me when he sold me a can of meat, the day after my return. After twelve years of exile, I confess that I did not expect this. And when I mentioned it to my friends, they blamed "the Process." Neither did

I expect the dictatorship to be called Process. *The language was, and perhaps still is, sick from fear.* They have lost the healthy custom of calling a spade a spade.

THE TASK

Our land of free men is hurt but alive. The military dictatorship that for twelve years forced it to shut up, to lie, to distrust, was unable to sour its soul: *"They weren't able to turn us into them,"* a friend told me, after the years of terror. And I believe it.

But fear survives disguised as prudence. Be careful, be careful: democracy is fragile, and it will break if you jostle it. From the viewpoint of the owners of an unjust system, one that strikes fear in order to perpetuate itself, all creative audacity is thought to be a terrorist provocation. A responsible government is an immobilized government; its duty is to keep the *latifundios* and the repressive machinery intact, to forget the dictatorship's crimes and to pay punctually the interest on the foreign debt. The officers left the country in ruins, and in ruins it remains. In the villages, the old people water flowers among the tombs.

And the young people? The policy of collective castration was aimed above all at them. The dictatorship tried to drain them of their consciences and of everything else. The system that denies them work and obliges them to leave is directed against them, above all against them. Will they be creative enough, insolent enough, and tough enough to confront the system that denies them? Will they realize in time that for the country to remain democratic it cannot remain paralyzed? Or will the oxygen of liberty make them repent their youth and keep the fear of specters in their hearts? Will they embrace with fatal resignation the destiny of sterility and solitude that those specters offer the country? Or will they act to transform it—

even if they do it all wrong—using their capacity for enthusiasm and beautiful madness? Will the country be a fountain of life or an elephant's graveyard?

(1986)

Democratorship:
Latin American Democracy
Held Hostage

The will of the people, plenty of will of the people: such is the diet needed by Uruguayan democracy, it is that anemic and sickly. And no wonder: it eats fear. To condemn it to impotence the masters of the country give it nothing to eat but fear: fear for breakfast, fear for dinner, and for supper, fear.

Signatures for the referendum will, in the coming days, be the first possible popular response to the swindle committed by those who had promised justice and ended by voting, in the name of fear, for impunity.

Confronted by this treachery, the people can recover the usurped word and speak out of their own mouth: say yes to democracy, no to "democratorship"—which is democracy mortgaged by dictatorship—democracy nullified, bent double, watchdogged, submitted to a regime of conditional freedom under the shadow of bayonets.

BEHIND THE THRONE

Democratorship is imposed as an imperial formula of change in face of the inevitable twilight of the military dictatorships in Latin America. The civilian presidents recently come to office

194

have no right to take their positions very seriously: the formula gives them the function of hostages of the military power structures and of the economic system over whose good health these military structures preside. Censorship stopped, the curtain rises, the public applauds; but watch out! That beautiful young lady named Democracy might be a transvestite: she strips, and a colonel is revealed.

The so-called third world consumes more weapons than food. The process of growing militarization gone mad does not necessarily require military governments. The new civilian governments of Latin America, which Uncle Sam has pulled out of his repertoire, spend more on arms than the military dictatorships that preceded them. The problem of Nicaragua is to blame, they say, although it is more Nicaragua's solution, a dangerous and contagious example of a people that lost patience. To guard a criminal social order, the neighbor governments are forced into armed insomnia. With good reason they feel themselves threatened, but threatened by their own peoples, who may find out that they'd be better off making history from below and from inside than continuing to suffer history made by others from above and from outside.

Under the new imperial formula, the place of the military is not on the throne, but behind it. They see to it that the civilian governments that start by wanting changes end up working to avoid them. The civilian governments govern but do not rule: in the name of realism they make themselves impotent. They survive by paying the price of paralysis: they can mention agrarian reform but not make it; they can promise justice but not practice it; they can talk but not say; they can act, but not do.

NOTHING NEW

Our country could well be said to have been one of the few exceptions until a few years ago, because the truth is that there is nothing new about this formula in contemporary Latin American history: almost all Latin American countries have hovered between dictatorship and democratorship up to now in the twentieth century. Since long before the doctrine of national security was officially formulated, the armed forces have played a tutelary role, armored guardian angels of the established order and, whenever necessary, executed the imperial veto on any revolution, reform or whisper thereof that implied danger or whisper thereof to private property and foreign investments.

One need but recall what happened when the governments of Arbenz in Guatemala, Goulart in Brazil, Bosch in the Dominican Republic, or Allende in Chile overstepped the mark. Or go further back in time—to 1932, for example. In that year the Communist Party won elections in El Salvador. Then General Maximiliano Hernández Martínez, who said he communicated telepathically with the White House, annulled the elections and killed thirty thousand people.

VOTE OF OBEDIENCE

In Guatemala, a country neighboring El Salvador, I witnessed a bloodbath twenty years ago, and it certainly didn't happen under military dictatorship. It was a lawyer, not a general, who started the long dirty war that has turned Guatemala into a slaughterhouse. Julio César Méndez Montenegro, the civilian president, was not overthrown by any coup, nor did he suffer any visible or invisible invasion from the north. He gave no cause for complaint: protected by the mantle of democratic legality, and under the pretext of struggle against guerrillas, the military launched the systematic and massive application of the technique of "disappearances" and other forms of state terrorism previously tried out in Vietnam, later to be profusely applied in Latin America.

Recently another civilian showed up in the government of

Guatemala, after a sinister rosary of military dictatorships. This prisoner, who wears not a striped uniform but a presidential sash, is named Vinicio Cerezo. Cerezo accepted the same humiliation that had made possible Méndez Montenegro's entry to the palace: he committed himself, like Méndez Montenegro, not to touch the landlords or the hangmen. No agrarian reform, no justice, in a country where a reverse agrarian reform has been in process for years, with the most atrocious results in all America.

The expulsion of indigenous communities and the destruction of their villages, provoked by big-landowner expansionism and the voracity of mining companies, have, according to Amnesty International and Americas Watch, left a total of forty thousand Guatemalans "disappeared" and one hundred thousand murdered.

The disappearances and killings have not stopped with the government of Cerezo. With the executioners unpunished and the machinery of crime intact, they have no reason to stop.

In Brazil, a prodigious circus pirouette brought to a halt the military cycle begun in 1964. The political head of the dictatorship, José Sarney, suddenly turned into the political head of democracy. In Brazil, too, civil stability demands absolution of those responsible for state terrorism and untouchability for the land: the Brazilian style of not introducing agrarian reform consists of much talking about it. In the past year, over 200 campesinos were murdered by big landlords and their goons in various episodes of struggle for the land. Not one landlord, not one hired killer, has yet been brought to trial.

In our country the vote of obedience to the generals seems symmetrical with the vote of obedience to the big ranchers. The government acts in such a way that the exhibition of electric cattle prods at military parades is all that's lacking; and at the same time shrugged shoulders respond to twenty thousand applications by peculiar Uruguayans who don't want to be public functionaries but to work the land. The big landlords, who use the country and destroy its fields, are violators of lands: they enjoy the same impunity as the violators of human rights and the violators of chained female prisoners.

ALTARS OF MONEY

The military humiliation of the Malvinas (Falklands) made possible for the Argentine government a better performance than the others in the field of justice. In Argentina too the dictatorship fell by its own weight, without any popular revolution overthrowing it; but it was the only dictatorship that fell at the end of a war which unmasked it and put in scandalous limelight the generals who only know how to kill compatriots.

This is not to imply any minimization of the trials and sentences of officers who committed the systematic horrors of state terrorism. After all, with or without swimming pool, General Videla is in prison for life. Yet at the first word, or perhaps at the second, President Alfonsin's will for justice has reached full stop.

Yet no full stop has been put to the injustice. The economic policy that made the military dictatorship possible and necessary continues more or less the same, at the service of an imperial power system that lends you what it steals from you and strangles you with your own rope. This economic policy cracks down on wages and rewards speculation, concentrates wealth and forces workers to turn into ants: it generates violence, generates madness. Do the Buenos Aires opinion polls exaggerate? The polls show that of every four inhabitants, one has "mental disturbances" and two want to get out. A friend who returned after a long absence to the big city, Latin America's Babylon, tells me his friends have said to him: "You have us worried. You seem so serene."

The liberal or neoliberal economic policy always comes pregnant with repression. It is not out of place to recall what happened in the Dominican Republic three years ago. Not under Trujillo's dictatorship, but in full democracy, the people erupted in spontaneous demonstrations against the sudden price rises of bread, oil, beans—rises dictated by the International Monetary Fund—and the ground was littered with eighty bodies, or one hundred, or two hundred, nobody knows: the bodies of the poor don't get counted or are counted by the heap.

Applying the same economic policy, which sacrifices human freedom on the altars of the freedom of money, the civilian and democratic government of Victor Paz Estenssoro is achieving in Bolivia what various military dictatorships had tried and failed to achieve; Dr. Paz, docile ally of the most gorillalike generals, is breaking the spine of the Bolivian labor movement.

THE STRAITJACKET

Nor has the ascent of a civilian government in our country implied essential changes in economic policy. The results of that continuity are plain to see. According to the government, the economy could hardly be in better shape. For the people, on the other hand, it could hardly be worse.

Democracy has defrauded the expectations of change that it had awakened. In two years it has not offered the youth any alternative to exile or despair, which is what happens when hope tires of hoping.

For democracy to be democracy, one must start by letting it out of the cage. Deep changes are loudly demanded by this country which was once kissed by the gods, before the politicos and the generals ruined it; but no real change will be possible while democracy remains strapped in the straitjacket that forces it to be a democratorship and nothing more.

(1987)
Translated by Cedric Belfrage

In Defense of Nicaragua

The pitiless, ever-growing siege and blockade are not taking place because democracy does not exist in Nicaragua, but so it never will. They are not taking place because a dictatorship exists in Nicaragua, but so one may again. They are not taking place because Nicaragua is a satellite, a sad pawn on the chessboard of the great powers, but so it may be one again.

Ever since it became rather clear that the Sandinista revolution was serious and that it planned to break out of the straitjacket of neo-colonialist capitalism, the system made up its mind to wipe it out. Since wiping it out is impossible because it would imply the extermination of the majority of the population, the system tries to deform it at least. Deforming the revolution would be, in the end, wiping it out: *deforming it to such a degree that no one could recognize himself in it*. If it survives, let it survive mutilated, and mutilated in its essential parts.

The four points of the compass are regaled once more with the cruel story of another revolution that has betrayed its aspirations. This propaganda wears the mask of disappointment. Relief for cynics, consolation for deserters, alibi for the greedy:

let no one bother himself with the belief that change is a possible venture.

Nicaragua spends 40 percent of its budget on defense and police, but Nicaragua is at war with the leading power in the world. Uruguay, a respected democracy, spends the same percentage on its armed forces, much smaller than the swelling columns of militia and people's army in Nicaragua, and it should be noted that no foreign power is invading Uruguay or threatening it on its frontiers.

"We are forced to die and we are forced to kill," Tómas Borge, founder of the Sandinista Front has explained. Armed resistance to aggression reveals in a painful way the collective dignity of a people *forced into violence from without.* And although it is quite true that the rules of war impose an inevitable verticalism, and in the trenches orders take the place of explanations, it is no less true that an armed people is a proof of democracy. The fact that there are three hundred thousand Nicaraguans, soldiers and militiamen, armed with rifles, some in exchange for a meager salary and the majority in exchange for nothing, shows that this strange Sandinista tyranny *is not afraid to arm the people, who, according to the enemy, are anxious to overthrow it.*

There is no government in the Americas or in Europe, democracy or dictatorship, democraship or dictatorcy, that doesn't feel authorized to propose, discuss, and perhaps impose some kind of *solution* for the *problem* of Nicaragua, which is the same thing as saying the *problem* of Central America. It gives the impression that when it took on the transformation of Nicaragua, the Sandinista revolution had brought about an unforgivable cataclysm that challenges the powerful and violates the law of universal balance: if it weren't for Nicaragua, Central America would be enjoying peace and happiness, or, at least, would cease disturbing the good order of the world. Calling for a change is permitted, proclaiming it to the sky may even turn out necessary, but making a change, transforming reality, that scandalizes the gods.

Everybody has been giving Nicaragua the Democracy test. With or without a dictatorship, in most Latin American countries the people vote but don't elect, and the ceremonies of official political life are projected, like the deceitful shadows of a magic lantern, over the background of an atrociously anti-democratic social reality.

Honest opponents, and they do exist, would have to recognize, at least, that during these eight years the Sandinista revolution has done the possible and the impossible in *laying the bases of justice and sovereignty necessary for democracy not to be a castle in the air*, not to be a pro forma tax paid to the reigning hypocrisy, a joke on people who have nothing and decide nothing.

—Nicaragua has put an end to poliomylitis and has reduced other illnesses, has vaccinated the entire population and has lowered infant mortality to such a degree that *today one out of three of the children who had previously died shortly after entering the world has survived*;

—For the first time in its history it has taught the population to read and write, and not only the Spanish-speaking population; it has taught reading and writing in indigenous languages and in English to 50,000 people. Nicaragua used to be a country of illiterates, and today *one out of every three Nicaraguans is studying*.

—Since the fall of Somoza, Nicaragua *has redistributed more land than all other Central American countries put together* through a prudent but true agrarian reform that has limited itself to the expropriation of non-productive lands and those that had belonged to the ruling dynasty. Approximately five million acres have been turned over to a hundred thousand families.

The people used to be very poor and they are still very poor, but something, something essential, has been changed. Now, for the first time, they are *doing something,* and for the first time they *believe in what they are doing.*

Nicaragua is part of the Third World. Nicaraguans are, therefore, *third-class people.* From the point of view of the opinion makers, they don't deserve respect: *third-class people are condemned to copy; they have a right to an echo but not to a voice.*

Everything that is happening in Nicaragua has been reduced to the geopolitics of blocs, a game of East versus West: the blame belongs to Moscow, which is sticking its nose in where it doesn't belong, and, in that way, is changing the delicate balance of power that guarantees world peace. The *contras* are not, therefore, mere paid mercenaries working for the restoration of the colonialist past and a dethroned dynasty; they aren't Business Fighters, but Freedom Fighters, heroes of a threatened civilization, Western Civilization, which, on the eve of the Apocalypse, turns to God and to the Rambos it can pay.

Not all the carnival masks in the world are enough to cover up so much hypocrisy. *Those who deny Nicaragua bread and butter condemn her for receiving them.* Those who condemn Soviet aid in the name of independence would do better to work for some other aid so as to broaden the freedom of movement of this young and besieged revolution.

For most Americans, Nicaragua has not been invaded but is the invader; they don't perceive her as a poor colony trying to be a country, but as a mysterious and dangerous power, threatening, lying in wait on the border. Few, very few Americans have been there and have seen the reality: *that in all of Nicaragua there's only one skyscraper, five elevators, and one escalator (which hasn't been working for over a year), that there are fewer Nicaraguans than there are inhabitants of the borough of Brooklyn in New York, and that because of hunger and disease they live twenty years less than if they'd been born in the United States.*

Nicaragua is not looking for walls to hide behind, but it needs shields with which to defend itself. These words I put down here, which have nothing neutral about them, are an attempt to give some of that help, even though it be of small import. Ambiguity and fog have become fashionable now, and taking sides is considered a sign of stupidity or poor taste. But this writer feels a joy in choosing and he confesses to being one of those antique creatures who still believe that joy gives meaning to the mysterious adventures of the human animal on this earth.

(1988)
Translated by Gregory Rabassa

The Structure of Impotence

"We are for democracy, but democracy is not for us," a resident of a Buenos Aires slum said recently in response to a public opinion poll. He is one of the many who wait on the table of the big city and are condemned to live on the leftovers.

In Latin America, the worst enemy of democracy is not the army, even though it does everything possible to make it seem that way. The worst possible enemy of democracy in Latin America is the entire structure of impotence, which the army safeguards, and which has its roots in the economic system. This system is part of a larger system, the international machinery of power. One of the devices of this vast and complex machinery is the demochrometer, which measures the greater or lesser degree of democracy in each country. As a general rule, the mass media—which fabricate world opinion—disseminate the measurements of this little apparatus and convert them into the unappealable verdicts of the West.

However, what it true for the demochrometer, the truth of the system, may be a lie for its victims. I don't think the eight million abandoned children who wander the streets of Brazil's cities believe in democracy. I don't think they believe in it because democracy doesn't believe in them. They have no democracy in which to believe: Brazilian democracy was never meant for them, nor does it function on their behalf, although it fulfills certain formal requirements that the demochrometer demands for its approval.

"NOTHING OF IMPORTANCE," SAID THE KING

Democracy is not what it is but what it appears to be. Ours is a culture of packaging. The packaging culture holds the contents in contempt. Words are what count, not deeds. There is no death penalty in Brazil, nor will there ever be according to the new constitution, but the death penalty is meted out all the time: every day a thousand children are killed by starvation, and who knows how many men are shot to death in the violent outskirts of the cities or on the plantations. Slavery has supposedly been outlawed for a century, but a third of Brazil's workers earn little more than a dollar a day and the social pyramid is white at the peak and black at the base: the richest are the whitest, and the poorest the blackest. Four years after abolition, back in 1892, the Brazilian government ordered that all documents related to slavery be burned, account books of the slavers, receipts, regulations, ordinances, etc., as if slavery had never existed.

For something to not exist, one merely has to decree that it does not exist. On July 14, 1789, Bastille Day, King Louis XVI wrote in his diary: "Nothing of importance." The Guatemalan dictator Manuel Estrada Cabrera decreed in 1902 that all of the volcanoes in the country were dormant, while violent eruptions from the Santa María volcano were burying more than a hundred villages in the vicinity of Quetzaltenango under avalanches of lava and mud. The Congress of Colombia enacted a law in 1905 determining that no Indians lived in San Andrés de Sotavento and other districts where oil gushers had suddenly sprouted; the Indians living there were thus made illegal, and the oil companies could kill them with impunity and seize their lands.

THE "AS IF"

In Uruguay, the Statute of Limitations for Punitive Claims, enacted at the end of 1986, declares that the tortures, kidnappings, rapes, and murders committed by the recent military dictatorship are to be forgotten, *as if* these terrorist acts perpetrated by the state had never taken place. The people of Uruguay preferred to call it the Law of Impunity and intervened with a petition of protest containing more than 600,000 signatures. Shortly before this law absolving the torturers was passed, the government of Uruguay signed and ratified the International Convention Against Torture, which obliges it to punish them. This also happened in Argentina. The convention explicitly denies the right to claim to have been following orders. The Argentine government signed and ratified it and went right on to whitewash the tortures carried out at the direction of the high command. In our countries, international conventions carry the same legal weight as national laws. *But the fact is that some laws call for human rights to be respected while other authorize their violation: some pretend to exist, others exist in fact.*

The history of Latin America teaches *the distrust of words.* In 1965, the military dictatorship of Brazil, the military dictatorship of Paraguay, the military dictatorship of Honduras, and the military dictatorship of Nicaragua all invaded Santo Domingo, along with the U.S. Marines, to save a democracy threatened by its people. In the name of democracy, those nostalgic for the Batista dictatorship landed on Cuban shores at the Bay of Pigs in 1961. Now, in the name of democracy, those nostalgic for the Somoza dictatorship attack Nicaragua. The president of Colombia speaks of democracy, and during 1987 state terrorism killed with impunity more than a thousand members of the political and trade-union opposition, following the instructions of the army counterinsurgency manual for setting up para-military organizations.

Official rhetoric raves deliriously, and its delirium is the norm of the system. "There will be no devaluation," say the finance ministers on the eve of the currency's collapse. "Agrarian reform is our principal objective," say the agriculture ministers while the *latifundios* grow. "There is no censorship," proclaim the ministers of culture in countries where the immense majority are prohibited from reading books by price or illiteracy.

A MOMENT OF PERFECT ABSURDITY

The system applauds infamy if it succeeds, and punishes it if it fails. It rewards those who steal large sums and punishes those who steal little. It invokes peace and practices violence. You are told to love thy neighbor and at the same time you are forced to survive by devouring him. Schizophrenic language achieves a moment of perfect absurdity when it confuses freedom of money with freedom of people, thus linking elements which simple common sense suggests are in blatant contradiction. Anyone can see this absurdity is not innocent. Yet there is no shortage of intellectuals disposed to walk into this trap, as evidenced recently after private banks were nationalized in Peru. There are those who consider the free expression of poets equivalent to the free speculation of bankers. But in Latin America and throughout the Third World, business freedom not only has nothing to do with the freedom of people, the two are mutually incompatible. In order to grant full freedom to money, military dictatorships put people in jail. Much blood, too much, has been spilled over the centuries for this to be a shocking revelation.

We are trained not to see. Education uneducates, the mass media isolate and separate. And education and the media numb us into allowing the wool to be pulled over our eyes.

THE STRUCTURE OF IMPOTENCE

THE USURPATION OF REALITY

*Even maps lie. We learn world geography on a map that doesn't
show the world as it is, but rather as its owners would have it.*
In the conventional projection, the one used in schools and
virtually everywhere, the equator is not located in the middle:
the Northern Hemisphere takes up two-thirds and the Southern
Hemisphere one-third. Scandinavia appears to be larger than
India when in reality it is less than a third the size; the Soviet
Union seems twice the size of Africa, when in reality it is considerably smaller. Latin America encompasses less area on the
world map than Europe and much less than the United States
and Canada put together, when in reality Latin America is twice
as large as Europe and substantially larger than the United States
and Canada.

The map that makes us small is symbolic of everything else.
Stolen geography, plundered economy, falsified history, daily
usurpation of reality: the so-called Third World, inhabited by
third-class peoples, encompasses less, eats less, remembers less,
lives less, says less.

And it doesn't only encompass less on the map; it takes up
less room in the papers, on TV, on the radio. Less, that is, as
a figure of speech: it hardly takes up any at all. At times, for
example, Latin America becomes fashionable. Momentarily, as
with all fashion, intellectuals from the North toss us fleeting
glances of adoration. At the end of the fifties it was Cuba's turn.
At the end of the seventies it was Nicaragua's. Between one
fascination and the other, illusions of immaculate revolutions,
there was the guerrilla struggle of Che Guevara and other romantic deeds. Such explosive passions lead fatally to disenchantment and public abomination. As in the sixteenth century,
reality defrauds the illusory promise of El Dorado. Reality is
what it is and not what some would like it to be. There are

those who would first confuse it with heaven in order to then have the right to confuse it with hell—and then damn it to hell forever: *the hell of silence, the hell of contempt.* Fascination and malediction are two faces of the same attitude—one that ignores reality and disrespects it.

THE UNIVERSAL SYSTEM OF THE LIE

In an article I published years ago, written with evident sympathy for the workers' rebellion in Poland, I allowed myself an observation that was not well received. I continue to believe, however, that it was correct: I said that if Lech Walesa had been born in Guatemala, he would have been disemboweled during the first strike, and that his murder wouldn't have merited a fraction of an inch in the world's major dailies, nor a second of airtime on the TV networks.

Guatemala has suffered, since the invasion of 1954, the most prolonged and systematic butchery in Latin America. The opinion manufacturers who control the production and consumption of news on an international scale shrug their shoulders. Military terror and starvation are considered "natural." Earthquakes, on the other had, are not: in February 1976, when the earth shook and killed 22,000 Guatemalans, a multitude of journalists gathered from all around the world. Of those journalists a handful noticed the fact that more than 22,000 people had been murdered in Guatemala during the seventies, the work of death squads organized by the military. And practically nobody showed any interest at all in finding out about the more than 22,000 people who in just one year were murdered by hunger, which kills silently. An impoverished country, a country of Indians: horror is nothing extraordinary.

We are all neighbors in this world of multinational programs and simulcasts via satellite, but as Orwell would say, some are more neighbors than others. Communications are centralized.

Everything that happens on the planet gets translated in the centers of power, translated into the language of the Universal System of the Lie, and then returned to the world converted into sounds and images for mass consumption. Objectivity? *We distrust an objectivity that reduces us to objects.* The misery of the Third World is turned into a commodity. The wealthy nations consume it from time to time as a way of congratulating themselves on how well life has treated them. *The universal system of the lie practices amnesia.* The North behaves as if it had won the lottery. Its wealth, however, is not the result of good fortune, but of a long, very long historical process of usurpation, which goes back to colonial times and has been greatly intensified by today's modern and sophisticated techniques of pillage. The more resonant the speeches in international forums extolling justice and equality, the more prices of Southern products fall on the world market, and the higher the interest climbs on Northern money, which loans with one hand and steals with the other. These techniques of pillage force the South to pay the bill for what the North squanders, including the broken dishes at the end of every party: the crises of the system's centers are unloaded onto the backs of the outskirts.

WHAT DO THEY TELL US?

In the dramatized versions of the Conquest of America still performed to this day by Indians of the Andes, the priests and conquistadores speak moving their lips but not uttering any sound. The conquerors speak, in indigenous theater, in a mute tongue. Today, the voices of the international system of power, broadcast by the dominant culture—what do they tell us? What do they tell us that has anything to do with our real needs? The dominant culture expressed through the educational system and above all through the mass media does not reveal reality; it masks it. It doesn't help bring about change; it helps avoid change. It doesn't encourage democratic participation; it induces passivity, resignation and selfishness. It doesn't generate creativity; it creates consumers.

There are ever more people whose opinions are made for them, and ever fewer who actually have opinions. The closer it gets to perfecting its instruments of intellectual irradiation, the more the dominant culture reveals its antidemocratic bent, reducing the public space for creativity and participation. The enslaving spread of television, for example, is injurious to popular culture and, I think, injurious in a particularly ugly way: its prolonged assault tries to turn all of Latin America into one vast suburb of Dallas. This is very serious, I believe, because in Latin America popular culture is the most authentic national culture. They say correctly that every small-town person that dies is a library that burns. Thanks to popular culture, which inherits and enriches collective memory, we Latin Americans have been able to preserve certain fundamental keys to our identity. Official culture, sterile and parroting, a foolish echo of the dominant culture, ignores these keys or, if it acknowledges them, belittles them. Or perhaps in its heart it fears them: these keys are reminders of dignity and imagination and other enemies of those who own wealth and power.

VALIUM TO DEADEN THE MIND

Popular culture is by its very nature a culture of participation. It is by nature democratic, passed along above all by oral tradition. Technological progress reduces the meeting places that nurture its growth: plazas, cafés, bandstands, gossip corners, markets. Television confines, separates, isolates: it transmits in just one direction, travels one way without coming back, from the mechanical transmitter to the human receiver, and the human receiver snacks on imported emotions as if they were canned sausages.

The struggle against structures hostile to democracy, structures of impotence, requires the development of a liberating national culture, capable of unleashing people's creative energy and capable of washing the cobwebs from their eyes so that they might see themselves and the world. The messages that television radiates into our countries, symbols that the dominant culture sells to the dominated one, symbols of the power that humbles us—these do not contribute much to the development of a liberating culture. But don't misunderstand me. Television per se should not be condemned, only television as a socially acceptable drug, Valium to deaden the mind. By the same token, neither should the messages be condemned simply because they come from the United States or other foreign countries.

A REACTIONARY BLUNDER

Nationalism of the right, which enters history ass-backwards, believes that national culture is defined by the origin of its components.

If this were so, to take a concrete example, there would be no Andalusian culture, because the patios typical of Andalusia come from imperial Rome, the grills and iron gates from Renaissance Florence, and the flowered silk shawls from Ming Dynasty China; "churro" pastries are Arabic and *cante jondo* music comes from Gypsy tunes, Arabic melodies, and Hebrew chants. It was a German who invented the concertina in the last century, as a kind of portable harmonium for playing sacred music in processions in his country. But the concertina escaped from Germany, and before falling into the hands of Aníbal Triolo it had already become the mainstay of the tango in the River Plate. No one knows for sure where Carlos Gardel, the most important tango singer, was born, but very probably it was in the French city of Toulouse. The very Cuban daiquiri comes from sugarcane brought by Columbus, limes that arrived from Spain, and foreign techniques for making sugar and ice.

National culture is defined by its content, not by the origin of its components. And when it is alive, it changes ceaselessly, challenges itself, contradicts itself, and receives outside influences that sometimes harm it, sometimes help it grow, and usually work simultaneously as threat and stimulant. The rejection of that which negates us doesn't have to imply the rejection of that which nourishes us. Latin America has no reason to renounce the creative fruits of cultures that flourished to a large degree thanks to a material abundance certainly connected to the pitiless exploitation of America's people and lands. To do so would be to commit the sin of denying reality, and to commit a reactionary blunder. Anti-imperialism also has its infantile disorders.

But the fact is that Latin America is still an enigma in its own eyes. What image does the mirror reveal? A broken one. Pieces. Pieces disconnected from each other: a mutilated body, a face to be put together. And we are trained to spit in the mirror.

THE FALSE PARTHENONS
OF A STERILE CLASS

The dominant cultures, cultures of dominant classes themselves dominated from the outside, have shown themselves to be pathetically incapable of offering either roots or wings to the nations they claim to represent. They are tired cultures, as if they had accomplished so much. *Despite their fraudulent polish, they express the dullness of the local bourgeoisies, still skilled at copying but ever less capable of creating. After cluttering our lands with false Parthenons, false palaces of Versailles, false castles of Loire, and false cathedrals of Chartres, today they squander the national wealth imitating North American models of ostentation and splendor.* Fortified in great harbors and Babylonesque cities, they neglect and scorn national realities, or at least those aspects that contradict their point of view. In practice, they limit themselves to serving as conveyor belts for foreign powers. Children come from Paris carried in the beaks of storks, and truth comes from Los Angeles or Miami in videocassettes.

Most of the time such assembly-line culture seeks to wipe out Latin America's memory and castrate its fertility, so that it will not know its own reality, nor recognize its own potential. Such culture induces Latin America to consume and reproduce passively the signs of its own curse. Its messages lend moral legitimacy to the atrocious law of might makes right, and teach us that if we are bad off, it's our fault: because we offer fertile soil for the communist seed from which only the thorny bramble sprouts, and above all because we are fools, loafers, clumsy oafs, and cowards. *The bottom line of our plight is that it is the fate we deserve.*

The powerful, very powerful structure of impotence begins with the economy, but it doesn't end there. In reality, that is what underdevelopment is: not just a question of statistics, not just a society of violent contradictions, oceans of poverty, tiny islands of opulence, no, not just these things. *Underdevelopment is above all a structure of impotence, set up to prevent subjugated peoples from thinking with their own heads, feeling with their own hearts, and walking with their own legs.*

THE KIDNAPPING OF HISTORY

For those who are starving, the system denies them even the nourishment of memory. So that they don't have a future, it steals their past. *Official history is told by, for, and of the rich, the white, the male, and the military.* Europe is the universe. We learn little or nothing of America's pre-Columbian past, not to mention Africa, of which we know only from old Tarzan movies. *The history of America, the true, betrayed history of*

America, is a story of endless dignity. On every single day some overlooked episode of resistance to power and wealth took place. But official history makes no mention of the uprisings of indigenous peoples or the rebellions of black slaves—or it mentions them in passing, when it mentions them at all, as episodes of misconduct. And it never ever mentions that some were led by women. The great processes of economic and social change do not exist, not even as a backdrop. These are made to disappear so that "developing countries" don't suspect that they are not moving toward development, but away from it, because throughout their long history they have been underdeveloped by the development of those countries that were squeezing the juice out of them. The important thing is to learn by heart the dates of the battles and exact birthdays of the founding fathers. Dressed up for a ball or perhaps a parade, these bronze men acted on their own by divine inspiration, followed by the faithful shadow of a self-effacing spouse: behind every great man is a woman, so we are told—dubious praise that reduces women to the backs of chairs. In the duel between good and evil, the people play the passive role of spear-carriers. The people form a confused rabble of anxious mental deficients led by overbearing chiefs, and periodically they gobble down the red poison like candy.

THE ALIEN PRESENCE IS CAPITALISM

The demonization of the forces of change, agents of alien ideologies, traffickers in cocaine, Marxism, and other drugs, requires the previous flushing out of historical memory. *In reality, the alien presence in America is capitalism*, which was not invented by Manco Cápac or Moctezuma, but imposed from outside and above by sixteenth-century invaders from Europe. The Conquest commercialized American life, imposed the so-much-in-exchange-for-so-much, while the Church proffered by divine order the law of profit and the law of fear: if you obey, your reward will be in heaven; if you disobey, hell will punish you. *On the other hand, there is no older tradition in America than the communitarian mode of production and way of life.* In addition to being the oldest tradition, the community is also the most persistent and the most obstinately vital, despite having suffered unceasing persecution for the last five centuries. It may well be said, then, that socialism comes from within and from below, from the most authentic and profound depths of the memory of our lands.

In the same sense, it's worth mentioning that *democracy was not a novelty that the barbarous Indians received from the European monarchies or from its civilized Inquisition.* Outside of Cuzco and Tenochtitlán, which were centers of hereditary despotism, the chronicles of the epoch describe revealing anecdotes that took place in a number of places: the Indians asked who elected the king of Spain or the king of England, because they elected their leaders in assemblies—in which women, it should be said, also expressed their opinions and voted.

THE RIFLE BARREL IS TWISTED

Official history, key link in the chain of dominant culture, also serves as an instrument of separation. We are taught histories that are divorced from one another. The history of each part of Latin America has little or nothing to do with that of the other parts: these handfuls of the same earth only meet in battle. Thus we are induced to quarreling and we are trained to shoot at our flanks. The gaucho Martín Fierro, a worldly man, said that the unity of brothers is the first rule, because while they are fighting among themselves, outsiders will devour them. The list of suspicions and resentments is endless: Uruguayans and Argentines,

Argentines and Chileans, Chileans and Peruvians, Peruvians and Ecuadorians . . .

Latin America's newly reborn democracies must not mistake their friends for enemies, nor leave their rifle barrels twisted. When all is said and done, our countries emerged from dictatorships cast in the same mold. If the model for repression had not been assembled elsewhere, a single model with multiple applications, there would be no way to explain the curious fact that with minor variations the very same straitjacket was applied successively in Brazil, the largest country in South America, and in Uruguay, the smallest; in Argentina, the most developed, and in Bolivia, the least. This model of repression was used to serve the interests of ruling classes that usually do not get along, *yet know how to work together when the potatoes catch fire.* That's when the system violates human rights, because it must do so in order to assure the continuity of the right of inheritance and the duty of obedience in countries that provide cheap labor, cheap raw materials, and open markets.

WE HAVE MADE SOME PROGRESS

The consciousness of shared roots, the knowledge of a historical process intimately intertwined, should open new doors leading out of reciprocal incommunication—or at least help to do so. Common challenges demand common responses, and I believe we have made some progress in that direction. The foreign debt and, above all, the crisis in Central America are demonstrating this. With great difficulty, a Latin American united front against the bankers is beginning to take shape. The world's usurers were most generous with the military dictatorships that multiplied our foreign debt to buy arms, finance luxuries, and send capital fleeing abroad. Now the democracies are becoming aware of the need to adopt a common strategy against their demands. As far as the crisis in Central America is concerned, it should suffice to recall the ease with which the U.S. government got the Organization of American States to expel Cuba and to invade the Dominican Republic. A quarter century later, things have changed quite a bit. Despite threats and bribes, not only has President Reagan failed to obtain OAS support to wipe out Nicaragua, but he has had to swallow the bitter pill of the recent peace accords, leaving him alone with his dreams of annihilation. *In the White House they keep acting as if they had bought Latin America in a supermarket; but these lands are beginning to unite to demand respect.*

"NATIONAL SECURITY IS LIKE LOVE," SAID THE GENERAL

Democracy and social justice have gotten divorced. Whoever would marry them lets loose the storm.

This is the Sandinista revolution's greatest crime in Nicaragua. The agrarian reform, the nationalization of the banks, the literacy campaign, and the popular health programs, which are saving the lives of half of the children who before were dying, these are threatening the national security of the West.

"National security is like love: there is never enough," said the chief of dictator Pinochet's secret police, General Humberto Gordon. But it is not only dictators who praise national security with such ardor. This doctrine, the doctrine of war from within, war against the people, war against the forces of change, does not miraculously end when the military leaves the government in civilian hands. The repressive apparatus in Uruguay, for example, has a budget fifteen times greater than that of the university, and continues functioning in the service of national security: maintaining a watchful vigilance, subjecting democracy to continual extortion. Democracy is treated like a child who may not go out without permission, and then must walk around on tiptoes, begging pardon for having disturbed anyone.

THE FACES AND THE MASKS

Formal liberty, built on real-life contradictions, serves the ends of the foxes who demand freedom of action in the henhouse. The Western demochrometer describes a culture of appearances: the marriage contract is more important than love, the funeral more important than the dead, the clothes more important than the body, and the mass more important than God. The Democracy Show is more important than democracy.

Latin American democracies want to be real democracies. They are not resigned to be democratorships, democracies mortgaged to dictatorships, even though the demochrometer doesn't give much importance to this detail. As far as the structure of impotence is concerned, any dynamic democracy, one capable of transforming reality, is dangerous. It is well known what happened to Salvador Allende and thousands of Chileans when Chile took democracy seriously.

Fifteen years after the tragedy of Chile, Nicaragua is resisting. Its feet planted firmly, this experience in popular participation, collective will, and national dignity is withstanding the evil winds. In Nicaragua, it is not only the people's army that is facing down the rented soldiers invading their country. Standing beside it is the energy of human creativity facing down the cursed legacy of underdevelopment, ignorance, passivity, irresponsibility, the fear of change, the fear of being, and the fear of accomplishment. And fear, as the Mothers of the Plaza de Mayo have said so eloquently, is a prison without bars.

The Sandinistas have discovered much more in the last few years than the Spanish conquistadores four and a half centuries before them. Nicaragua is "Nicaraguanizing"; Nicaragua is beginning to discover itself. A blind country washes its eyes and is astonished to see itself for the first time, illuminated by the insurgency of a people that has ceased to bear witness to its own disgrace.

And one asks oneself: What dazzling image will rise up after centuries of fear, when reality ceases to be a mystery and hope a consolation? When power and the words and our lands belong to all, what will people say? Since every battle against the structure of impotence illuminates an astounding possible future, every triumph, small as it might be, wins laurels: not laurels to crown the head of military heroes or courtesan-poets or the gods of some Olympus, but those that enhance the flavor and pleasure of the steaming, bubbling, rising kettle of the people.

(1987)

The Body as Sin
or Celebration

Nearly five centuries have passed since we were Discovered. I feel it wouldn't be a bad idea that one of the central themes of the celebration should be homage to the sexual freedom that formerly existed in America, or at least in a good part of America, before she got that name and when no one had yet done her the favor of discovering her. Priests like Bartolomé de Las Casas or Vasco de Quiroga preached in America the word of a God in love with the human condition, but it was not that God who was imposed on our lands, but a universal Chief of Police who entered with fire and sword to teach sin and castigate freedom in the Great Beyond and the Here and Now.

Not a bad idea, I say, such homage to the most ancient memory of America, which is a memory of freedom. Nor would the idea be inopportune, now that the developed countries are suffering the pangs of castrating morality, under the influence of growing panic about AIDS.

AIDS, a new and contagious disease still without a vaccine or sure remedy, could be the perfect alibi of the sex police; and it already is. Would that I were wrong, but I have the impression, not to say certainty, that we are seeing the development of the best possible culture medium for enemies of the unforgivable joys of the body. What has just happened, for example, with

Gary Hart, so thunderously denounced and condemned, did not occur in other times when Franklin Delano Roosevelt and John Kennedy were protagonists of almost identical situations.

PURITANISM IN ACTION

Recently the newspapers of Europe and the United States have given page-one headlines to the Gary Hart scandal. The journalists of the *Miami Herald*, dedicated to the noble task of spying under beds, brought to light an amorous adventure of the potential alternative to Reagan. Whatever urge I had to applaud Hart vanished when I read his painful explanations, unworthy of the least worthy of those accused by the Holy Office of the Inquisition.

In any case, the *Miami Herald* denunciation, which ended Hart's political career, conveniently displaced to inside pages the simultaneous revelations of President Reagan's diversion of illegal funds to murder Nicaraguans. The Puritan tradition, which stems from the colonial era and not from earlier, has hung Hart from the mainmast of the *Mayflower*. From the viewpoint of a system that customarily uses the double standard, double language, and double accounting, he has undoubtedly committed a worse crime than the atrocities committed by the Contras for and on behalf of the United States.

A CRUSADE AGAINST SEX

While in the North of America the wind of hypocrisy swung the political corpse of Hart, in Europe prudish neomoralism had its own field day.

In Paris, the ministers of the interior and of culture fired new propaganda broadsides in their censorship campaign against eroticism, known as pornography. On a beach in Cádiz, two women sunbathing in the altogether, or nearly, were sent to prison for three days, something that hasn't happened in Spain for years if I remember rightly. All nudity is sinful because it harks back to the original sin, said Saint Augustine, and in Florence his devotees screamed to high heaven about the announced exhibition of Masaccio's *Adam*, whose subject for the first time could show his terrible original nudity. The technicians had succeeded in undressing Adam, and now he is as Masaccio presented him to the world, without the fig leaf that the Church had stuck on him. And in the Vatican, meanwhile, the Pope, newly returned from America and Germany, sharpened his castration scissors.

THE ABODE OF SATAN

In Chile, in the National Stadium of sinister memory, the Pope had personally confirmed the persistence of a demonic pagan tradition. When His Holiness exhorted young Chileans to repudiate sex, they answered him with an orotund and unanimous *No-o-o-o*. Some years earlier, General Pinochet had issued a decree-law against another very demonic pagan tradition: a decree-law against the Mapuche Indian's communitarian way of producing and living. At the time of the conquest these two had been precisely the basic proofs of America's perdition, or of its need for salvation. Clearly, too, the Indians smelled of sulfur for their tendency to worship idols and offer them bloody ceremonial sacrifices, but the most irrefutable proofs that the New World was the abode of Satan were two: free love and the absence of private property.

A DANGEROUS MEMORY

Love was free in most of the American space, although sexual life was submitted to relatively rigid rules in the vast dominated areas from the Cuzco Valley to the Lake of Texcoco, where the Incas and the Aztecs held sway—societies of slaves and masters vertically vertebrated by the state. But these relatively rigid rules look very flexible if one compares them with what came later. After all, in all America there was divorce, in the sense that nobody was condemned to perpetual wedlock, and nowhere in America was the woman's virginity of the slightest importance.

In the Caribbean and other regions, homosexuality was considered normal. It was in Panama in 1513 that Vasco Nuñez de Balboa performed one of his exorcising ceremonies, throwing to the carnivorous dogs fifty homosexual Indians, who until then had enjoyed freedom and respect among their people. On the Colombian coast of the Caribbean in 1599, the Tairona Indians rose in defense of their sexual customs, the free practice of divorce, homosexuality, and incest, and eighty communities were virtually exterminated by the repression when order—the order of prohibitions—was restored.

It is stimulating to evoke this memory of freedom. In the world of our time, homosexuality is still considered a crime in many penal codes, and a crime or a disease in nearly all moral codes. And paradoxically, because history enjoys black humor, the Caribbean region is one of the worst with respect to macho prejudice against homosexuals and women.

VINDICATION OF JOY

At the rate we are going, the AIDS terror could become terrorism. This plague seems to confirm scientifically all the gruesome curses that Jehovah, according to the Old Testament, laid upon homosexuals and all those who in one way or another keep biting at the forbidden apple, which is as we know the most tasty and dangerous of the fruits of the kingdom of this world.

Worse than the plague of AIDS is the plague of fear. For this reason it would be a good thing that the commemoration of the Discovery should give us a little help. Put in this way, it seems a bit crazy, and for this reason I say it: that we need to break through this rising wave of castrating puritanism, which threatens to drain the electricity from life and reduce it to virtuous, aseptic, inoffensive boredom. And if this was done, we wouldn't have to approach the celebrations as an homage to the Catholic Monarchs, founders of the Inquisition in Spain and champions of intolerance and obscurantism in America. On the contrary, the historic birthday could be approached as universal applause for the beautiful people who, despite so much persecution and so much scorn, have known how to keep alive the two oldest traditions of America: the tradition of freedom and the tradition of community. Then it would be an homage (for example) to the Maya communities of Guatemala, which have survived innumerable annihilation campaigns and which are still able to choose solidarity and scorn property, and which still call the act of love "play." Or it would be a celebration (for another example) of the Huichol way of giving birth. When they are about to give birth, the Huichol women in Mexico's Nayarit mountains do not think about the Biblical curse which condemned woman to beget in pain. They concentrate on the memory of that night nine months earlier, so that the child to be born may be worthy of the joy that made it.

(1987)
Translated by Cedric Belfrage

The Blue Tiger
and the Promised Land

Fine words and pretty ceremonies are about to descend upon us: The five hundredth anniversary of the so-called Discovery is approaching. I think Alejo Carpentier was right when he called this the greatest event in the history of humankind. But it seems strikingly clear to me that America wasn't discovered in 1492, just as Spain was not discovered when the Roman legions invaded it in 218 B.C. And it also seems clear as can be that it's high time America discovered itself. And when I say America, I'm talking first and foremost about the America that's been despoiled of everything, even its name, in the five-century-long process that put it at the service of foreign progress: our Latin America.

This necessary discovery, a revelation of the face hidden behind the masks, rests on the redemption of some of our most ancient traditions. It's out of hope, not nostalgia, that we must recover a community-based mode of production and way of life, founded not on greed, but on solidarity, age-old freedoms, and identity between human beings and nature. I believe there is no better way to honor the Indians, the first Americans, who from the Arctic to Tierra del Fuego have kept their identity and message alive through successive campaigns of extermination.

Today they still hold out vital keys to memory and prophecy for all of America, not just our Latin America. Simultaneously, they bear witness to the past and cast the light of fresh fires on the path ahead. If the values they embody were of only archae-ological interest, the Indians would no longer be objects of bloody repression, nor would the powerful be so anxious to separate them from the class struggle and from the people's liberation movements.

I am not one to believe in traditions simply because they are traditions. I believe in the legacies that multiply human freedom, and not in those that cage it. It should be obvious, but it can never be too obvious: when I refer to remote voices from the past that can help us find answers to the challenges of the present, I am not proposing a return to the sacrificial rites that offered up human hearts to the gods, nor am I praising the despotism of the Inca or Aztec monarchs.

On the contrary, I am applauding the fact that America can find its most youthful energies in its most ancient sources: the past tells us things that are important to the future. A system lethal to the world and its inhabitants, that putrefies the water, annihilates the land, and poisons the air and the soil, is in violent contradiction with cultures that hold the earth to be sacred because we, its children, are sacred. Those cultures, scorned and denied, treat the earth as their mother and not as a raw material and source of income. Against the capitalist law of profit, they propose the life of sharing, reciprocity, mutual aid, that earlier inspired Thomas More's *Utopia* and today helps us discover the American face of socialism, whose deepest roots lie in the tradition of community.

Halfway through the last century, an Indian chief named Seattle warned officials of the United States government: "After several days, the dying man does not smell the stench of his own body. If you continue polluting your bed, one night you will die suffocated by your own wastes." Chief Seattle also said, "Whatever happens to the earth, happens to the sons of the earth." And I have just heard this same phrase, exactly the same, from the lips of one of the Maya-Quiché Indians in a documentary filmed recently in the mountains of Ixcán, Guatemala. This is how the Mayas explain why their people are hunted down by the army: "They kill us because we work together, eat together, live together, dream together."

What dark threat emanates from the Indians of the Americas, what threat treacherously lives on despite the centuries of crime and scorn? What ghosts are the executioners exorcising? What fears?

To justify usurping the lands of the Sioux Indians at the end of the last century, the United States Congress declared that "community property is dangerous to the development of the free enterprise system." And in March 1979, a law was promulgated in Chile requiring the Mapuche Indians to divide up their lands and turn themselves into small landowners with no links among them; the dictator Pinochet explained that the communities were incompatible with the nation's economic progress. The U.S. Congress was right. So was General Pinochet. From capitalism's point of view, communal cultures that do not separate human beings from one another or from nature are enemy cultures. But the capitalist point of view is not the only one.

The official story of the conquest of America has been told from the perspective of mercantile capitalism in expansion. It takes Europe as its center and Christianity as its only truth. This is essentially the same official story, after all, that is told of the "reconquest" of Spain by Christians against "Moorish" invaders, a way of disqualifying Spaniards of Muslim culture who had been living in the peninsula for seven centuries when they were expelled. The expulsion of these supposed "Moors," who had nothing Moorish about them, along with Spaniards of Jewish faith, signaled the triumph of intolerance and sealed the ruinous history of the very Spain that discovered and conquered America. A few years before friar Diego de Landa cast the books of the Mayas into the flames in Yucatán, Archbishop Cisneros had burned the Islamic books in Granada, in a great bonfire of purification that blazed for several days.

The official story repeats the ideological alibis of the usurpers of America, but in spite of itself it also reveals the reality that it contradicts. That reality, burned, banned, and falsified, emerges in the shock and horror, the outrage and also the awe of the chroniclers of the Indies when they came face to face with those beings that Europe, the Europe of the Inquisition, was in the process of "discovering."

The Church acknowledged in 1537 that the Indians were persons, endowed with soul and reason, but it blessed the crime and pillage: the Indians were persons, but persons possessed by the devil and therefore without any rights. The conquistadores acted in the name of God, to root out idolatry, and the Indians gave continuous proof of their irremediable perdition and irrefutable causes for condemnation. The Indians did not know private property. They did not use gold or silver as money, but to adorn their bodies or pay homage to their gods. Those false gods were on the side of sin. The Indians went around naked: the spectacle of nudity, warned Archbishop Pedro Cortés Larraz, causes "much injury to the brain." Indissoluble marriage bonds did not exist anywhere in America, and virginity had no value. On the Caribbean coasts and in other areas, homosexuality was unrestrained, and this offended God as much as or more than the cannibalism of the Amazon jungle. The Indians had the unwholesome habit of bathing every day, and, to cap it all, they believed in dreams. Thus the Jesuits were able to confirm the influence of Satan on the Canadian Indians: Indians so diabolical they had interpreters for the symbolic language of dreams, because they believed that the soul speaks while the body sleeps and that dreams express unfulfilled desires. The Iroquois, Guaraní, and other American Indians elected their chiefs in open meetings, where women took part as men's equals, and removed them from office if they became overbearing. No doubt possessed by the Devil, Chief Nicaragua asked who had elected the king of Spain.

"Good fishing gets boring after a while, but sex is always fun," said, and say, the Mehinaku Indians of Brazil. Sexual freedom gave off an unbearable odor of sulfur. The chronicles of the Indies abound in the scandal of these infernal lusts that lurked in every corner of America beyond the valleys of Mexico and Cuzco, which were sanctuaries of puritanism. The official story reduces pre-Columbian reality largely to the centers of the two civilizations with the highest level of social organization and material development. Incas and Aztecs were at the height of their imperial expansion when they were overthrown by the European invaders, allied with peoples subjected by those empires. In those two societies, dominated hierarchically by kings, priests, and warriors, rigid codes of behavior held sway; their taboos and prohibitions left little or no space for freedom. But even in those centers, the most repressive in America, what came later was worse. The Aztecs, for example, punished adultery with death, but they allowed divorce at the wish of the man or woman. Another example: the Aztecs had slaves, but the children of slaves were not born slaves. Marriage for life and hereditary slavery were European products that America imported in the sixteenth century.

In our time, the conquest continues. The Indians go on expiating their sins of community, freedom and other affronts. The purifying mission of Civilization no longer masks the plunder of gold or silver: Under the banner of Progress, onward march the legions of modern pirates, without hooked hands, eye patches, or wooden legs, the multinationals that swoop down on the uranium, petroleum, nickel, manganese, tungsten. The Indians suffer, as before, the curse of the wealth of the lands they inhabit. They were driven toward arid soil; technology has discovered, beneath those soils, fertile subsoils.

"The conquest isn't over," gaily proclaimed the advertisements published in Europe eleven years ago, offering Bolivia to foreigners. The military dictatorship held out to the highest bidder the richest land in the country, while treating the Indians the same as in the sixteenth century. In the first phase of the conquest, Indians were compelled to describe themselves in public documents, "I, wretched Indian . . ." Now the Indians only have the right to exist as servile labor or tourist attractions.

"Land is not sold. Land is our mother. You don't sell your mother. Why don't they offer one hundred million dollars to the Pope for the Vatican?" a Sioux chief asked recently in the United States. A century earlier, the Seventh Cavalry had ravaged the Black Hills, sacred territory to the Sioux, because they held gold. Now multinational corporations mine its uranium, although the Sioux refuse to sell. The uranium is poisoning the rivers.

A few years ago, the Colombian government told the Indians of the Cauca valley, "The subsoil does not belong to you, but to the Colombian nation," and immediately turned it over to the Celanese Corporation. After a time, part of the Cauca had been turned into a lunar landscape. A thousand hectares of Indian land were made barren.

In the Ecuadorian Amazon, oil is dislodging the Auca Indians. A helicopter flies over the jungle, with a loudspeaker announcing in the Auca language, "It's time to leave now. . . ." And the Indians obey the will of God.

From Geneva, in 1979, the United Nations Human Rights Commission warned: "Unless the Brazilian government alters its plans, we can expect that the largest of the surviving tribes will cease to exist in twenty years." The commission was referring to the Yanomami, in whose Amazonian lands tin and rare minerals had been discovered. For the same reason, the Nambiquara Indians now number fewer than two hundred, and they were fifteen thousand at the beginning of the century. Indians die like flies when they come in contact with unknown bacteria brought by the invaders, as in the days of Cortés and Pizarro —a process now speeded up by Dow Chemical's defoliants, sprayed from the air. When the commission launched its pathetic warning from Geneva, FUNAI, the official body for the protection of Brazil's Indians, was run by sixteen colonels and employed fourteen anthropologists. There has been no change in the government's plans since then.

In Guatemala, in the lands of the Quichés, the largest oil deposit in Central America has been found. The 1980s were a long slaughter. The army—mestizo officers, Indian soldiers—has been busy bombing villages and evicting communities so that Texaco, Hispanoil, Getty Oil, and other companies can survey and exploit the oilfields. Of every ten Guatemalans, six are Indians, but in Guatemala the word "Indian" is an insult.

When I first arrived in Guatemala City, I sensed I was in a country foreign to itself. In the capital, I found only one house that was truly Guatemalan, with beautiful wooden furniture, native blankets and rugs, handmade glass and earthenware. Just one house had not been invaded by Miami-style plastic kitsch: it belonged to a French teacher. But you only had to travel a little way outside the capital to find the green branches of the old Mayan trunk, rising miraculously despite the implacable ax blows suffered year after year, century after century. The ruling class, ruled by bad taste, considers the beautiful indigenous clothing ridiculous disguises appropriate only for carnival or the museum, just as they prefer hamburgers to tamales and Coca-Cola to fresh fruit juice. The official country, which lives off the real country but is ashamed of it, would like to erase it. It regards the native tongues as mere guttural noises, and the native religion as pure idolatry, because for the Indians all land is a place of worship and every wood a sanctuary.

When the Guatemalan army passes through the Mayan villages, destroying homes, harvests and animals, it reserves its best efforts for the systematic slaughter of children and old people. Children are killed the same way cornfields are burned: down to the root. "We're going to leave them with no seed," Colonel Horacio Maldonado Shadd explains. And in every old person there lurks a transmitter for the unpardonable community tradition and the no less unpardonable tradition of identifying with nature. The Mayas still ask forgiveness of a tree when they have to cut it down.

The repression is a cruel ceremony of exorcism. You only have to look at the photographs, the features of the officers and their sturdy build: these grandchildren of Indians, deserters from their culture, dream of becoming George Custer or Buffalo Bill, and they long to turn Guatemala into a gigantic supermarket. And the soldiers? Don't they have the same faces as their victims, the same skin color? They are Indians trained for violence and humiliation. In the barracks the metamorphosis is worked: first they are turned into cockroaches, then into birds of prey. Finally they forget that all life is sacred and are convinced that horror is the natural order of things.

Racism is not the sorry privilege of Guatemala. Throughout America, from north to south, the dominant culture acknowledges Indians as objects of study, but denies them as subjects of history: the Indians have folklore, not culture; they practice superstitions, not religions; they speak dialects, not languages; they make handicrafts, not art.

Perhaps the approaching celebration of the five hundredth anniversary could help turn things around, so topsy-turvy are they now. Not to confirm the world, adding to the self-importance, the self-glorification of the masters of power, but to denounce and change it. For that we shall have to celebrate the vanquished, not the victors. The vanquished and those who identified with them, like Bernardino de Sahagún, and those who lived for them, like Bartolomé de Las Casas, Vasco de Quiroga, and Antonio Vieira, and those who died for them, like Gonzalo Guerrero, the first conquered conqueror, who ended his days fighting at the side of the Indians, his chosen brothers, in Yucatán.

And perhaps in this way we could get a bit closer to the day of justice than the Guaraní, pursuers of Paradise, have always been awaiting. The Guaraní believe that the world wants to be different, that it wants to be born again, and so the world entreats the First Father to unleash the blue tiger that sleeps beneath his hammock. The Guaraní believe that someday that righteous tiger will shatter this world so that another world, with neither evil nor death, guilt nor prohibitions, can be born from its ashes. The Guaraní believe, and I do too, that life truly deserves that festival.

(1987)
Translated by Liz Heron

You Didn't Die When They Killed You: A Speech Delivered in the Monster's Belly

[*Readers of Eduardo Galeano's books may be startled to learn that the Uruguayan writer was invited to Chile to receive the José Carrasco Tapia Prize (named after a journalist murdered in 1986 by the Pinochet dictatorship) and spoke these words at the presentation ceremony in Santiago.*

Asked to explain for Americans confused by Latin American torture regimes how all of this was possible in today's Chile, Galeano replied from Montevideo to translator Cedric Belfrage:" I don't know how it could happen, but it happened."]

Last September in Peru, a fortune-teller read my fortune. She told me: "Within a month you will receive a distinction." I laughed. I laughed at the word "distinction," which has something comic about it, and because it brought to mind an old acquaintance who was foolish but on target and who used to say, admonishing me with his finger: "Sooner or later writers turn into hamburgers."

So I laughed at the fortune-teller's prophecy, and my laugh made her laugh.

Exactly one month later, I received a telegram in Montevideo. It said that in Chile I had been awarded a distinction (the telegram, like the fortune-teller, said "distinction"). It was the

José Carrasco Tapia Prize. I jumped for joy—joy undarkened by any shadow of doubt, because no prize bearing that name can be a reward for repentants, for the tamed, for the yea-sayers.

Nor did the smallest doubt about the nature of the prize darken my joy. I knew, I know, I wasn't being invited to a funeral ceremony.

We live in a world that treats the dead better than the living. We the living are askers of questions and givers of answers, and we have other grave defects unpardonable by a system that believes that death, like money, improves people.

Nothing of that sort. This is an homage to the passion for life, illuminated by the living memory of a murdered compañero, and this is a celebration of the joy of believing in certain things that death cannot kill.

The system, which wants us to be blind, wants us to be dumb, wants us to be deaf, doesn't help us to keep being born as we live. The system trains us to keep dying as we live, and killing as we live: killing what is outside, because every neighbor is a competitor and possible enemy—and above all killing what is inside, killing the best that each of us has alive in himself.

When I was a kid, the priests scared me with the Devil. Now I believe that the Devil, that chief cook in hell, doesn't exist. But at the same time I have proof that the Devil of Fear does exist. The Devil of Fear disguises himself to deceive us. The deceiver offers cowardice as if it were prudence, and betrayal as if it were realism. And we must realize that the great trickster operates quite successfully among us. Lining up before the Devil of Fear are those who would surrender freedom for security. Many of our laws carry his unmistakable signature. For example, the Argentinian law that authorizes torture and killing, always provided it's done by superior order. For example, the Uruguayan law that bids us forget tortures and crimes, always provided they were committed by people in uniform. Those are two laws of the impunity of power. The impunity of power brings general putrefaction of customs.

In a dictatorship or a democracy, democracy or democratorship, the Devil of Fear doesn't act alone. In Uruguay, at least, I almost always see him accompanied by a friend. He goes around with his partner the Devil of Greed. This is another devil in disguise. The Devil of Greed commits his crimes in the name of God and with the blessing of the Holy Father, who sprinkles holy water on the profit motive, the practice of usury, and the right to live off the labor of others.

The Devil of Greed tells us that if we sell him our soul we'll prosper and end up like Hong Kong. He dictated the political economy that the military regime imposed on my country, which the civilian regime has carried on without much change. That political economy condemns workers to live like fakirs. Work isn't worth anything, the money won't stretch, you do twice the work for half the pay. What do our countries produce? Cheap labor. The reality is black humor:

"You have to tighten your belt."

"I can't. I ate it yesterday."

Furthermore, this political economy forces producers to become speculators. It's the day of the opportunist: to survive you must get smart. Society is divided into fuckers and fucked. It's not good business to work or to produce; creation is a crime. Dignity isn't quoted on the market. The society pages show swindlers arm in arm with hangmen. The day of the chameleon: no one has taught humanity as much as this humble creature.

The system, which does everything backward, encourages plagiarists and discourages creators, rewards the infamous and punishes those who say what they believe and believe in what they do. Roguery is raised to the level of economic doctrine and pompously rebaptized "modernization." A friend remarked to me the other day that if we go on this way we'll have to replace the statue of our national hero, General José Artigas, in Independence Plaza. Instead of Artigas, my friend said, we'll have to put up Lazarillo de Tormes.*

---

* The title character of an anonymous Spanish classic, a streetwise urchin who lives by his wits, and whose name has become synonymous with "rogue."

The recent flood of signatures by the Uruguayan people against the impunity law, which tells us to forget the military dictatorship's atrocities, implies a yearning for justice far beyond rejection of that law. The signatures also, I think, express refusal of a whole way of life based on a self-centered conformity, an attitude of who cares, of what are you going to do about it, of you stay out of this, of every man for himself. The people have signed up against the visible terrorist crimes of the state, but also against the invisible ones: to show that the national will to solidarity, the popular capacity to believe and to create, and the dangerous and marvelous passion for liberty, are alive—badly wounded but alive.

Wasn't this also the fight of Pepe Carrasco? Isn't this, with allowance for distance of time and place, the fight of all Chileans who here are breaking lances with the Devil of Greed and the Devil of Fear?

I am not a Chilean, but it's just as if I were one. My favorite song is a Chilean song, a song that gives thanks to life. That song moves my lips when I wander in the labyrinths of doubt or discouragement, and singing it puts me back on track. Singing it, I recover the desire to thank life, which has given me so much love of flight and so much hatred of cages.

This love and this hate form the two profiles of the same certainty, more powerful than doubt or discouragement. There are certainties like this that bump into me every time I get lost, and raise me up each time I fall. I owe them to people I care about. They were a gift from people I care about.

I'm not a Chilean, but it's as if I were. One of my most invulnerable certainties is the certainty that it's worthwhile to die for things without which it's not worthwhile to live. And this faith I owe to a Chilean friend whose name was, is, Salvador Allende.

Today we have gathered to celebrate a certainty that upsets the bureaucrats and the generals. Technocrats can't decipher it, merchants can't buy it, the police can't police it. Recently, at the end of a conference, I tried to define this certainty with these words: Creating and fighting are our way of saying to the fallen compañeros: You didn't die when they killed you.

This certainly has nothing to do with the Great Beyond. It has to do with the Great Here and Now, with the joy of the continuing human adventure on earth. We have the joy of our joys, and we also have the joy of our sorrows, because the painless life that consumer civilization sells in the supermarkets doesn't interest us, and we're proud of the price of so much pain that we pay for so much love. We have the joy of our errors, stumblings that prove the passion of moving and of love along the road. And we have the joy of our defeats, because the fight for justice and beauty is also worthwhile when it is lost. And above all, above all we have the joy of our hopes, with a full measure of disenchantment. When disenchantment has become an article of mass and universal consumption, we go on believing in the astounding power of the human embrace.

So here we join together, and in this spirit. And joining together we say to Pepe Carrasco and those who fell as he did, in Chile or anywhere else, to each and every one of those who have staked all and life itself for dignity: No, no, no, you didn't die when they killed you.

(1988)
Translated by Cedric Belfrage

We Say No

[*From July 11 through July 16, 1988, two months before the plebiscite on General Piochet's rule, three hundred intellectuals and artists participated in Chile Creates, an international meeting of art, science, and culture in support of democracy in Chile.*

This is the opening speech that Eduardo Galeano delivered, in the name of all those invited, on Monday evening, July 11, 1988.]

We have come from different countries, and we are here—reunited under the generous shade of Pablo Neruda—to join the people of Chile, who say no.

We also say no.

We say no to the praise of money and of death. We say no to a system that assigns prices to people and things, within which he who has the most is hence he who is most worthy, and we say no to a world which spends two million dollars each minute on arms for war while each minute it kills thirty children with hunger or curable illnesses. The neutron bomb, which saves things and annihilates people, is a perfect symbol of our times. To the murderous system that converts the stars of the night sky into military objectives, the human being is no more than a factor of production and of consumption and an object of use; time, no more than an economic resource; and the entire planet a source of income that must yield up to the last drop of its juice. Poverty is multiplied in order to multiply wealth, and the arms that guard this wealth—the wealth of very few—are multiplied and keep all others on the brink of poverty. Meanwhile, solitude is also multiplied: we say no to a system that neither feeds its people nor loves them, that condemns many to a hunger for food and many more to a hunger for the embrace.

We say no to the lie. The dominant culture, which the mass media irradiates on a universal scale, invites us to confuse the world with a supermarket or a racetrack, where one's fellow man can be merchandise or competition, but never a brother. This culture of lies, which vulgarly speculates with human love in order to extract its appreciation, is in reality a culture of broken bonds: its gods are its winners, the successful masters of money and of power, and its heroes are uniformed "Rambos" who use their influence while applying the Doctrine of National Security. By what it says and what it fails to say, the dominant culture lies when it claims that the poverty of the poor is not a result of the wealth of the wealthy, but rather the daughter of no one, originating in a goat's ear or in the will of God, who created the lazy poor and the donkey. In the same way, the humiliation of some men by others does not necessarily have to motivate shared indignance or scandal, because it belongs to the natural order of things: let us suppose that Latin American dictatorships form part of our exuberant nature and not of the imperialist system of power.

Disdain betrays history and mutilates the world. The powerful opinion-makers treat us as though we do not exist, or as though we are silly shadows. The colonial inheritance obliges the so-called Third World—populated by third-class people—to accept as its own the memory of the victors who conquered it and to take on the lies of others and use them as its own reality. They reward our obedience, punish our intelligence, and discourage our creative energy. We are opinionated, yet we cannot offer our opinions. We have a right to the echo, not to the voice, and those who rule praise our talent to repeat parrot fashion. We say no: we refuse to accept this mediocrity as our destiny.

We say no to fear. No to the fear of speaking, of doing, of being. Visible colonialism forbids us to speak, to do, to be. Invisible colonialism, more efficient, convinces us that one cannot speak, cannot do, cannot be. Fear disguises itself as realism: to prevent realism from becoming unreal, or so claim the ideologists of impotence, morals must be immoral. Confronted with indignity, misery, lies and deceit, we have no alternative other than that of resignation. Marked by fatality, we are born irresponsible, violent, stupid, picturesque, and condemned to military bondage. At best, we can aspire to convert ourselves into model prisoners, to be able to conscientiously pay our share of a colossal foreign debt contracted to finance the luxury that humiliates us and the club that beats us.

And within this framework, we say no to the neutrality of the human word. We say no to those who invite us to wash our hands of the crucifixions we witness daily. To the bored fascination of an art that is cold, indifferent, contemplative of its mirrored reflection, we prefer a warm art, one that celebrates the human adventure in the world and participates in this adventure, an art that is incurably enamored and pugnacious. Would beauty be beautiful if it were not just? Would justice be just if it were not beautiful? We say no to the divorce of beauty and justice, because we say yes to the powerful and fertile embrace they share.

As it happens, we are saying no, and by saying no we are saying yes.

By saying no to dictatorships, and no to dictatorships disguised as democracies, we are saying yes to the struggle for true democracy, one that will deny no one bread or the power of speech, and one that will be as beautiful and dangerous as a poem by Neruda or a song by Violeta.*

By saying no to the devastating empire of greed, whose center lies in North America, we are saying yes to another possible America, which will be born of the most ancient of American traditions, the communitarian tradition that the Chilean Indians have defended, desperately, defeat after defeat, during the last five centuries.

In saying no to a peace without dignity, we are saying yes to the sacred right of rebellion against injustice and its long history, as long as the history of popular resistance on the long map of Chile. By saying no to the freedom of money, we are saying yes to the freedom of people: a mistreated and wounded freedom, a thousand times defeated as in Chile and, as in Chile, a thousand times arisen.

To say no to the suicidal egotism of the powerful, who have converted the world into a vast barracks, we are saying yes to human solidarity, which gives us a universal sense and confirms the power of a brotherhood that is stronger than all borders and their guardians: the force that invades us, like the music of Chile, and like the wine of Chile, embraces us.

And by saying no to the sad charm of disenchantment, we are saying yes to hope, the famished and crazy and loving and loved hope of Chile, the obstinate hope, like the sons of Chile shattering the night.

(1988)
Translated by Cedric Belfrage

* Violeta Parra, Chilean songwriter and artist.

Salgado: Light is a Secret of Garbage

[*This essay appears in a book of photographs by the acclaimed Brazilian photographer Sebastião Salgado.*]

1

Are these photographs, these figures of tragic grandeur, carvings in stone or wood by a sculptor in despair? Was the sculptor the photographer? Or God? Or the Devil? Or earthly reality?

This much is certain: it would be difficult to look at these figures and remain unaffected. I cannot imagine anyone shrugging his shoulder, turning away unseeing, and sauntering off, whistling.

2

Hunger looks like the man that hunger is killing. The man looks like the tree the man is killing. The trees have arms, the people, branches. Withered bodies, gnarled: trees made of bones, the people of knots and roots that writhe under the sun. The trees and the people, ageless. All born thousands of years ago—who knows how many?—and still they are standing, inexplicably standing, beneath a heaven that forsakes them.

3

This world is so sad that the rainbows come out in black and white and so ugly that the vultures fly upside down after the dying. A song is sung in Mexico:

> *Se va la vida por el agujero*
> *Como la mugre por el lavadero.*
> (Life goes down the drain
> Like dirt in the sink.)

And in Colombia they say: *El costo de la vida sube y sube y el valor de la vida baja y baja.* [The more the cost of living goes up the less life is worth.]

But light is a secret buried under the garbage, and Salgado's photographs tell us that secret.

The emergence of the image from the liquid of the developer, when the light becomes forever fixed in shadow, is a unique moment that detaches itself from time and is transformed into forever. These photographs will live on after their subjects and their author, bearing testimony to the world's naked truth and hidden splendor. Salgado's camera moves about the violent darkness, seeking light, stalking light. Does the light descend from the sky or rise up out of us? That instant of trapped light—that gleam—in the photographs reveals to us what is unseen, what is seen but unnoticed; an unperceived presence, a powerful absence. It shows us that concealed within the pain of living and the tragedy of dying there is a potent magic, a luminous mystery that redeems the human adventure in the world.

4

The mouth, not yet dead, fixed to the spout of a pitcher. The pitcher, white, glowing: a breast.

This neck, a child's, a man's, an old man's, rests on someone's hand. The neck not yet dead, but already given up for dead, can no longer bear the weight of the head.

5

Salgado's photographs, a multiple portrait of human pain, at the same time invite us to celebrate the dignity of humankind. Brutally frank, these images of hunger and suffering are still respectful and seemly. Having no relation to the tourism of poverty, they do not violate but penetrate the human spirit in order to reveal it. Salgado sometimes shows skeletons, almost corpses, with dignity—all that is left to them. They have been stripped of everything but they have dignity. That is the source of their ineffable beauty. This is not a macabre, obscene exhibitionism of poverty. It is a poetry of horror because there is a sense of honor.

In Andalusia I was once told of a very poor fisherman who went about peddling shellfish in a basket. This poor fisherman refused to sell his shellfish to a young gentleman who wanted the entire catch. He offered to pay the fisherman whatever price he asked, but the fisherman refused to sell for the simple reason that he took a dislike to the young gentleman. And he simply said to him:

"I am the master of my hunger."

6

A little dog stretched out upon his friend's grave. His head high, he keeps a vigil over him in his sleep between the lighted candles.

An automobile among ruins, inside it a black woman in a bridal gown looking at a flower made of cloth.

Impossible ships in the midst of the infinite wilderness of sand.

Tunics—or banners—of sand lashed by the wind.

Cactuses like swords of the earth, armored arms of the earth.

In the factories pipelines that are intestines or voracious boa constrictors.

And on the earth, out of the earth, there are peasant feet: feet of earth and time.

7

Salgado photographs people. Casual photographers photograph phantoms.

As an article of consumption, poverty is a source of morbid pleasure and much money. Poverty is a commodity that fetches a high price on the luxury market.

Consumer-society photographers approach but do not enter. In hurried visits to scenes of despair or violence, they climb out of the plane or helicopter, press the shutter release, explode the flash: they shoot and run. They have looked without seeing and their images say nothing. Their cowardly photographs soiled with horror or blood may extract a few crocodile tears, a few coins, a pious word or two from the privileged of the earth, none of which changes the order of their universe. At the sight of the dark-skinned wretched, forsaken by God and pissed on by dogs, anybody who is nobody confidentially congratulates himself: life hasn't done too badly by me, in comparison. Hell serves to confirm the virtues of paradise.

Charity, vertical, humilates. Solidarity, horizontal, helps. Salgado photographs from inside, in solidarity. He remained in the Sahel desert for fifteen months when he went there to photograph hunger. He traveled in Latin America for seven years to garner a handful of photographs.

8

The miners of Serra Pelada: bodies of clay. More than fifty thousand men in northern Brazil buried in clay, hunting for gold. Loaded down with clay they scale the mountain, slipping sometimes and falling, each fallen life no more important than a pebble that falls. A host of miners climbing. Images of the pyramid builders in the days of the Pharaohs? An army of ants? Ants, lizards? The miners have lizard skins and lizard eyes. Do the wretched of the earth live in the world's zoo?

Salgado's camera moves in to reveal the light of human life with tragic intensity, with sad tenderness. A hand, open, reaches out from nowhere to the miner struggling up the slope, flattened by his burden. The hand, like the hand in Michelangelo's fresco, touching the first man and, in touching, creating him. The miner on his way to the top of Serra Pelada—or Golgotha—leans, resting, on a cross.

9

This is stripped-down art. A naked language that speaks for the naked of the earth. Nothing superfluous in these images, miraculously free of rhetoric, demagogy, belligerence.

Salgado makes no concessions, though it would be easy and, unquestionably, commercially advantageous for him to do so. The profoundest sadness of the universe is expressed without offering consolation, with no sugar coating. In Portuguese, *salgado* means "salty."

The picturesque, studiously avoided by Salgado, would cushion the violence of his blows and foster the concept of the Third World, as, after all, just "another" world: a dangerous, lurking world but at the same time *simpático*, a circus of odd little creatures.

10

Reality speaks a language of symbols. Each part is a metaphor of the whole. In Salgado's photographs, the symbols expose themselves *from the inside to the outside*. The artist does not extract the symbols from his head, to generously offer them to reality, requiring that they be used. Rather, reality selects the precise moment that speaks most perfectly for it: Salgado's camera denudes it, tears it from time and makes it into image, and the image makes itself symbol—a symbol of our time and our world. These faces that scream without opening their mouths are "other" faces no longer. No longer, for they have ceased being conveniently strange and distant, innocuous excuses for charity that eases guilty consciences. We are all those dead, going back centuries or millennia, who nevertheless remain stubbornly alive—alive down to their profoundest and most painful radiance, who are not pretending to be alive for a photograph.

These images that seem torn from the pages of the Old Testament are actually portraits of the human condition in the twentieth century, symbols of our one world, which is not a First, a Third, or a Twentieth World. From their mighty silence, these images, these portraits, question the hypocritical frontiers that safeguard the bourgeois order and protect its right to power and inheritance.

11

Eyes of a child looking on death, not wanting to see it, unable to look away. Eyes riveted on death, snared by death—death that has come to take those eyes and that child. Chronicle of a crime.

12

I have spent five minutes searching for words as I gaze at a blank sheet of paper. In those five minutes, the world spent $10 million on armaments and 160 children starved to death or died of curable illness. That is to say, during my five minutes of reflection, the world spent $10 million on armaments *in order that* 160 children could be murdered with utter impunity in the war of wars, the most silent, the most undeclared war, the war that goes by the name of peace.

Bodies out of concentration camps. Auschwitzes of hunger. A system for purification of the species? Aimed at the "inferior races" (which reproduce like rabbits), starvation is used instead of gas chambers. And for the same price, a method of population control. The epoch of peace by fear was ushered in with the atom bombs at Hiroshima and Nagasaki. For want of world wars, starvation checks population explosion. Meanwhile, new bombs police the hungry. A human being can die only once, as far as we know, but the number of nuclear bombs currently stockpiled provides the option of killing everyone twelve times.

Sick with the plague of death, this world that eradicates the hungry instead of hunger produces food enough for all of humanity and more. Yet, some die of starvation and others of overeating. To guarantee that the usurpation of bread shall endure, there are twenty-five times as many soldiers as doctors in the world. Since 1980, the poor countries have increased military spending while expenditures for public health were cut back by half.

A Grenadian economist, Davison Budhoo, resigned from the International Monetary Fund. In his farewell letter he wrote: "The blood is so much, you know, it runs in rivers. It dries up too; it cakes all over me; sometimes I feel that there is not enough soap in the whole world to cleanse me from the things that I did do in your name."

13

Houses like the empty skins of dead animals. The blankets are shrouds and the shrouds dry shells that encase shriveled fruits or deformed beings.

People bearing bundles, bundles bearing people. Bearers scarcely able to walk the mountains, bowed under timbers large as coffins that they carry on their shoulders, becoming part of their shoulders. But they walk on the clouds.

14

The Third World—the "other" world—worthy only of contempt or pity. In the interest of good taste, not often mentioned.

Had AIDS not spread beyond Africa, the new plague would have gone unnoticed. It hardly would have mattered if thousands or millions of Africans had died of AIDS. That isn't news. In what is known as the Third World, death from plague is a natural death.

If Salman Rushdie had stayed in India and written his novels in Hindustani, Tamil, or Bengali, his death sentence would have attracted no attention. In the countries of Latin America, for example, several writers have been condemned to death and executed by recent military dictatorships. The European countries recalled their ambassadors from Iran in a gesture of indignation and protest against Rushdie's death sentence, but when the Latin American writers were sentenced—and executed—the European countries did not recall their ambassadors. And the reason they were not recalled was that their ambassadors were busy selling arms to the murderers. In the Third World, death by bullets is a "natural" death.

From the standpoint of the great communications media that uncommunicate humanity, the Third World is peopled by third-class inhabitants distinguishable from animals only by their ability to walk on two legs. Theirs are problems of nature not of history: hunger, pestilence, violence are in the natural order of things.

15

A Way of the Cross with statues of stone. A Way of the Cross with people of flesh and blood. Is that tattered child wandering the dunes of the desert gentle as Jesus? Does he possess Jesus' anguished beauty? Or *is* he Jesus on the way to the place where he was born?

16

Hunger lies. It simulates being an insoluble mystery or a vengeance of the gods. Hunger is masked, reality is masked.

Salgado was an economist before he found out he was a photographer. He first came to the Sahel as an economist. There, for the first time, he tried to use the camera's eye to penetrate the skins reality uses to hide itself.

The science of economics had already taught him a great deal about the subject of masks. In economics, what appears to be, never is. Good fortune through numbers has little or nothing to do with the greater good. Let us postulate a country with two inhabitants. That country's per capita income, let us suppose, is $4,000. At first glance, that country would seem to be doing not at all badly. Actually, however, it turns out that one of the inhabitants gets $8,000 and the other zero. Well might the other ask those adept in the occult science of economics: "Where do I collect my per capita income? At which window do they pay?"

Salgado is a Brazilian. How many does the development of Brazil develop? The statistics show spectacular economic growth over the last three decades, particularly through the long years of military dictatorship. In 1960, however, one out of every three Brazilians was malnourished. Today, two out of every three are. There are sixteen million abandoned children. Out of every ten children who die, seven are killed by hunger. Brazil is fourth in the world in food exports, fifth in area, and sixth in hunger.

17

Caravans of pilgrims wander the African desert, dying, searching futilely for a blade of grass, an insect to eat. Are they people— or mummies that move? Are they walking statues, disfigured by the wind, in the last throes or asleep, perhaps alive, perhaps dead, perhaps at once dead and alive?

A man carries his son—or bones that were his son—in his arms and that man is a tree, rigid and tall, rooted in the solitude. Rooted in the solitude, an amazing tree caresses the air, swaying its long branches, the foliage a head leaning over a shoulder or a breast. A dying child manages to move its hand in a final gesture, the gesture of a caress, and caressing, dies. Is that woman who walks, or drags herself, against the wind a bird with broken wings? Is that scarecrow with arms thrown open in solitude a woman?

(This text is dedicated to Helena Villagra, who saw with me.)

(1990)
Translated by Asa Zatz

Words about Memory
and about Fire

AN ANGEL'S ASTONISHMENT

One day, God pointed at the Americas and asked an angel of heaven to prepare a report. God wasn't curious, nor was he bored. God was worried. He had heard that in Latin America people were dying by the thousands, from hunger or bullets, and that they held him responsible. He had heard that people were saying he wished it so.

The little angel, a civil servant of the Great Beyond, began by studying a map of the Here and Now. On the map, Latin America was smaller than Europe, and much smaller than the United States and Canada. The winged bureaucrat then discovered that what he could see did not coincide in the least with the map. When he consulted official history books, he got the same result. In history, as on the map, Latin America shrinks.

A WRITER'S ASTONISHMENT

Latin America is gravely ill with foolishness and "copyitis." For five centuries she has been trained to spit in the mirror; to ignore and despise the best of herself.

The true history of America, all of America, North and South, is a source of astonishing dignity and beauty. Yet dignity and beauty, the Siamese twins of humiliation and horror, are rarely mentioned in official histories. The victors, who invoke the right of inheritance to justify their privilege, impose their own memory as the only memory allowed. Official history, the wardrobe where the system keeps its old costumes, deceives by what it says and even more by what it keeps silent. This parade of masked heros reduces our dazzling reality to a small, ridiculous show: the victory of the rich, the white, the male, and the military.

A HUNTER OF VOICES

White and male, yet neither uniformed nor wealthy, I wrote *Memory of Fire* to combat the amnesia that consumes what is worth remembering.

I am not a historian; I am a writer challenged by enigmas and lies, who would like the present to stop being a painful atonement for the past, who would like to imagine the future rather than accept it: a hunter of scattered voices, lost and true.

Any memory that merits rescue has been pulverized, blown to a thousand tiny bits.

THE ELEPHANT

When I was a child, my grandmother told me the fable of the blind men and the elephant.

Three blind men were standing by an elephant. One of them squeezed its tail and said, "It's a rope."

Another caressed the elephant's leg and said, "It's a column."

The third blind man rested his hand on the elephant's side and said: "It's a wall."

That's us: blind to ourselves and to the world. Since birth we are trained to see only fragments. The dominant culture, a culture of disconnection, breaks up the past like it breaks up the present. And keeps us from putting the pieces together.

WINDOWS

The brief chapters of *Memory of Fire* are the windows of a house; there are as many possible houses as there are readers. These spaces open to time help the reader discover the time-that-was as if it were happening now, a past that becomes present through the story-windows the trilogy recounts.

"The branch has its faithful birds," wrote the poet Salinas, "because it does not bind, it offers." The reader comes and goes at will in this house of words. He can start at the beginning or at the end, read straight through or back and forth, at random or however. The house is indeed the reader's own.

YESTERDAY AND TODAY

Memory of Fire is written in the present tense, as though past history were occurring in the present, because the past is alive even if it's been buried by error or infamy. The divorce of past and present is as disastrous as the divorce of soul and body, or mind and heart.

THE INCESSANT METAPHOR

I found it in a book. When black slaves escaped from the plantations of Surinam in the seventeenth century, the women filled their luxuriant tresses with seeds. When they arrived in the jungle, they shook their heads to fertilize the free land.

Memory of Fire recounts a thousand brief moments of history. Brief moments such as this one, which reveal the marvel or the terror of the human adventure in America. Because each situation symbolizes many others, grand events are revealed through small ones, and the universe is viewed through a keyhole. Reality, the unsurpassable poet, speaks in a language of symbols.

I began to write this trilogy the day I realized something that now seems to me to be self-evident: that history is an incessant metaphor.

THE EBB AND FLOW OF MYTH

Myths, collective metaphors, collective acts of creation, offer answers to the challenges of nature and the mysteries of human experience. Through myths, memory lives on, recognizes itself, and acts.

Throughout the pages of the trilogy, historic experience is interwoven with myth, as it is in life. The first part of *Memory of Fire*, however, is based exclusively on indigenous myths transmitted from parents to children by oral tradition. I found no better way to approach the America that existed prior to Columbus's arrival. In any event, practically all documentation of this period ended up in the bonfires of the conquistadores.

These indigenous myths, keys to the most ancient memories of America, perpetuate the dreams of the conquered—lost dreams, scorned dreams—and return them to a history that is alive: they come from history, and to history they return.

In 1572, when the Spaniards cut off the head of Túpac Amaru, the last king of the Inca dynasty, a myth was born among the Indians of Peru. This myth proclaimed that the severed head would one day be rejoined to the body. Two centuries later, the myth returned to the reality from which it came, and prophecy became history: José Gabriel Condorcanqui took the name

Túpac Amaru and led the largest indigenous revolt of all time. The severed head found its body.

VOICES OR ECHOES?

Soon we will celebrate the five hundredth anniversary of the arrival of Columbus, and it's high time America begins to discover herself. Rescuing the past is part of this urgent task of revelation. But where are the resounding voices, obstinately alive, that help us to exist? Above and outside? Or below and within? In "civilization" or in "barbarism"?

Way back in 1867, Ecuador sent a collection of paintings by her greatest artists to the Paris World's Fair. These paintings were exact copies of certain masterworks of Europe. The official catalogue praised the artists' talent in the art of reproduction.

THE CHORUS

Those from above, who copy those from outside, despise those from below and within: The people are but the hero's chorus. The "ignorant" do not make history; they receive it ready-made.

Indigenous rebellions, which did not let up from 1493 on, receive little or no mention in the texts that teach America's past. Equally ignored are the continuous black slave revolts, which began from the moment Europe gloriously founded hereditary slavery in America.

For usurpers of memory and thieves of the word, this long history of dignity is no more than a chain of delinquent acts. The fight for freedom is reduced to the forefathers raising their swords for independence: reduced to a battle that ended when the new masters of each newly born nation drafted a noble constitution which denied all rights to the same people who had given up their lives in the name of liberty.

THE WOMEN

"Behind every great man is a woman. . . ." Frequent homage, doubtful tribute. It reduces women to chair backs.

In her traditional role, a woman is a devoted daughter, unselfish wife, self-sacrificing mother, and exemplary widow. She obeys, decorates, consoles, and remains silent. In official histories this loyal shadow merits only silence. At most, a mention of the wives of our founding fathers. But in real history, another woman looks out between the bars of this prison cell, and at times it is impossible to deny her existence. Such is the case of the Mexican nun and poet Sor Juana Inés de la Cruz, who could not avoid her own great and disturbing talent, or of Simón Bolívar's lover and companion Manuela Sáenz and her shining life. Nevertheless, no mention is made—even in passing—of certain black and Indian captains, women who gave a tremendous beating to the colonial troops long before the wars of independence. There is one honorable exception to this law of silence: recently Jamaica recognized Nanny as a national heroine. Two and a half centuries ago, Nanny—a fierce slave, half woman, half goddess—led the Windward maroons to freedom, leaving the British army defeated and humiliated.

THE PIOUS MAN AND THE MADMAN

As a child I was taught in school to revere Francisco Antonio Maciel, "the Father of the Poor," and founder of the Caridad Hospital in Montevideo. Years later, I discovered that this pious gentleman earned his living selling human flesh: he was a slave trader.

For all the statues that are superfluous in our towns and cities, an equal number are lacking. I came across much infamy in my research for *Memory of Fire*, but I also discovered marvels of which I had never heard.

Simón Rodríguez was one of the most amazing revelations. Few know of him in Venezuela, where he was born; in the rest of Latin America, practically no one has heard of him. He is vaguely remembered, if at all, for having been the childhood tutor of Simón Bolívar. Yet in these lands he was the most audacious thinker of his time, and now, a century and a half later, his words could have been spoken a week ago. Simón Rodríguez preached in the desert from the back of a mule. He was taken for a madman, and called El Loco, because he chided the owners of power who were powerless to do anything but import ideas and merchandise from Europe and the United States. "Imitate originality," Don Simón would say, "since you copy everything else!" This was the first of his unpardonable sins: he was original. The other: he wasn't an officer.

THE NOBEL AND THE NOBODY

Past history is topsy-turvy because present history is upside down. Not only in South America, but in North America as well.

Who in the United States has not heard of Teddy Roosevelt? This national hero preached the glories of war and waged it against the weak. War purifies the soul, Roosevelt proclaimed, and betters the human race. And for this, he was awarded the Nobel Peace Prize.

But who in the United States has heard of Charles Drew? It's not that history has forgotten him; it never met him. A scientist whose research on the storage and transfusion of blood saved millions of lives, Drew was director of the American Red Cross. In 1942, it refused to use blood from African-American donors for transfusions. Drew, who was black, resigned.

THE EARTH IS FLAT

Amnesia is not the sad privilege of poor nations alone. Wealthy nations also teach oblivion. Official history does not mention—among many other things—the source of their wealth. No wealth is innocent of another's poverty. Every day, Europe confirms with impunity that the earth is not round. The forefathers were right: the earth is flat, the horizon an abyss at the bottom of which lies Latin America and the rest of the Third World.

DRY GRASS, DAMP GRASS

An African proverb opens *Memory of Fire*, and explains its title. Slaves brought these words to America: "The dry grass will set fire to the damp grass."

Those slaves also brought from Africa the ancient truth that we all have two memories. Individual memory is vulnerable to time and passion and, like us, is condemned to die. Collective memory, like us, is destined to survive.

WITH ONE'S BACK TO LIFE

Those who hold power find refuge in the past—believing it lies still, believing it is dead—in order to deny the moving, changing present, and to exorcise the future. Official history invites us into a museum full of mummies. No danger: you can study the Indians who died centuries ago and at the same time despise or ignore the Indians alive today. You can admire the extraordinary ruins of ancient temples, while crossing your arms and contemplating the poisoned rivers and devastated forests where Indians live today.

The Conquest continues in all of the Americas, from north to south. The Indians who survive still suffer eviction, plunder, and murder. They still suffer scorn: the mass media teach self-hate to the vanquished. In the age of television, Indian children play cowboys and Indians, and it's hard to find anyone who wants to play the Indian.

VOICES OF YESTERDAY AND TOMORROW

The mute past bores me. *Memory of Fire* would like to multiply the voices that fly at us from the past but sound like the present, and speak to the future.

Ancient Indian cultures are the most futuristic of all. After all, they have kept alive the essential identity between man and nature, while the rest of the world insists on committing suicide. These supposedly uncultured cultures refuse to rape the land or to reduce it to a commodity, an object to use and abuse. The sacred earth is not a thing.

After all, community, the community-based mode of production and life, stubbornly heralds another possible America. This prophetic voice speaks from the most ancient of times, and still resounds despite five centuries of attempts to impose an obligatory silence. Community is the oldest and the most obstinate of all American traditions. As much as it pains those who decry socialism as a foreign notion, our deepest roots are in community: communal property, communal labor, shared lives, lives based on solidarity. Private property, on the other hand, a way of life and work based on greed and selfishness, is indeed an import, brought by the conquistadores since 1492.

A FEAST OF CREATION

Elitism, racism, militarism, and machismo prevent America from recognizing in her mirrored reflection her own luminous and multiple faces. As we work toward our own undoing, we are fascinated by and dedicated to our own negation. Not only Latin America, but also successful North America, where doubtful prosperity masks mutilations of the soul.

But Latin America is the main subject of *Memory of Fire*. In these lands I recognize the best of my joy and sorrow. Writing is my way of helping Latin America reveal her astonishing identity. Her true history, her true reality, is a feast of creation.

FURIES AND LOVES

Memory of Fire, fashioned from furies and loves, is a subjective history, written by one who neither believes in objectivity nor pretends to practice it. As I wrote it, I felt as though I were conversing with America, as if she were a person, a woman who told me her secrets, the acts of love and violation from which she was born. And I felt that I was conversing with myself. In some mysterious way, all that had occurred in America had happened to me, although I hadn't realized it. The characters of her history were people I myself had loved, or hated, and forgotten (or at least I thought so). It was a long trip from the "I" to the "we." Speaking to America, I was talking to myself. Discovering America, I was discovering myself.

THE INCESSANT BIRTH

The third volume of the trilogy is built around the figure of Salvadoran revolutionary Miguel Mármol, his eleven deaths and eleven resurrections. Miguelito, so many times killed and reborn, is the most telling metaphor of Latin America.

Our collective memory remains stubbornly alive: a thousand times slain, a thousand times reborn in the hiding places where she licks her wounds.

(1989)

Impunity U.

This university, odd as it seems, is not for the privileged few. Impunity U. caters to all of Latin America's youth, rich and poor, learned and illiterate. Reality gives the practical courses. Television takes care of theory.

HOW TO DISCREDIT DEMOCRACY

The effectiveness of the pedagogy is beyond question. The classes that teach the impunity of politicians, for example, are rapidly achieving the massive alienation of our youth. If discouragement continues to be sown at this pace, soon no one will believe in anyone. The most instructive case is that of Carlos Menem, who became president of Argentina with 46 percent of the vote. The next day Menem claimed as his own the platform of Alvaro Alsogaray, who had obtained 6 percent, and ever since, Menem has been doing the complete opposite of what he had promised. Such usurpation of the collective will contributes greatly to discrediting democracy in a country that has seldom known it and in a society overwhelmed by the weight of the army and the Church.

Impunity U. offers instruction in lack of scruples and teaches moral irresponsibility. On occasion, its courses are illustrated with statistics. Those tiny numbers are used, for example, in the course on relations between economics and politics in the newborn, or reborn, democracies of Latin America. The economy is increasingly antidemocratic. The people proceed from enthusiasm to desperation, and more than one defrauded citizen identifies democracy with fraud. The civilian governments continue with impunity the neoliberal economic policies—free market, free money—imposed by the military dictatorships. The results are evident. The contradictions between political democracy and social dictatorship have never been so apparent. According to the Economic Council on Latin America, a regional UN agency, four out of every ten Latin Americans "live in a state of absolute misery." Their destiny is not written in the stars: it's written in the system.

The trap of hunger and the trap of consumption operate with impunity, and thus the gap separating the trappers from the trapped grows wider and wider: an ever greater gulf between the vast majority that needs much more than it consumes and the tiny minority that consumes much more than it needs.

HOW TO DISCREDIT THE STATE

Another subject offered in Impunity U. deals with politicians and the state. The same politicians that with impunity squeezed the the last drop out of the state now discover that the state is useless and ought to be tossed on the trash heap. Over the course of many years they turned citizens' rights into political favors, put the public at the service of public services, and made the state a labyrinth full of parasites strolling about aimlessly. Franz Kafka surely would have picked another subject had he experienced the bureaucracy in these countries of ours where there's no water during the day and no electricity at night, where the telephones don't work, letters don't arrive, and dossiers bear offspring.

And now the traditional politicians who made the patient ill want to sell us the hospital. Back in government after the sun set on the military, they intone psalms to the glory of monetary freedom, and sacrifice public enterprises on the altar of the marketplace.

The impunity of the owners of the world. Let the will of the rich countries be done, even though the rich countries are rich precisely because they preach economic freedom but do not practice it. Our good conduct is measured by the punctuality of our payments and our capacity to obey. The creditors pound the table and our civilian governments bow their heads and swear they will privatize everything. Those tiny numbers prove that in Latin America monetary freedom favors flight not roosting, and thus speculation mocks production and the economy becomes a roulette wheel. Yet trumpets herald private capital as if the cavalry were coming to the rescue.

Our governments do indeed want to privatize everything, and they begin by hanging bargain-sale signs in areas central to national sovereignty: communications, energy, transport. Privatize everything and, where possible, the hospitals, schools, cemeteries, jails, and zoos as well. Everything except the armed forces, which incidentally take the lion's share of every public budget. In the new state, the National Security State, the military bureaucracy is sacred. If not, who will take care of the "social cost" of the "adjustment programs"? The impunity of money, which in our countries kills with hunger or bullets, demands that the welfare state give way to the judge-and-gendarme state: a judge susceptible to bribes and threats, an implacable gendarme of the poor.

HOW TO DISCREDIT JUSTICE

Military impunity is the most intensive course at Impunity U. The speed with which civilian power throughout Latin America is being discredited shows the extent of its success.

This course is based on the acceptance of might makes right as a natural law. Slandering the jungle, urban culture calls the law that governs our civilized life "the law of the jungle." Every day in the vertigo of competition, in the struggle for money and power, the market economy and the imperial order confirm the morals of the military: humiliation is the destiny the weak deserve—weak countries, weak companies, weak governments, weak people.

The military dictatorships, which in recent years fouled us with filth and fear, left democracy mortgaged twice over. The civilian governments accepted that accursed inheritance without a word: the payment of their debts and the forgetting of their crimes. Now we all work to pay the interest and we all live in a state of amnesia.

Did the military debts, which civilian governments socialized, finance development projects? The nuclear power plant at Angra dos Reis, Brazil, is a good example: it cost several billion—no one knows how many—and emits no more light than a lightning bug. And did the absolution of military and paramilitary terrorism granted by civilian governments consolidate democracy? Or did it in fact legalize arrogance, encourage violence, and identify justice with vengeance or madness? We are all equal before the law, the constitution says. But our constitutions, mediocre works of surrealist fiction, are unaware that in this world justice, like democracy and welfare, is a privilege of rich nations.

Military debt, translated into overwhelming foreign debt, is not the price of development. Military debt is the price of terror, and impunity keeps us from realizing this, because it forbids us to remember. Our professors in this subject are way beyond Freud. To pass the exams, you repeat this lesson: a poor memory is a sign of good health.

HOW TO DISCREDIT HUMAN LIFE

At this rate, Latin America is well on its way to becoming an immense breeding ground of Frankensteins. Colombia offers us an example of alarming fertility.

For years now in Colombia, those in power have taught that crime pays. In the shadow of power and nourished by it, paramilitary groups rain death on the country. The international press attributes all responsibility to drug traffickers and guerrillas, but violence is really the child of National Security Doctrine, which authorizes the armies to kill their compatriots. In any case, money from the cocaine mafias was not considered dirty as long as it was used to clean up the reds. And of the seventy-five massacres that took place in 1988, butcheries that bathed Colombia in blood, only five were the direct work of the traffickers. Under the cover of self-defense groups formed to fight guerrilla kidnappings, the death squads were born, grew, and multiplied with impunity over the course of many years. With impunity, the army participated; with impunity, the government tolerated it. In 1983, the attorney general indicted fifty-nine military officers and policemen, members of a gang responsible for more than a hundred murders and disappearances. Military justice handled the matter: it was never heard of again. In 1988, the assassinations of politicians, union leaders, and intellectuals of the left totaled seven times the lives lost in confrontations between the guerrillas and the army. That year, workers in the cement industry went on strike—and not over salaries: they were demanding the right to bear arms. Twelve of their leaders had been murdered. To Amnesty International's charges, the Ministry of Defense responded with a list of military torturers who had been sanctioned. The ministry neglected to mention that the sanction consisted of forty-eight hours detention.

Today, Colombia is worse off than Chicago in the times of Al Capone and Prohibition. In eight months, three presidential candidates have fallen, riddled with bullets. A precocious graduate of the College of Impunity, a fifteen-year-old boy from the slums of Medellín, assassinated the leader of the United Left, Bernardo Jaramillo, for $650. Normally, they get much less. As the Mexican *corrido* puts it, life is worth nothing. People die of *bulletosis* and the social sciences have produced a new kind of specialist, the *violentologist*, who attempts to decipher what has happened. Some restrict themselves to confirming an old adage: in addition to being dolts and loafers, the poor are violent if born in Colombia. Others, however, refuse to believe that Colombians bear the mark of violence on their brows. It is not a function of genes: this violence is the child of fear; this tragedy is the child of impunity.

HOW TO DISCREDIT NATIONAL SOVEREIGNTY

Like all our armed forces, the Colombian military obeys a foreign power through the Inter-American Defense Council. This obligatory obedience supersedes its sworn loyalty to its own nation. The dominant foreign power trains it in the arts of impunity, transmitting a know-how of the highest level, tested and proven.

The latest public spectacle in this discipline was the invasion of Panama, a resounding success. This operation, intended to capture a CIA agent who had been unfaithful to the Company, cost seven thousand lives and $7 billion in damages. But almost all the victims were poor and so were the neighborhoods razed, making it no hardship for the whole world to shrug its shoulders and leave it at that. With utter impunity, the United States imposed a new administrator for the Panama Canal to prevent the treaty from being fulfilled, and a new president for the country. The new president, the obese Endara, spends his days on hunger strikes protesting the fact that Rome doesn't pay its traitors, while Panama suffers with impunity the daily humiliation of foreign occupation.

From its headquarters and through its many branch offices, Impunity U. induces us to stop loving and to stop believing, both each other and ourselves. Its professors invite us to forget the past so we will be incapable of remembering the future. Every day, we learn to resign ourselves in order to survive. But a short while ago, on a wall in a neighborhood in the city of Lima, a rebellious student wrote: *"We don't want to survive. We want to live."* He spoke for many.

(1990)

Funeral for the Wrong Corpse

A crane pulls down Lenin's statue in Bucharest. An eager multitude lines up outside McDonald's in Moscow. The odious Berlin Wall is sold off in souvenir-size chunks. In Warsaw and Budapest, the ministers of economy sound just like Margaret Thatcher—in Beijing, too, while tanks crush students. The Italian Communist Party, the largest in the West, announces its forthcoming suicide. The Soviets cut back aid to Ethiopia and Colonel Mengistu suddenly discovers that capitalism is good. The Sandinistas, mainstay of the finest revolution in the world, lose at the polls. The headlines proclaim: "The Nicaraguan Revolution Is Over."

It seems the only place left for revolution is the display case of an archaeological museum. Nor is there room for the left, except for the repentant left willing to sit down with the bankers. We are all invited to the burial of socialism. The funeral procession, they claim, will include all of humanity.

I must confess, I don't believe it. This funeral is for the wrong corpse.

IN NICARAGUA, THE RIGHTEOUS PAY FOR THE SINNERS

Perestroika burst the seams of an unbearable straitjacket with a passion for freedom. Everything is exploding. There is no reason why social justice should be the enemy of freedom or efficiency. The people were at the end of their rope, fed up with a bureaucracy that was as powerful as it was useless, that in the name of Marx forbade them to say what they thought, to live what they felt. Spontaneity of any kind was an act of treason or insanity.

Socialism? Communism? Was it all nothing but a grandiose fraud? From the vantage point of Latin America I ask myself: If this was the case, or might have been, why should we be the ones to pay? Our face was never in that mirror.

National dignity was the loser in the recent Nicaraguan elections. It was vanquished by hunger and war; but it was vanquished as well by the winds buffeting the left around the world. The righteous paid for the sinners. The Sandinistas are not to blame for either war or hunger. Nor do they bear the slightest responsibility for what happened in the East. Paradox of paradoxes: a democratic, pluralistic, independent revolution that copied nothing from the Soviets, the Chinese, the Cubans, or anybody else paid for the plates that others had broken, while the local Communist Party voted for Violeta Chamorro.

Those responsible for the war and hunger now celebrate an outcome that will further punish their victims. The day after the elections, the United States lifted its economic embargo, just as it did years ago after the military coup in Chile. The day after President Allende's death, the price of copper rose miraculously on the world market.

Actually, the revolution that overthrew the Somoza family dictatorship did not have a moment's respite over ten long years. Every day Nicaragua was invaded by a foreign power and its hired criminals. It faced unrelenting siege from the bankers and the commercial masters of the world. In spite of all this, it managed to be more civilized than the French Revolution, not having guillotined or executed anybody, and more tolerant than that of the United States, having granted in the midst of war freedom of expression (with some restrictions) to the local spokespeople of the colonial overlord.

The Sandinistas brought literacy to Nicaragua, reduced infant mortality significantly, and distributed land to the peasantry. But the country was bled white by war. War damage amounted to one and a half times the country's gross domestic product. This means that Nicaragua was destroyed one and a half times. The magistrates of the International Court of Justice at The Hague found against U.S. aggression, but their decision had no effect. Nor were the congratulations of the United Nations specialized organizations for education, food, and health of any avail. One cannot eat praise.

The invaders rarely attacked military objectives. Farm cooperatives were their favorite targets. How many thousands of Nicaraguans were killed or wounded over the past decade by order of the U.S. government? Proportionately, in the United States it would be equivalent to three million. Yet, many thousands of North Americans were welcomed in Nicaragua during those years, and nothing ever happened to any of them. Except for one. He was killed by the Contras. (He was very young, an engineer, and a clown. Everywhere he went a swarm of children followed. He organized Nicaragua's first clown school. The Contras killed him as he was measuring the water in a stream for a dam. His name was Ben Linder.)

CUBA'S TRAGIC SOLITUDE

But what about Cuba? Didn't the same thing happen there as in the East? A divorce between power and the people? Aren't people there, too, fed up with one party, one press, one truth?

Fidel Castro said: "If I am Stalin, my dead are enjoying good health." And that, to be sure, is not the only difference. Cuba did not import a prefabricated model of vertical power from Moscow, but was obliged to transform itself into a fortress to keep from ending up on the dinner plate of its all-powerful enemy. And even under these conditions this tiny developing country made astonishing strides. There is less illiteracy and less infant mortality today in Cuba than in the United States. Furthermore, in contrast to a number of Eastern countries, Cuban socialism was not orthopedically imposed from above and without but was born deep within and grew from the very bottom. The many Cubans who died for Angola or gave the best of themselves for Nicaragua, expecting no recompense, did so from the dictates of their hearts, not submissively following the orders of a police state. No one ever deserted and there was always fervor to spare.

Now is a time of tragic solitude for Cuba. A time of danger. The invasion of Panama and the disintegration of the so-called socialist camp are, I am afraid, influencing its domestic politics in the worst way, abetting bureaucratic obduracy, ideological rigidity, and the militarization of society.

NEW TIMES: THE TWO SIDES OF THE COIN

With respect to Panama, Nicaragua, or Cuba, the U.S. government invokes democracy as the Eastern governments invoked socialism—as an alibi. Latin America has been invaded by the United States more than a hundred times in this century. Always in the name of democracy and always to impose military dictatorships or puppet governments to rescue money in danger. The imperial system does not want democracies. It wants vassals.

The invasion of Panama was scandalous, with its seven

thousand victims among the ruins of the poor barrios leveled by the bombings. But more scandalous than the invasion was the impunity with which it was carried out. Impunity encourages repetition. President Mitterand greeted this crime against sovereignty with discreet applause, and the whole world, after paying the tithe of a statement here and there, crossed its arms.

In this context, silence and even thinly disguised complaisance on the part of some of the Eastern countries speaks eloquently. Does liberation there give a green light to oppression in the West? I never agreed with those who condemned imperialism in the Caribbean but applauded or kept their mouths shut when national sovereignty was trampled in Hungary, Poland, Czechoslovakia, or Afghanistan. The right to self-determination is sacred in all places at all times. Those who point out that Gorbachev's democratic reforms were possible because the Soviet Union ran no risk of being invaded by the Soviet Union are right. So are those who note that the United States is safe from military coups and dictatorships because there is no U.S. embassy in the United States.

Without the shadow of a doubt, freedom is always good news—for the East now living it with due jubilation, and for the entire world. But at the same time, are the paeans to money and the virtues of the market good news? The idolatry of the American way of life? The naive illusion of joining the International Club of the Rich? The bureaucracy, nimble only for stepping into a better position, is rapidly adapting to the new situation. The old bureaucrats are beginning to transform themselves into new bourgeois.

From the standpoint of Latin America and the so-called Third World, the defunct Soviet bloc had at least one fundamental virtue: it did not get fat by feeding off the poor, did not take part in the international capitalist gang rape. On the contrary, it helped fund justice in Cuba, Nicaragua, and many other countries. I suspect that in the not-very-distant future this will be recalled with nostalgia.

A NIGHTMARE COME TRUE

For us capitalism is not a dream to be pursued, but a nightmare come true. Our challenge lies not in privatizing the state but in deprivatizing it. Our states have been bought up at bargain prices by the owners of the land, the banks, and everything else. And for us, the market is nothing more than a pirate ship—the greater its freedom, the worse its behavior. The local market and the world market. The world market robs us with both hands. The commercial hand keeps buying from us ever cheaper and selling to us ever dearer. The financial hand, which lends us our own money, keeps paying us less and charging us more.

We live in a region of European prices and African wages, where capitalism acts like the kind man who says, "I'm so fond of poor people that I never think there are enough of them." In Brazil alone, for example, the system kills a thousand children a day by disease or hunger. With or without elections, capitalism in Latin America is antidemocratic—most people are prisoners of need, doomed to isolation and violence. Hunger lies, violence lies: they claim to be part of nature, they pretend to belong to the natural order of things. When that "natural order" becomes disorderly, the military steps in, hooded or barefaced. As they say in Colombia: "The cost of living goes up and up, and the value of life goes down and down."

STEP BY STEP

The elections in Nicaragua were a very cruel blow. A blow like hatred from God, as the poet said. When I heard the result, I was a child lost in the storm. A lost child I remain, but I'm not alone. We are many. Throughout the world, we are many.

Sometimes I feel as though they have stolen even our words.

The term "socialism" is applied in the West as makeup for injustice; in the East it evokes purgatory or maybe hell. The word "imperialism" is out of fashion and is no longer to be found in the lexicon of mainstream politicians, even though imperialism does exist and pillage and kill. And the term "militance"? And the very fact of militant fervor? For the theoreticians of disenchantment it is a ridiculous old relic. For the repentant, a trick memory likes to play.

In a few months we have witnessed the clamorous shipwreck of a system that usurped socialism, that treated people like children who never grew up, dragging them by the ear. Three or four centuries ago, the Inquisitors slandered God by saying that they were carrying out His orders; but I believe that Christianity is not the Holy Inquisition. In our time, the bureaucrats have stigmatized hope and besmirched the most beautiful of human adventures; but I also believe that socialism is not Stalinism.

Now, we must begin all over again. Step by step, with no shields but those borne by our own bodies. It is necessary to discover, to create, to imagine. In a speech shortly after his defeat, Jesse Jackson championed the right to dream: "Let us defend that right," he said. "Let us not permit anyone to take that right away from us." And today more than ever we must dream. Together we must dream dreams that undream themselves and come to life in mortal matter, as another poet put it, wished it. My best friends live fighting for that right; and for it, some of them have given their lives.

This is my testimony. The confession of a dinosaur? Perhaps. In any case, it is the affirmation of one who believes that the human condition is not doomed to selfishness and the obscene pursuit of money, and that socialism did not die because it had not yet been. Today is the first day of the long life ahead of it.

(1990)

Scorn as Destiny

1

The end of history? That's nothing new for us. Five centuries
ago, Europe decreed memory and dignity to be crimes in America. The new owners of these lands banned the remembrance
of history, as well as the making of it. Since then, all we can do
is accept it.

2

Black skins, white wigs, crowns of lights, cloaks of silk and
jewels: at the Rio de Janeiro carnival the starving dream together
and for a while are kings and queens. For four days the most
musical people in the world live out their collective delirium.
And on Ash Wednesday, at midday, the party is over. The police
arrest anyone who stays in costume. The poor take off their
feathers and paint, rip off the visible masks, the masks that
unmask, masks of fleeting freedom, and put on different masks,
invisible ones that negate the human face: the masks of routine,
obedience, and misery. Until the next carnival, the queens go
back to washing dishes and the princes to sweeping the streets.

They sell newspapers they cannot read, sew clothes they cannot wear, polish cars they will never own, and build homes

where they will never live. They built Brasilia, and from Brasilia were expelled. They build Brazil each day, and Brazil is their land of exile.

They cannot make history. They are condemned to suffer it.

3

The end of history. Time is pensioned off, the world stops turning. Tomorrow is another name for today. The places at the table are laid, and Western civilization denies no one the right to beg for crumbs.

Ronald Reagan wakes up one days and says: "The Cold War is over. We've won." And State Department functionary Francis Fukuyama achieves sudden notoriety by discovering that the end of the Cold War is also the end of history. In the name of liberal democracy, capitalism becomes the last port of call for all journeys, "the final form of human government."

Hours of glory. Class struggle is no more, and to the East lie allies, not enemies. The free market and consumer society win universal consensus, a consensus delayed only a bit by the communist mirage. As the French Revolution wished, we are all now free, equal, and fraternal. Property owners, too. Kingdom of greed, paradise on earth.

Like God, capitalism has no doubts about its own immortality.

4

The fall of the Berlin Wall was most welcome, writes Peruvian diplomat Carlos Alzamora, in a recent article. But the other wall, he adds, the wall that separates the poor world from the opulent one, is higher than ever. Universal apartheid: acts of racism, intolerance and discrimination erupt with ever greater frequency in Europe, punishing all intruders who scale that wall to reach the citadel of prosperity.

It's plain to see. The Berlin Wall died a timely death. But it lived no more than thirty years. The other wall will soon be celebrating its five hundredth anniversary. Unequal exchange, financial extortion, capital bleeding away, monopoly over technology and information, cultural alienation—these are the bricks that are laid day by day, as wealth and sovereignty drain ever faster from the South to the North.

5

Money and people work in opposite ways. The freer money is, the worse for people. Economic neoliberalism—the only and ultimate system imposed by the North on the South as the end of history—consecrates oppression under the banner of freedom. In the free market the victory of the strong is natural, the annihilation of the weak is legitimate. Racism rises to the status of economic doctrine. The North confirms divine justice: God rewards the chosen people and castigates inferior races, condemned by biology to laziness, violence, and inefficiency. In a single day, a worker from the North earns more than one from the South could in half a month.

6

Starvation wages, low costs, ruinous prices on the world market.

Sugar is one of Latin America's products condemned to instability and decline. For many years there was just one exception: the Soviet Union paid (and still pays) a steady price for Cuba's sugar. Now, in its euphoria capitalism triumphant rubs its hands with glee. There are plenty of signs that this commercial pact will not last much longer. No one thinks that this exemplary exception could point the way to a new, fairer international order, an alternative to the systematic plunder that technicians call "deteriorating terms of trade." No. If the Soviets still pay a good price for Cuban sugar, that only demonstrates the diabolical designs that guided Moscow's steps, in the days when it sported horns, a trident, and a tail.

The prevailing order is the only one possible: thieving commerce is the end of history.

7

Worried by cholesterol, hunger long forgotten, the North still practices charity. Mother Theresa of Calcutta is more efficient than Karl Marx. The North's aid to the South amounts to much less than the alms solemnly pledged at the United Nations, but it allows the North to dump its war junk, its surplus goods, and development projects that underdevelop and spread the hemorrhage to cure the anemia.

Meanwhile, over the last five years, the South has donated to the North an infinitely larger sum, the equivalent of two Marshall Plans at constant prices, in the form of interest payments, profits, royalties, and all kinds of colonial tribute. Northern banks have gutted the debtor states of the South, and ended up owning our public enterprises in exchange for nothing.

Just as well that imperialism does not exist. No one mentions it anymore, so it does not exist. That history, too, has ended.

8

But if empires and their colonies have come to rest behind glass in the museum of antiquities, why are the dominant countries still armed to the teeth? Because of the Soviet threat? Not even the Soviets believe that alibi anymore. If the Iron Curtain has melted away and the bad guys of yesterday are the good guys of today, why do the powerful continue to manufacture and sell weapons and fear?

The budget of the U.S. Air Force exceeds the sum total of the elementary education budgets of the entire so-called Third World. A waste of resources? Or resources to defend waste? If the countries and the social classes that have bought up the world disarmed, could the unequal organization of the world, which portrays itself as eternal, be sustained a single day longer?

This system, sick with consumerism and arrogance, so voraciously intent on the destruction of land, sea, air, and sky, now mounts guard at the foot of the high wall of power. It sleeps with one eye open, and with good reason.

The end of history is its message of death. The system that sanctifies a cannibalistic international order tells us: "I am everything. After me, nothing."

9

At a computer screen, the fate, for good or ill, of millions of human beings is decided. In the era of supercompanies and supertechnology, some people are merchants and others are merchandise. The magic of the market fixes the value of things and people.

Latin American products are worth less every day. So are we, the Latin Americans.

The Pope in Rome forcefully condemned the brief blockade, or threatened blockade, of Lithuania. But the Holy Father never uttered a word against the blockade of Cuba, now in its thirtieth year, or of Nicaragua, which lasted a decade. That's normal. And since we Latin Americans are worth so little alive, it's normal too that the value placed on our dead should be a hundred times less than that on the victims of the now disintegrated Evil Empire. Noam Chomsky and Edward Herman took the trouble to measure the space we merit in the leading U.S. media. Jerzy Popieluszko, the priest murdered by state terror in Poland in 1984, took up more space than the sum total of one hundred priests murdered by state terror in Latin America in recent years.

They imposed scorn on us as custom. And now they sell us scorn as destiny.

10

The South learns its geography from world maps that reduce it
to half its actual size. Will future maps blot it out altogether?
  Until now, Latin America was the land of the future.
  Cold comfort. But it was something.
  Now we are told that the future is the present.

(1990)

To Be Like Them

(To Karl Hubener)

Dreams and nightmares are made of the same material. But this nightmare purports to be the only dream we're allowed: a development model that scorns life and idolizes things.

CAN WE BE LIKE THEM?

Promise of politicians, rationale of technocrats, fantasy of the forsaken: the Third World will become like the First World, rich, cultured, and happy, if only it behaves itself and does what it's told without kidding around or asking embarrassing questions. In the final episode of the soap opera called History, prosperity will reward the good behavior of those dying of hunger. *We can be like them*, announces the gigantic neon sign that lights the pathway to the development of the underdeveloped and the modernization of the backward.

But *what can't be, can't be, and besides it's impossible*, as Pedro the Cock, a bullfighter, put it. If poor countries rise to the level of production and waste of the wealthy, the planet will die. Our unlucky planet is already in a coma, poisoned by industrial civilization and squeezed to the next to the last drop by consumer society.

In the last twenty years, while humanity tripled in number, erosion killed off the equivalent of all the arable land in the United States. The world, transformed into market and merchandise, is losing fifteen million hectares of forest each year. Of these, six million become desert. Nature has been humiliated and subordinated to the accumulation of capital. Land, water, and air are being poisoned so that money will generate more money without a drop in the rate of profit. Efficient is he who earns more in less time.

In the North, acid rain from industrial smoke is killing off woods and lakes, while toxic wastes poison rivers and seas. And in the South, export agribusiness marches on, obliterating trees and people. North and south, east and west, people are sawing away with delirious enthusiasm at the very branch on which they sit.

From forest to desert: modernization, devastation. The incessant bonfire of the Amazon consumes half a Belgium a year. In all of Latin America, land is peeling away and drying up—twenty-two hectares of forest die *every minute*, most of it sacrificed by the companies that produce meat or wood on a grand scale to be consumed elsewhere. Costa Rican cows turn into McDonald's hamburgers. Half a century ago, trees covered three-quarters of that small country; few are left today. At the current rate of deforestation, Costa Rica will be bald by the end of the century. Costa Rica exports meat to the United States, and imports from the same place pesticides that the United States bans from its own soil.

A few countries squander resources that belong to everyone. Crime and delirium of the society of waste: the richest 6 percent of humanity devours a third of all the energy and a third of all the natural resources consumed in the world. Statistical averages show that one North American consumes as much as fifty Haitians. Of course, such averages can't summon up a resident of Harlem or Baby Doc Duvalier, but it's still worth asking: What would happen if the fifty Haitians suddenly consumed as much as fifty North Americans? What would happen if the immense population of the South devoured the world with the voracious impunity of the North? What would happen if luxury goods and automobiles and refrigerators and TV sets and nuclear power plants and electrical generating stations proliferated in the South in such a crazy fashion? In ten years all the oil in the world would be used up. And what would happen to the climate, which is already close to collapse from global warming? What would happen to the land, the little bit left after erosion? And the water, which a fourth of humanity is already drinking contaminated by nitrates and pesticides and industrial waste laced with mercury and lead? What would happen? It wouldn't happen. We would have to move to another planet. This one, worn so thin already, couldn't handle it.

The precarious equilibrium of the world, which teeters on the brink of the abyss, depends on the perpetuation of injustice. The misery of many makes possible the extravagance of the few. For a few to continue consuming more, many must continue consuming less. And to make sure the many don't cross the line, the system multiplies the weapons of war. Incapable of fighting poverty, the system fights the poor, and its culture—dominant and militarized—blesses the violence of power.

The American way of life, founded on the right to waste, can only be lived by dominant minorities in dominated countries. Its adoption en masse would be the collective suicide of humanity.

It's not possible. But would it be desirable?

DO WE WANT TO BE LIKE THEM?

In a well-organized anthill, the queens are few and the workers many. Queens are born with wings and can make love. Workers, who neither fly nor love, work for the queens. The police ants keep watch over the workers and the queens.

Life is what happens to you while you're busy making other plans, said John Lennon. In our age, marked as it is by the confusion of means and ends, people don't work to live: they live to work. Some work more and more because they need more than they consume; and others work more and more to continue consuming more than they need.

It seems quite normal that in Latin America the eight-hour day belongs to the dominions of abstract art. Second jobs, which official statistics rarely admit, are the reality for very many who would otherwise go hungry. But is it normal that people at the peak of development should work like ants? Does wealth bring freedom, or does it intensify the fear of freedom?

To be is to have, says the system. And the system is a trap: the more you have, the more you want; people end up belonging to things and working for them. Consumer life-style, which is becoming the only life-style anywhere, makes time a scarce and expensive resource: time is sold, rented, invested. But who is the owner of time? Automobiles, television sets, VCRs, personal computers, cellular phones, and all the other countersigns of happiness. Machines, created *to save time* or *to pass the time*, seize control of time. Take the case of the automobile: not only does it rule urban space, it rules human time. In theory, cars *economize time*, but in practice they devour it. A good portion of work time goes to paying for transportation to and from the job, which in itself takes up more and more time because of the traffic jams in our modern Babylons.

You do not have to be an economic genius. Common sense tells us that technological progress, by increasing productivity, diminishes the time that must be devoted to work. But common sense didn't foresee the fear of *free time*, or the traps of consumerism, or the manipulative power of advertising. In Japan, people have worked forty-seven hours a week for the past twenty years. Europe's workdays have shrunk, but very slowly, at a pace that has nothing to do with the accelerated development of productivity. In automated factories, there are ten workers where once there were a thousand, but instead of broadening the arena of freedom, technological progress generates unemployment. The freedom *to waste time*: consumer society doesn't allow for such waste. Even vacations, organized by the large companies that industrialized tourism, have become an exhausting pursuit. *To kill time*: modern vacation spots reproduce the vertigo of daily life in the urban anthill.

According to the anthropologists, our Paleolithic ancestors worked no more than twenty hours a week. According to the newspapers, our contemporaries in Switzerland voted at the end of 1988 on a measure to reduce the work week to forty hours without cutting salaries. And the Swiss voted it down.

Ants communicate by touching antennae. TV antennae communicate with the centers of power in the modern world. The little screen offers us the urge to own, the frenzy to consume, the excitement of competition, and the anxious yearning to succeed, just as Columbus offered baubles to the Indians. Successful merchandise. Advertising fails to tell us, however, that according to the World Health Organization, the United States consumes *nearly half of all the tranquilizers sold on the planet.* In the last twenty years, the work week in the United States *increased.* During that period the number of people suffering from stress *doubled.*

THE CITY AS GAS CHAMBER

A peasant is worth less than a cow and more than a hen, I'm told in Caaguazú, Paraguay. And in the northeast of Brazil: *He who plants has no land, he who has land does not plant.*

Our fields empty out, Latin America's cities become hells as large as countries. Mexico City grows at the rate of half a million people and thirty square kilometers *per year*; it already has five times as many inhabitants as all of Norway. By the end of the century, the capital of Mexico and the Brazilian city of São Paulo will be the largest cities in the world.

The great cities of the South are like the great cities of the North viewed through a warped mirror. Modernization by mimicry increases the model's defects. Latin America's raucous smoke-filled capital cities have no bicycle lanes or catalytic converters to filter out toxic fumes. Clean air and silence are so rare and expensive that not even the richest of the rich can buy them.

The Brazilian subsidiaries of Volkswagen and Ford make cars without catalytic converters for sale in Brazil and other Latin American countries. They make them with converters in Germany and the United States. Argentina produces unleaded gasoline for export and poisonous gasoline for the internal market. In all of Latin America, automobiles have the freedom to vomit lead from their exhaust pipes. From the cars' point of view, lead raises the octane level and the rate of profit. From people's point of view, lead damages the brain and the nervous system. Cars, the true owners of cities, pay no attention to the intruders.

The year 2000, memories of the future: people with oxygen masks, birds that cough instead of sing, trees that refuse to grow. Right now in Mexico City you see signs that say: *We beg of you not to bother the walls* and *Please don't slam the door.* There are still no signs that say: *Breathing not advisable.* How long will it be before such public health warnings appear? Cars and factories offer up to the atmosphere eleven thousand tons of enemy gases and fumes every day. There is a cloud of filth in the air, children are born with lead in their blood, and on more than one occasion, dead birds have rained down over this city which, until half a century ago, was *the most transparent region on earth.* Now this cocktail of carbon monoxide, sulfur dioxide, and nitrogen oxide can be as high as three times the maximum tolerable to human beings. What will be the maximum tolerable to urban beings?

Five million cars: the city of São Paulo has been defined as a sick person on the verge of a heart attack. A cloud of fumes masks it. Only on Sunday can you see, from the outskirts, the most developed city of Brazil. On downtown avenues, electric billboards warn the population every day:

Air quality: ruin

According to the testing stations, in 1986 the air was dirty or very dirty on 323 days.

In June 1989, for a few rainless and windless days, Santiago de Chile vied with Mexico City and São Paulo for the world pollution championship. San Cristóbal Hill in downtown Santiago was invisible, hidden behind a mask of smog. Chile's young democratic government took a few minimal steps to control the eight hundred tons of fumes that spew into the city's air each day. The cars and the factories screamed to the high heavens: those limitations violated business freedom and infringed on the right of property. Money's freedom, which scorns everyone else's, knew no bounds during the dictatorship of General Pinochet, and made a worthy contribution to poisoning everything. The right to pollute is a fundamental incentive to foreign investment, almost as important as the right to pay tiny salaries. And after all, General Pinochet never denied Chileans the right to breathe shit.

THE CITY AS JAIL

Consumer society, which consumes people, obliges people to consume, while television offers courses on violence to the learned and the illiterate alike. Those who have nothing may live far away from those who have everything, but every day they spy on them through the little screen. Television exhibits the obscene extravagance of the orgy of consumption, and at the same time teaches the art of shooting your way in.

Reality imitates TV, street violence is the continuation of television by other means. Street children practice private enterprise through crime, the only field open to them. Their only human rights are the right to rob and the right to die. Tiger cubs abandoned to their fate go on the hunt. On any corner they hit and run. Life comes to an early end, eaten up by glue and other drugs good for fooling hunger and cold and loneliness; or it ends when a bullet cuts it down.

To walk the streets of Latin America's large cities is risky, and so is staying home. *The city as jail*: he who is not a prisoner of need is a prisoner of fear. Those who have something, no matter how little, are condemned to live under threat, in terror of the next mugging. Those who have a lot live enclosed in secure fortresses. The great buildings and residential complexes are the feudal castles of the electronic era. It's true, they're missing the moats filled with crocodiles and the majestic beauty of the castles of the Middle Ages, but they've got the great raised bars, the high walls, the watchtowers, the armed guards.

The state, which is policelike rather than paternalistic, does not practice charity. Old-fashioned talk about reforming those who have gone astray by inculcating a belief in the virtues of study and work belongs to antiquity. In the epoch of market economies, the leftovers of the human breed are eliminated by hunger or the bullet. Street children, children of poor laborers, are not nor can they be *useful to society*. Education is the privilege of those who can pay for it; repression is the damnation of those who cannot.

According to the *New York Times*, between January and October 1990, the police murdered more than forty children in the streets of Guatemala City. The bodies of these children, beggar children, robber children, garbage-picking children, turned up without tongues, eyes, or ears, tossed in the dump. According to Amnesty International, during 1989, 457 children and adolescents were executed in the Brazilian cities of Rio de Janeiro, São Paulo, and Recife. These crimes, committed by death squads and other forces of the parapolice order, did not occur in backward rural areas, but in the most important cities of Brazil: they did not occur where capitalism is *lacking*, rather where there is *too much of it*. Social injustice and scorn for life grow along with the economy.

In countries where there is no death penalty, the death penalty is meted out every day in defense of the right of property. Opinion-makers tend to make apologies for crime. In the middle of 1990, in the city of Buenos Aires, an engineer shot two young thieves fleeing with the tape player from his car. Bernardo Neustadt, Argentina's most influential journalist, commented on television: *I would have done the same*. In the 1986 Brazilian elections, Afanásio Jazadji won a seat in the state congress of São Paulo in one of the greatest landslides in Brazil's history. Jazadji earned his immense popularity on the radio. His program loudly defended the death squads and preached in favor of torture and the extermination of delinquents.

In the civilization of savage capitalism, the right to own is more important than the right to live. People are worth less than things. In this sense, the laws of impunity are revealing. They absolved the state terrorism practiced by the military dictatorships of three countries in the South; they pardoned crime and torture; they did not pardon crimes against property. (Chile: decree law 2191 of 1978. Uruguay: law 15.848 of 1986. Argentina: law 23.521 of 1987.)

THE "SOCIAL COST" OF PROGRESS

February 1989, Caracas. Bus fares suddenly soar to the skies, the price of bread triples, and an enraged people explodes: in the streets three hundred lie dead, or five hundred, or who knows.

February 1991, Lima. A plague of cholera attacks the coasts of Peru, venting its fury on the port of Chimbote and the miserable slums of Lima and killing a hundred in a few days. The hospitals have no IV solution and no salt. The government's program of economic adjustment dismantled the little that was left of the public health system, and doubled in a flash the number of Peruvians living in extreme poverty. They earn less than the minimum wage, and the minimum wage is $45 *per month*.

Today's wars—electronic wars—take place on videogame screens. The victims are neither seen nor heard. Neither does laboratory economics hear or see the scorched earth or the hungry. Remote-control weapons kill without remorse. The international technocracy, which imposes on the Third World its development programs and adjustment plans, also murders from outside and from afar.

For more than a quarter of a century, Latin America has been dismantling the fragile barriers that held off the arrogance of money. The creditor-bankers bombarded those defenses with the sure-shot weapon of extortion, while the governing military officers and politicians dynamited them from within. One after another they fall, the protective barriers raised by the state in other times. Now the state is selling off nationalized public enterprises for nothing, or worse than nothing because the seller pays. Our countries hand the keys and everything else over to the international monopolies, now called *price-formation factors*, and become free markets. In its wisdom, the international technocracy counsels injections for wooden legs and says the free market is the talisman of wealth. Why is it that rich countries, who preach the free market, do not practice it? This shrine of the weak is the most successful export of the strong. It's made for the consumption of poor countries. No rich country has ever used it.

Talisman of wealth for how many? Official statistics from Uruguay and Costa Rica, the two countries where social strife used to be least evident: now one of every six Uruguayans lives in extreme poverty, and two of every five Costa Rican families is poor.

The doubtful matrimony of supply and demand, in a free

market that serves the despotism of the powerful, punishes the poor and generates a speculative economy. Production is discouraged, labor is scorned, consumption is deified. The blackboards in foreign exchange houses are watched as if they were movie screens, the dollar is spoken of as if it were a person:

"And how is the dollar?"

Tragedy repeats itself as farce. Since the times of Christopher Columbus, Latin America has suffered capitalist development elsewhere as a tragedy of its own. Now it repeats as farce this caricature of development: a dwarf pretending to be a child.

The technocracy sees numbers and does not see people, but it only sees numbers that are convenient. At the end of this long quarter-century, some successes of *modernization* are celebrated. The *Bolivian miracle*, for example, fulfilled by virtue and courtesy of drug money: the cycle of tin has closed, and with the fall of tin came the end of the mining towns and the most combative labor unions of Bolivia. Now the people of Llallagua, who don't have drinking water, have a parabolic television antenna high up on Calvary Hill. Or the *Chilean miracle*, from the wonderful wizard of Chile, General Pinochet, a success sold as a potion in the countries of the East. But what was the price of the Chilean miracle? And who are the Chileans who paid it and continue to pay it? Who will be the Poles and Czechs and Hungarians who will pay it? In Chile, official statistics proclaim the proliferation of loaves, even while confessing to the proliferation of the hungry. The cock crows victory; the cackling is suspect. Could it be that failure has gone to its head? In 1970, 20 percent of all Chileans were poor. Today it's 45 percent.

The numbers confess, but they do not repent. After all, human dignity depends on the weighing of costs and benefits, and sacrificing the poor masses is nothing more than the *social cost* of Progress.

What might be the value of that *social cost*, if it could be measured? At the end of 1990, *Stern* magazine made a careful assessment of the damage caused by development in Germany today. The magazine estimated, in economic terms, the human and material cost of automobile accidents, traffic jams, air and water pollution, food contamination, the deterioration of green areas, and other factors, and concluded that the value of these damages was equivalent to a quarter of the entire gross national product. The spread of misery obviously was not included among the damages, because for the past several centuries Europe has fed its wealth on foreign poverty, but it would be interesting to know how far such an assessment would go if it were applied to the catastrophes of *modernization* in Latin America. In Germany the state controls and limits, up to a certain point, the noxious effects of the system on people and the environment. What would be the damage in countries like ours, which swallowed the story of the free market and let money move like a tiger on the loose? The damage done to us now and in the future by a system that fills our heads with artificial needs so that we forget our real needs—how accurately can it be assessed? Can the mutilation of the human soul be measured? The spread of violence, the debasement of daily life?

The West is living the euphoria of victory. The collapse of the East served up the vindication: in the East it was worse. Was it worse? Rather, I think, one should ask whether it was essentially *different*. In the West: justice sacrificed in the name of freedom, on the altar of the god of Productivity. In the East: freedom sacrificed in the name of justice, on the altar of the god of Productivity.

In the South, we still have the chance to ask ourselves if that god deserves our lives.

(1990)

War of the Fallacies

1. FIRST DAY: SOME QUESTIONS

War. For what?

To prove that the right of invasion is a privilege reserved for the great powers? And that Hussein cannot do to Kuwait what Bush did to Panama?

So that the Red Army can with impunity beat up on the Lithuanians and the Latvians?

So that Arabs finance the butchery of the Arabs?

So that everyone understands the oil is not to be touched?

Or so that it remain absolutely essential for the world to continue wasting $2 million a minute on arms, now that the Cold War is over?

And what if one of these days, from so much playing at war, this world, turned into an arsenal, blows up?

Who sold the destiny of humanity to a handful of crazy, greedy killers?

Who will live to say that their crime was our suicide?

2. THIRD DAY: IMAGES

The most selling image: War as spectacle. The stars of Operation Desert Storm are the Dow Jones Average and the Price of Oil, with a supporting cast of Wasps, Vampires, missiles, antimissile missiles, anti-antimissile missiles, and many terrorized extras wearing Martian masks.

The most altered image: Saddam Hussein. He's the villian. He used to be the hero.

When the Berlin Wall fell, the West was left without enemies. The peacetime war economy, the basis of prosperity for the prosperous, demands enemies. If no one threatens, why must the world have a soldier for every forty inhabitants, while it has one doctor for every thousand? Hussein served the Free World against the Hitler of Teheran; the arms industry had no better client. Now he's the Hitler of Baghdad. Television shows us his crazy fanatical eyes; Iraqi fundamentalism replaces the threat of Iranian fundamentalism.

Hussein prays. Bush prays. The Pope prays. Everyone prays. All believe in God. And God, in whom does He believe?

The stoniest image: President Bush explains the war. Evoking the worldwide effort against Hitler, Bush speaks for the allies. The allies will liberate a small country humbled by an ambitious and powerful neighbor. Panama? No, the small country is called Kuwait.

But it seems that the invasion of Kuwait was not only an act of irresponsible thuggery. It was also an act of stupidity: by invading, Hussein served up on a silver platter the cover Bush needed. Now it's all against one: twenty-eight nations have joined in this glorious enterprise to save U.S. hegemony on the planet.

By the war, the United States seeks to shore up its threatened power. Threatened from within by recession and the highest foreign debt in the world. And threatened from without by the unstoppable competition of Japan.

The most revealing image: The reticence of Helmut Kohl, as telling as the near silence of the Japanese. The rivals of the United States depend on Persian Gulf oil that belongs to the United States—to the United States and to England, the loyal colony of its former colony.

The most painful image: Russian soldiers send a message from Moscow to Washington. They are veterans of the invasion of Afghanistan. They offer to volunteer for the invasion of Iraq.

The East is no longer a counterweight to the West. A new era: the United States can carry out with impunity its role as policeman of the world. We all know that this country, never invaded by anybody, has long had the habit of invading others. In a couple of centuries of independent life, more than two hundred armed aggressions.

The most eloquent image: Pérez de Cuellar in the shadows, with his face in his hands. Born for peace, the United Nations is now an instrument of war. The Security Council gave the green light. The Soviet Union said fine. China offered no opposition. Cuba and Yemen voted no.

Iraq is being punished because it failed to comply with a UN resolution. The United States refused to comply with several UN resolutions on Nicaragua. Israel refused to comply with several UN resolutions on the territories it occupies. And the world did not declare war on them.

The most sinister image: King Fahd and the emir of Kuwait, the richest men on earth, and the rest of the gangsters of the desert, monarchs from a comic opera who administer countries that the British Empire bought or invented in its day. These petro-cracies embody Democracy in this bloody soap opera. And in the ritual of sacrifice, they pay the bills. Oil can do it all.

The most euphoric image: Celebrations on Wall Street. On the third day of war, the New York Stock Exchange records one of the sharpest rises in history. Meanwhile the price of oil falls. In other words, the market returns to normality. More than half the world's oil reserves lie in the war zone, but the right of the consuming powers to go on burning up the planet's energy seems guaranteed. No, despite the worrying false alarm, Europe will not have to reduce its consumption by 7 percent. Auto-mobiles sigh with relief. Televisions as well. This war has broken all the records for ratings.

The most terrifying image: The technocrats of death. Art of war, cannibalism as gastronomy: the generals explain the unfolding of their plan of annihilation. We see maps without inhabitants, or video screens with little white crosses to show where the bombs fall like rain.

The most stimulating image: The antiwar demonstrations. Roses or lit candles in their hands. The television pretends they don't exist; but in some cities they are multitudes who march and believe. They believe that war is not our fate.

The most tragic image: That which is not broadcast. The absent image, censored in these first days: the dead, the wounded, the mutilated. Human lives. That detail.

The most anxious image: The days passing by. 1991, the only palindromic year of the twentieth century, was born with the

promise of good luck. Already he's been stained with the blood
and grime of war. Let's hope this little year can change his sign.
Let's hope they let him. He doesn't want to be a bum.

(1991)

Othercide: For Five Centuries the Rainbow Has Been Banned from America's Sky

The Discovery: October 12, 1492, America discovered capitalism. Christopher Columbus, financed by the king and queen of Spain and the bankers of Genoa, brought the good news to the islands of the Caribbean. In his diary, the admiral wrote the word "gold" 139 times, and fifty-one times the words "God" or "Our Lord." His eyes did not tire of seeing so much beauty on those beaches, and on November 27 he spoke prophetically: *On them, all of Christianity will do business.* Columbus thought Haiti was Japan and Cuba was China. And he believed that the inhabitants of China and Japan were Indians from India. But he wasn't wrong in that either.

After five centuries of business from all of Christianity, one-third of the American forest has been annihilated, a lot of once-fertile land is sterile, and over half of the population eats infrequently. The Indians, victims of the greatest thievery in world history, still suffer the usurpation of their remaining bits of land, and are still condemned to the negation of their *distinct* identity. They are still prohibited from living the traditional way; their right to be themselves is still denied. At first, pillage and "othercide" were carried out in the name of God in heaven. Now it is done in the name of the god of Progress.

However, in that outlawed and scorned identity, certain keys to another possible America still shine. America, blinded by racism, doesn't see them.

On October 12, 1492, Christopher Columbus wrote in his diary that he wished to take a few Indians back to Spain *so they could learn to speak* ("*que deprendan fablar*"). Five centuries later, on October 12, 1989, in a court of justice in the United States, a Mixtec Indian was considered "mentally retarded" because he did not speak proper Castillian. Ladislao Pastrana, a Mexican from Oaxaca, an undocumented bracero in the fields of California, was to be committed for life to a public asylum. Pastrana did not understand the Spanish interpreter, and the psychologist diagnosed "clear intellectual deficiency." Finally, anthropologists clarified the situation: Pastrana expressed himself perfectly well in his own language, Mixteco, spoken by the inheritors of a complex culture more than two thousand years old.

Paraguay speaks Guaraní. The only case of its kind: the language of the Indians, language of the vanquished, is the sole national tongue. However, according to the polls, most Paraguayans consider people who don't understand Spanish *to be like animals*.

One of every two Peruvians is Indian, and the constitution says that Quechua is as official a language as Spanish. The constitution says so, but reality doesn't listen. Peru treats Indians the way South Africa treats blacks. Spanish is the only language taught in the schools and the only one understood by judges and police and bureaucrats. (Spanish is not the only language on television, because television also speaks English.)

Five years ago, officials of the civil registry in the city of Buenos Aires refused to record the birth of a child. The parents, Indians from the province of Jujuy, wanted to name their child Qori Wamancha, a name in their language. The Argentine registry would not accept it because "it is a foreign name."

The Indians of the Americas live as exiles in their own land.

Language is not a sign of identity, it's a curse. It doesn't distinguish them, it betrays them. When an Indian gives up his language, he begins to become civilized. Does he begin to become civilized or to commit suicide?

When I was a child, in the schools of Uruguay we were taught that the country had been saved from the "Indian problem" thanks to the generals who in the nineteenth century exterminated the last Charrúas.

"The Indian problem": the first Americans, the true discoverers of America, are "a problem." And for that problem to be resolved, the Indians must stop being Indians. Wipe them off the map, or wipe out their souls, annihilate them or assimilate them: genocide or othercide.

In December 1976, Brazil's interior minister announced triumphantly that "the Indian problem will be completely resolved" at the end of the twentieth century: by then all the Indians will be integrated into Brazilian society, and they will no longer be Indians. The minister explained that the office charged with their protection (FUNAI, Fundação Nacional do Indio) will take care of civilizing them. That is, it will take charge of disappearing them. Bullets, dynamite, offerings of poisoned food, pollution of the waters, devastation of the forest, and the spread of virus and bacteria unknown to the Indians, all have accompanied the invasion of the Amazon by companies anxious to acquire the minerals, lumber, and everything else. But the long and ferocious stampede has not done the job. The domestication of the surviving Indians—to rescue them from barbarism—is necessary to clear the last obstacles from the pathway of conquest.

Kill the Indian and save the man, advised the pious U.S. colonel Henry Pratt. And many years later, Peruvian novelist Mario Vargas Llosa explained that there is no other way "to save" the

Indians from hunger and misery than to modernize them, even if their cultures must be sacrificed.

"Salvation" condemns Indians to work from dawn to dusk in mines and on plantations, in return for pay that won't even buy a can of dog food. To "save" the Indians also means to crush their communal sanctuaries and throw them on the rock heap of cheap labor in violent cities, where they lose their language, their names, and their style of dress, and end up as beggars and drunkards and whores. Or to "save" the Indians means putting them in uniform and sending them out gun in hand to kill other Indians or to die defending the system that negates them. After all, Indians are good cannon fodder: of the 25,000 U.S. Indians who fought in World War II, 10,000 died.

On December 16, 1492, Columbus announced it in his diary: the Indians were useful *for ordering and putting to work, farming and doing everything necessary, building houses and learning to wear clothes and use our customs.* Kidnapping the body, robbing the soul: since colonial times all America has referred to this operation with the verb "to reduce" (*reducir*). A "saved" Indian is a "reduced" one. They are "reduced" until they disappear: emptied of themselves, they become non-Indians, and are nobody.

The shaman of the Chamacoco Indians of Paraguay sings to the stars, to the spiders, and to the crazy woman Totila who wanders crying through the woods. And he sings what the sandpiper tells him:

"Don't be hungry, don't be thirsty. Climb up on my wings and we shall eat river fish and we shall drink the wind."

And he sings what the mist tells him:

"I have come to break the frost, so that your people do not feel the cold."

And he sings what the horses of the sky tell him:

"Put on our saddles and we shall seek the rain."

But the missionaries of an evangelical sect have obliged the shaman to set aside his feathers and rattles and chants, *because they are things of the Devil.* And he can no longer cure snake-bites, nor bring rain in times of drought, nor fly above the earth to sing what he sees. In an interview with Ticio Escobar, the shaman says: "*I stop singing and I get sick. My dreams don't know where to go and they torment me. I'm old, I'm wounded. In the end, what use is it to deny what is mine?*"

The shaman said this in 1986. In 1614 the archbishop of Lima ordered all the quenas and other Indian musical instruments burned. And he outlawed all their dances and songs and ceremonies *so that the demon can't continue playing his tricks.* And in 1625 the magistrate of the Royal Audience of Guatemala ordered anyone practicing Indian dances and songs and ceremonies to be punished with a hundred lashes, *because through them they make deals with demons.*

In order to steal the Indians' freedom and their possessions, their symbols of identity are stolen. They are forbidden to sing and dance and dream their gods, even though their gods sang and danced and dreamed them into being on the day of Creation so long ago. From the friars and functionaries of the colonial regime to the U.S. missionaries who today proliferate in Latin America, colonizers have crucified the Indians in the name of Christ: the pagans must be evangelized to save them from hell. The God of the Christians is used as an alibi for pillage.

Archbishop Desmond Tutu was speaking of Africa, but it is just as true of America:

"*They came. They had the Bible and we had the land. And they said: 'Close your eyes and pray.' And when we opened our eyes, they had the land and we had the Bible.*"

The doctors of the modern state, on the other hand, prefer the alibi of enlightenment: the ignorant barbarians must be civilized to save them from darkness. Before as now, racism converts colonial thievery into an act of justice. The colonized are sub-human. They have superstitions not religion, folklore not cul-ture: subhuman people deserve subhuman treatment, barely worth the low price of the fruit of their labor. Racism has legitimized colonial and neocolonial pillage throughout the cen-turies and throughout the various levels of successive humilia-tions. Latin America treats its Indians as the great powers treat Latin America.

Gabriel René-Moreno was Bolivia's most prestigious historian of the nineteenth century. One of Bolivia's universities is named for him. This father of national culture believed that *the Indians are asses that beget mules when they cross with the white race.* He weighed Indian and mestizo brains, and according to his scale they weighed five, seven, and even ten ounces less than the brains of the white race. He concluded that they were *cell-ularly incapable of conceiving of republican liberty.*

The Peruvian Ricardo Palma, a contemporary and colleague of Gabriel René-Moreno, wrote that *the Indians are an abject and degenerate race.* The Argentine Domingo Faustino Sar-miento praised the long struggle of the Araucanian Indians for freedom: *they are wilder, that is, more stubborn animals, less apt for Civilization and European assimilation.*

The most ferocious racism in Latin American history is to be found in the words of the most famed and celebrated intellec-tuals of the end of the nineteenth century and in the documents of liberal politicians who founded the modern state. Some of them were born Indians, like Porfirio Díaz, the author of cap-italist modernization in Mexico, who forbade the Indians to walk on main streets or sit in public plazas unless they changed their cotton pantaloons for European trousers and their sandals for shoes.

Those were the days of the piecing together of the world market led by the British Empire, when *scientific* scorn for Indians bestowed impunity on those who would steal their lands and their labor.

The market demanded coffee, for example, and coffee demanded more land and more hands. So, for example, Guatemala's liberal president, Justo Rufino Barrios, a progressive man, restored forced labor from colonial times and gave his friends plenty of Indian lands and Indian peons.

Racism becomes a blind rage in countries like Guatemala, where the Indians are still the clear majority despite frequent waves of extermination.

Today no labor is paid worse: Mayan Indians get 65 cents to pick a hundredweight of coffee or cotton or a ton of sugar cane. The Indians can't even plant corn without military authorization, and cannot move without a work permit. The army organizes massive labor roundups for the plantings and the harvests of crops for export. On the plantations they use pesticides fifty times as toxic as the maximum tolerable; mother's milk is the most contaminated in the Western world. Rigoberta Menchú: her younger brother Felipe and her best friend María died in childhood from the pesticides sprayed from crop dusters. Felipe died working on a coffee plantation; María in the cottonfields. With machetes and bullets, the army then killed off the rest of Rigoberta's family and the remaining members of her community. She survived to tell the story.

With happy impunity, the government admits that 440 Indian villages were wiped off the map between 1981 and 1983, during an extensive campaign of annihilation that murdered or disappeared many thousands of men and women. The *cleaning up* of the highlands, scorched earth, also cost the lives of innumerable children. The Guatemalan military is convinced that the vice of rebellion is passed on through the genes.

An inferior race, condemned to vice and laziness, incapable of order or progress—does it deserve a better fate? Institutional

violence, state terrorism, clears away any doubts. The conquistadores no longer use iron armor; they dress up in uniforms
from the Vietnam War. And they do not have white skin: they
are mestizos ashamed of their blood, or Indians rounded up by
force and obliged to commit crimes that kill them. Guatemala
scorns the Indians, Guatemala scorns itself.

Twelve hundred years before European mathematicians, this
inferior race had discovered the number zero. And it had learned
the age of the universe with astonishing precision, a thousand
years before today's astronomers.

The Mayas are still travelers in time:

What is a man in the road? Time.

They don't know that time is money, as Henry Ford taught
us. They consider time, founder of space, to be sacred, as are
its daughter the land and its son the human being: like the land,
like people, time cannot be bought or sold. Civilization continues doing all it can to show them they are wrong.

Civilization? History changes according to the voice that sings
it. In America, in Europe, or in any other place. What for the
Romans was *the invasion of the barbarians*, for the Germans was
the migration south.

It's not the voice of the Indians that has told, thus far, the
history of America. Just before the Spanish conquest, a Mayan
prophet, mouth of the gods, announced: *When greed is done
away with, the face will be untied, the hand will be untied, the
feet of the world will be untied.* And when the mouth is untied,
what will it say? What will the *other* voice say, the one never
heard?

From the point of view of the victors, which to date has been
the only point of view, Indian customs have always confirmed
their possession by demons or their biological inferiority. From
the earliest days of colonial life:

The Indians of the Caribbean commit suicide rather than
work as slaves? Because they're lazy.

They walk around naked, as if their entire bodies were faces? Because savages have no shame.

They know nothing of the right of property, and share everything, and have no desire to accumulate wealth? Because they are closer to monkeys than to man.

They bathe themselves with suspicious frequency? Because they are like the heretics of the sect of Mohammed, who are rightly burning in the fires of the Inquisition.

They never hit their children and they let them run free? Because they are incapable of punishing or educating.

They believe in dreams and obey their voices? By influence of Satan or pure stupidity.

They eat when they are hungry and not when it is time to eat? Because they are incapable of controlling their instincts.

They make love when they wish? Because the demon induces them to repeat the original sin.

Homosexuality is allowed? Virginity has no importance at all? Because they live on the outskirts of hell.

In 1523, Chief Nicaragua asked the conquistadores:

"And your king, who elected him?"

The chief had been elected by the elders of the communities. Had the king of Castile been elected by the elders of his communities?

Pre-Columbian America was vast and diverse, and it had forms of democracy that Europe was unable to see and of which the world remains ignorant. To reduce American Indian reality to the despotism of the Incan emperors or the bloody rites of the Aztec dynasty is like reducing the reality of Renaissance Europe to the tyranny of its monarchs or the sinister ceremonies of the Inquisition.

In Guaraní tradition, for example, chiefs were chosen in assemblies of men and women—and assemblies deposed them if they failed to carry out the collective mandate. In Iroquois tradition, men and women governed on an equal footing. The chiefs

were men, but it was the women who elected and deposed and
the council of women held decision-making power over many
fundamental aspects of the entire confederation. Around 1600,
when the Iroquois men went to war on their own, the women
went on a love strike. And before long the men, obliged to sleep
alone, submitted to shared government.

In 1919 the military chief of Panama in the islands of San Blas
announced his victory:

*"The Kuna Indians will no longer wear molas. They will wear
civilized dress."*

And he announced that Indian women must never paint their
noses, only their cheeks, as should be. And they must put their
gold rings in their ears, not their noses. As it should be.

Seventy years after that cock crow, Kuna Indian women still
wear gold rings in their painted noses, and they still wear
molas made of many-colored cloths that overlap with an ever-
astonishing display of imagination and beauty: they wear their
molas in life, and in them they are buried when they die.

In 1989, just before the U.S. invasion, General Manuel No-
riega assured the world that Panama was a country that respected human rights:

"We are not a tribe," the general said.

"Archaic techniques" in the hands of communities had made
the deserts of the Andes fertile. "Modern technologies" in the
hands of private export plantations have turned the fertile lands
of the Andes and everywhere into deserts.

It would be absurd to go five centuries back in technology;
but it is no less absurd to ignore the catastrophes caused by a
system that wrings people dry and demolishes the forest and
rapes the earth and poisons the rivers, all in order to make the
highest profit in the shortest time. Is it not absurd to sacrifice
Nature and people on the altars of the world market? We live

within that absurdity; and we accept it as if it were our only possible destiny.

The "primitive cultures" are still dangerous because they have yet to lose their common sense. Common sense that is, by natural extension, communal sense. If the air belongs to everyone, why must the land have an owner? If from the earth we came and to the earth we return, isn't any crime against the earth also killing us? The earth is cradle and grave, mother and companion. It is offered the first sip and the first bite; it is given rest, protection from erosion.

The system scorns what it ignores, because it ignores what it fears discovering. Racism is also a mask of fear.

What do we know of indigenous cultures? What we've been told in Westerns. And what do we know of African cultures? What we've been told by Professor Tarzan, who was never there.

A black poet from the interior of Bahia says: *First they stole me from Africa. Then they stole Africa from me.*

The memory of America has been mutilated by racism. We still act as if we were children of Europe, and no one else.

At the end of the last century, a British doctor, John Down, identified the syndrome which now carries his name. He believed that an alteration of the chromosomes implied *a return to inferior races*, which begot *Mongolian idiots, Negroid idiots,* and *Aztec idiots.*

Simultaneously, an Italian doctor, Cesare Lombroso, attributed to *the born criminal* the physical features of blacks and Indians.

At that time, the suspicion that Indians and blacks by nature tended toward crime and mental weakness was given a scientific basis. Indians and blacks, traditional instruments of labor, became from then on *objects of science.*

In the same period as Lombroso and Down, a Brazilian doc-

tor, Raimundo Nina Rodrigues, began studying the black problem. Nina Rodrigues, who was mulatto, arrived at the conclusion
that *the mixing of bloods perpetuates the characteristics of inferior
races*, and thus *the black race in Brazil has always constituted
one factor contributing to our inferiority as a people.* This psy-
chiatrist was the first to research the African culture of Brazil.
He studied it as a clinical case: black religions as pathology;
trances as manifestations of hysteria.

Some time later, an Argentine doctor, the socialist José Ingenieros, wrote that *blacks, opprobrious scum of the human race,
are closer to anthropoid monkeys than to civilized whites.* And
to demonstrate their incorrigible inferiority, Ingenieros offered
proof: *blacks have no religious ideas.*

In reality, "religious ideas" had crossed the sea with the slaves.
A proof of the obstinacy of human dignity: on the American
coasts only the gods of love and war arrived. The gods of fertility,
on the other hand, who would have multiplied the harvests and
slaves of the bosses, fell into the water.

The fighting and loving gods who completed the trip had to
put on disguises. They had to disguise themselves as white saints
to survive and help the millions of men and women violently
taken from Africa and sold as things. Ogum, the god of iron,
snuck by as Saint George or Saint Anthony or Saint Michael.
And Shangó, with all his thunder and fire, became Saint Barbara.
Obatalá became Jesus Christ, and Oshún, the goddess of fresh
waters, became the Virgin of La Candelaria . . .

Outlaw gods. In the Spanish and Portuguese colonies and in
all the rest: in the English islands of the Caribbean, *after* the
abolition of slavery it was still forbidden to play drums or flutes
in the African style. And simply having an image of any African
god was cause for a jail term.

Outlaw gods, because they dangerously excite human passions, and through humans they come alive. Friedrich Nietzsche
once said:

"I could only believe in a god that knows how to dance."

Like José Ingenieros, Nietzsche knew nothing of African gods. If they had known them, perhaps they would have believed in them. And perhaps they would have changed some of their ideas. Nietzsche anyway.

Dark skin indicates incorrigible defects. Thus, outrageous social inequality, which is also racial, finds an alibi in hereditary tares.

Humboldt noted it two hundred years ago, and in all America it hasn't changed: the social pyramid is black at the base and white at the top. In Brazil, for example, racial democracy consists of having the whitest on top and the blackest below. James Baldwin, on the blacks of the United States:

"When we left Mississippi to come north we did not come to freedom. We came to the bottom of the labor market, and we are still there."

An Indian from the north of Argentina, Asunción Ontiveros Yulquila, still remembers the trauma that marked his childhood:

"Good and pretty people were those that looked like Jesus and Mary. But my father and mother didn't look anything like the images of Jesus and Mary that I saw in the church at Abra Pampa."

One's own face is an error of Nature. One's own culture, proof of ignorance or guilt to be expiated. To civilize is *to correct*.

Biological fatalism, stigma of *inferior* races congenitally condemned to indolence and violence and misery, not only keeps us from seeing the real causes of our historic misadventure. Racism also keeps us from knowing or recognizing certain fundamental values that scorned cultures have miraculously kept alive, and that they bring alive, rightly or wrongly, despite centuries of persecution, humiliation, and degradation. Those fundamental values are no museum pieces. They are factors of history, essential ingredients of our inevitable creation of an America without rulers or ruled. Those values *accuse* the system that denies them.

Some time ago, the Spanish priest Ignacio Ellacuría told me that to him the notion of the Discovery of America seemed absurd. The oppressor is incapable of discovery, he told me:

"It is the oppressed who discovers the oppressor."

He believed that the oppressor couldn't even discover himself. The true reality of the oppressor can only be seen from the point of view of the oppressed.

Ignacio Ellacuría was shot down for believing in that unpardonable capacity of revelation, and for taking the risks implied by his faith in the power of prophecy.

Did the Salvadoran military kill him? Or was it a system that cannot tolerate the gaze that gives it away?